THE CRUCIFIED JEW

Rabbi Dr Dan Cohn-Sherbok received a doctorate from Cambridge University and has taught Jewish theology at the University of Kent since 1975. He is the author of *The Jews of Canterbury*; *On Earth as it is in Heaven: Jews, Christians and Liberation Theology*; *The Jewish Heritage*; *Jewish Petitionary Prayer: A Theological Exploration*; *Holocaust Theology*; *Rabbinic Perspectives on the New Testament*; *Blackwell's Dictionary of Judaica*; *Issues in Contemporary Judaism* and the *Dictionary of Judaism and Christianity*. He is also the editor of numerous volumes and has contributed more than a hundred articles to books and scholarly journals.

Also by Dan Cohn-Sherbok

A Dictionary of Judaism and Christianity
Dictionary of Judaica
Holocaust Theology
Issues in Contemporary Judaism
Jewish Petitionary Prayer: A Theological Exploration
On Earth as it is in Heaven: Jews, Christians and Liberation Theology
Rabbinic Perspectives on the New Testament
The Jewish Heritage
The Jews of Canterbury
A Traditional Quest: Essays in Honour of Louis Jacobs (editor)
Problems of Contemporary Jewish Theology (editor)
Exploring Reality (editor)
Islam in a World of Diverse Faiths (editor)
Religion in Public Life (editor)
The Canterbury Papers: Essays on Religion and Society (editor)
The Salman Rushdie Controversy in Interreligious Perspective (editor)
The Sayings of Moses (editor)
Tradition and Unity: Sermons Published in Honour of Robert Runcie (editor)
Using the Bible Today: Contemporary Interpretations of Scripture (editor)
World Religions and Human Liberation (editor)

THE CRUCIFIED JEW

TWENTY CENTURIES OF
CHRISTIAN ANTI-SEMITISM

Dan Cohn-Sherbok

Fount

An Imprint of HarperCollins*Publishers*

Fount Paperbacks is an Imprint of
HarperCollins*Religious*
Part of HarperCollins*Publishers*
77–85 Fulham Palace Road,
Hammersmith, London W6 8JB

First published in Great Britain in 1992
by HarperCollins*Religious*
and this edition in 1993 by Fount Paperbacks
1 3 5 7 9 8 6 4 2

A catalogue record for this book is
available from the British Library

ISBN 0 00 627604 0

Set in Ehrhardt

Printed and bound in Great Britain by
HarperCollinsManufacturing Glasgow

For Lavinia

Contents

Acknowledgements		xi
Introduction		xiii

1 THE GRECO-ROMAN WORLD — 1

Pagan Anti-Judaism — 1
The Spiritualization of the Torah — 4
Revival Movements in the Greco-Roman World — 6
The Impact of Gnosticism — 8
Pharisaism and the Spiritualization of Judaism — 10

2 ANTI-JUDAISM IN THE NEW TESTAMENT — 12

The True Israel — 12
Jesus and the Leaders of the Nation — 15
The Abrogation of the Law — 17
Paul's Mission to the New Israel — 20
Anti-Jewish Antitheses in Hebrews and the Gospel of John — 22

3 THE CHURCH FATHERS AND JEWISH HATRED — 25

The Iniquity of the Jews — 25
The Jews and the Future Church — 28
Divine Election — 30
Jewish Rejection and Exile — 32
The Fulfilment of the Law — 34

4 MEDIEVAL PERSECUTIONS, RITUAL MURDER AND THE TALMUD — 38

Western Jewry in the Middle Ages — 38
Persecution and Christian Opinion — 41
Ritual Murder — 43

The Badge and the Talmud 45
The Black Plague and the Jewish Response 48

5   THE DEMONIC IMAGE OF THE JEW 51

The Vile Jew 51
The Devil and the Jews 53
The Jew as Sorcerer 55
The Truth behind the Myth 58
Persecution of the Demons 61

6   POST-MEDIEVAL ANTI-SEMITISM IN FRANCE,
    ENGLAND AND GERMANY 64

French Jewry in the Post-Medieval Period 64
The French Vilification of the Jews 68
Agitation against the Jews in England and Germany 70
Martin Luther's Diatribe 72
After Luther 75

7   SPANISH PERSECUTION AND THE INQUISITION 77

Jewish Persecution in Spain 77
Attack on the Jews and the Decline of the Aljamas 79
The Conversos 82
The Inquisition and the Marranos 84
Torture and Expulsion 87

8   THE DISPERSION OF THE MARRANOS 89

The Marranos of Portugal 89
The Dispersion of the Marranos 91
The Marrano Duke of Naxos 94
The Shabbatean Movement 96
Spinoza and Anti-Judaism 98

9   ANTI-SEMITISM IN EASTERN EUROPE 101

Polish Jewry 101
Scholarship in Poland 103
The Chmielnicki Massacres 105
Hasidism and Later Polish Anti-Judaism 108
Russian Jewry 109

Contents

10 WESTERN JEWRY IN THE EARLY MODERN
    PERIOD   113

German Jewry   113
French Antipathy to the Jews   116
Jews in Great Britain   118
Jewry in the New World   120
Life in the Jewish Community   122

11 THE ENLIGHTENMENT IN ENGLAND, FRANCE
    AND GERMANY   125

English Free Thinkers   125
The French Protestant Reaction   127
The Jews and the French Enlightenment   129
Stirrings in Germany   132
The Berlin Haskalah   135

12 THE EMANCIPATION OF THE JEWS   139

The French Experience   139
German Emancipation   142
Jews and the Russian Empire   144
The Jewish Reaction   146
The Gentile Response   148

13 JUDEOPHOBIA IN THE EARLY NINETEENTH
    CENTURY   152

The English View   152
French Hatred   154
The Wandering Jew and French Socialism   157
German Racism and Metaphysical Thought   160
Richard Wagner   162

14 MODERN IMAGES OF THE JEW IN GERMANY,
    FRANCE AND RUSSIA   165

German Anti-Semitic Campaigns   166
Before Dreyfus   168
The Dreyfus Affair and Zionism   170
Russian Protests   173
Revolution and Ritual Murder   175

15   PRELUDE TO THE HOLOCAUST   179
  The German Reaction   180
  Russian Hostility   182
  British Anti-Semitism   185
  Anti-Semitism in the United States   188
  French Judeophobia   192

16   THE DEATH CAMPS   195
  Hitler and the Jews   195
  The Destruction of Polish and Russian Jewry   197
  The Death Camps   199
  Jewish Resistance   202
  The Final Stage of Terror and Christian Responsibility   205

17   ANTI-SEMITISM IN A POST-HOLOCAUST
     WORLD   210
  The German and Austrian Reaction   210
  Judeophobia in Britain and America   212
  French Hostility   214
  Polish Anti-Semitism   217
  Jewish Hatred in Russia   219

18   TOWARD RECONCILIATION   222
  Church Statements   222
  Jesus the Jew   225
  God's Covenant and the Jewish People   227
  Christian Mission   229
  The Holocaust   231

Conclusion   234
Further Reading   242
General Index   245
Index of Names   253

Acknowledgements

I would like to acknowledge my indebtedness to Leon Poliakov's multi-volume *History of Anti-Semitism*, London, 1974 which provided a quarry for information as well as most of the source material quoted throughout this book. Students who wish to gain a deeper knowledge of the subject are strongly recommended to read this monumental work. Thanks are also due to Rosemary Radford Reuther's excellent study *Faith and Fratricide: The Theological Roots of Anti-Semitism*, New York, 1974 which served as the basis for the discussion of Jews, pagans and Christians in the ancient and early Christian world in Chapters 1–3. In addition I would like to acknowledge my use of source material from a number of important studies: Joshua Trachtenberg's *Jewish Magic and Superstition*, New York, 1961 in Chapter 5; Martin Gilbert's *The Holocaust: The Jewish Tragedy*, London, 1986 in Chapter 16; Harry James Cargas' *Shadows of Auschwitz*, New York, 1990 in Chapter 16; Robert Wistrich's *Anti-semitism: The Longest Hatred*, London, 1991 in Chapter 17; and Marcus Braybrooke's *Time to Meet: Towards a deeper relationship between Christians and Jews*, London, 1990 in Chapter 18. I am most grateful as well to Giles Semper of HarperCollins for his encouragement, and to Mollie Roots and her staff in Rutherford College secretarial office for their help in typing the manuscript.

NOTE ON TERMINOLOGY:
Some writers distinguish between the terms "anti-Semitism", "anti-Jewish", and "anti-Judaism". In this study "anti-Semitism" (spelled with a hyphen) is used as a generic term, designating hostility toward both Judaism and the Jewish people.

Introduction

Recently as I was sitting drinking a cup of coffee in our house in Canterbury, a glossy leaflet dropped through our letterbox, entitled *The Ultimate Blasphemy: Revelations from the Talmud*. With a sense of horror I read the opening paragraph:

> The *Talmud* is the Jewish law consisting of binding precepts (the *Mishnah*) handed down by Jewish "sages" with their commentaries. It is the codification of ancient oral laws – a body of rabbinic literature which is of prime importance in Jewish religious practice. Buried in the *Talmud* is some vicious mud slinging, or rather *Talmud* slinging where the mud is replaced by excreta. You are the target!

As I read on I could see that this tract echoed similar treatises produced in previous centuries to inflame Christian hatred against the Jewish community. Various statements were allegedly quoted from the *Talmud* and other rabbinic sources. They included such horrid pronouncements as: "He who sheds the blood of the *goyim* is offering a sacrifice to God"; "Jews are human beings; the other peoples of the world are not human beings, but beasts"; "It is always a meritorious deed to get hold of a gentile's possessions"; "A Jew may lie and perjure to condemn a Christian. The name of God is not profaned when lying to Christians"; "It is a good deed for every Jew to burn and destroy the non-Jewish church or whatever belongs to it or is done for it, and to throw the ashes into the four winds"; "A Jew may violate but not marry a non-Jewess."

The author of this leaflet declared that such "filthy rubbish" blasphemes against the Christian faith; in response Christians must ask themselves a series of questions: Are we more revolting than Zionist thugs who kill and maim young Palestinians seeking their heritage from the bandit State of Israel? Can we be a greater disaster than the strident vengeful Jews who try to change our laws? Such questions are of course rhetorical. The purpose of such anti-Jewish sentiment is to poison Christian minds and turn gentiles against Jews. Not surprisingly both Jews and Christians in Canterbury who received this leaflet were outraged and deeply troubled. This manifestation of contemporary Christian anti-Semitism is however not an isolated incident. In recent years similar outbreaks of anti-Jewish hatred have taken place in Europe and elsewhere. Why is it that the flames of racial hatred have been kept alive five decades after millions of Jews were murdered in the most brutal fashion by the Nazis? Have the lessons of the twentieth century not been sufficient to ensure that such Jewish suffering shall never happen again?

The answers to these questions are complex; anti-Semitism has arisen as a result of numerous causes: political, religious, social, cultural and economic. Over the years numerous writers have attempted to account for this hatred and trace its history in multi-volume works, shorter expositions, and specialized studies. These various publications provide a terrifying account of Jewish antipathy, persecution, and massacre through the centuries. Yet although most of these investigations refer to the Christian contribution to the problem of Jew-hatred, they do not focus on the underlying Christian hostility to Judaism and the Jewish people. Recently however a number of Christian and Jewish theologians have drawn attention to the persistence of Christian anti-Judaism from New Testament times to the present day. Such studies as Rosemary Radford Reuther's *Faith and Fratricide: The Theological Roots of Anti-Semitism*, Harry James Cargas' *Shadows of Auschwitz*, Franklin Littell's *The Crucifixion of the Jews*, Edward Flannery's *The Anguish of the Jews*, John Roth and Richard Rubenstein's *Approaches to Auschwitz* and Robert Wistrich's *Antisemitism: The Longest Hatred* have stressed that the seeds of anti-Semitism were sown in Christian sources and nurtured throughout the history of the Church.

Drawing on this observation, this volume sets out to illustrate that for twenty centuries Christian anti-Semitism has generated hostility toward the Jewish faith and the people of Israel. Chapter 1 begins with a discussion of ancient pagan animosity to the Jewish faith. Wherever Greeks were dominant, the common view was that anything non-Greek was uncivilized. In this context Judaism was regarded with contempt. When the Church emerged in the first century AD it drew upon Hellenistic ideas that had penetrated into the Jewish religion. In this way Christianity absorbed pagan hostility to the Jews and utilized aspects of Judaism in the Hellenistic and Roman period to distance itself from the faith from which it had evolved.

In Chapter 2 the development of Christian anti-Jewish attitudes is traced in detail. According to the writers of the Gospels, Jesus attacked the leaders of the Jewish nation for their hypocrisy. For the Church what is required is faithfulness to Christ rather than obedience to the Law. In proclaiming this Christian message Paul stressed that the Jewish nation had been rejected by God, and the new covenant had superseded the old. Such an antithesis is highlighted in the Epistle to the Hebrews; here Christ is depicted as the eternal Temple in contrast to the earthly cult in Jerusalem. Such a conflict is also found in the Fourth Gospel which distinguishes between the fulfilled spiritual domain of Christianity and the fallen world of darkness associated with Jews and Judaism. In these various ways the New Testament laid the foundations for later Christian hostility to the Jewish nation.

This New Testament tradition served as the basis for the early Church's vilification of the Jews, as is illustrated in Chapter 3. According to the Church Fathers, the Jewish people are lawless and dissolute. For this reason, God's promises now apply to the Christian community. Having rejected Christ, the Jewish people have been excluded from God's grace and are subject to his anger. The Church thus constitutes the elect – this is the culmination of the messianic vision of the return of all nations to Zion. Christians are to serve as God's instruments for bringing all humanity to knowledge of God, but the Jews are to suffer rejection and misery as they wander in exile.

Chapter 4 continues with a discussion of the medieval tradition of anti-Jewish hostility which evolved from the *Adversos Judeos* teaching of the early Church Fathers. During the Crusades Christian mobs massacred Jewish communities. Jews were charged with killing Christian children to use their blood for ritual purposes, blaspheming Christ and Christianity in the Talmud, and bringing about the Black Plague by poisoning wells. Such Christian animosity and persecution evoked Jewish denunciations of the Christian faith and pleas for divine vengeance. When besieged by their enemies, many Jews of this period went to their deaths as martyrs to the Jewish faith, persuaded that God would punish their Christian tormentors for their sins.

As Chapter 5 illustrates, Jewry was detested throughout the Middle Ages and the image of the demonic Jew became a feature of Western

Christendom. Continually Jews were accused of satanic activities and viewed as a sub-species of the human race. The belief that the Jewish population could work miracles against the Christian community inflamed the Church and served as the basis for the accusation that Jews defamed the Host and committed acts of ritual murder.

Although Jews, like their Christian neighbours, did practise magic during this period, their intentions were invariably benevolent – thus Christian attacks on Jews were based solely on fear and ignorance.

The next Chapter highlights the fact that during the post-medieval period negative Christian stereotypes of the Jews continued to play an important role in Western European culture. In France catechisms, lives of Jesus, and canticles depicted the Jews in the most terrible light. Similarly in England Jews were vilified as they were in Germany. Such attitudes were most forcibly expressed in Martin Luther's diatribes against the Jews in which he echoed previous Christian denunciations. These tracts were subsequently followed by similar Christian publications which denounced Judaism and the Jewish nation. Hence the legacy of Christian hostility towards the Jews continued to the early modern era.

Chapter 7 continues this account of Christian anti-Jewish sentiment by surveying the attitude of the Church toward Spanish Jewry. Although the Spanish Jewish community flourished during the Middle Ages, by the fourteenth century it came to be regarded with suspicion and contempt. In order to escape Christian attack, many Jews converted to the Christian faith. Yet such mass conversion paved the way to a new form of persecution in the fifteenth century. Under King Ferdinand and Queen Isabella the Christian Inquisition was inaugurated to seek out those converts suspected of practising Judaism in secret. Throughout the country tribunals were established – those found guilty were punished, and many who refused to confess were burned at the stake. In 1492 an Edict of Expulsion was promulgated to rid the country of the entire Jewish population.

Chapter 8 outlines the saga of the Marrano dispersion to other countries. Many sought refuge from their Christian tormentors in Portugal where they lived outwardly as Christians while covertly observing Judaism. None the less, here too the Inquisition sought out those who allegedly betrayed the Christian faith. Meanwhile a number of Marranos attempted to escape from Christian persecution by fleeing to other lands. In these domains these former Jews returned to their ancestral faith; some gained positions of importance while others awaited the coming of the Messiah to deliver them from Christian oppression.

The following chapter demonstrates that in the late medieval and early modern period Polish Jews – like their co-religionists in Western Christian lands in previous centuries – were subject to intense Christian anti-Semitic sentiment. In the mid–seventeenth century a Cossack onslaught led by the hetman Bogdan Chmielnicki led to the death of thousands of Jews. Similarly, when Polish territories were annexed to Russia in the nineteenth century the Christian population viewed the Jewish inhabitants with contempt, and eventually Jews were expelled from the villages where they resided.

As Chapter 10 explains, in the early modern period commercial interests were coupled with age-old Christian prejudice against the Jews. In Germany merchants maintained that Jewish trade would pollute the nation and undermine the economic vitality of the country. Similarly the French bourgeoisie resisted Jewish settlement as did the Christian population in Great Britain when Jewish naturalization was proposed. Thus despite the various advances made in the seventeenth and eighteenth centuries, the pattern of Jewish life did not alter radically from medieval times. Jews were stereotyped as strange and demonic, and even many enlightened Jews were unable to escape Christian anti-Jewish hostility.

During the Enlightenment, as Chapter 11 makes clear, English reformers sought to improve the condition of the Jewish community. Others, however, attacked Jewry on the basis of rationalist and scientific assumptions. In France Protestants influenced by the Enlightenment attempted to counter such charges, yet they too were unable to free themselves from traditional Christian attitudes regarding Jewish guilt and divine punishment. Similarly, within Germany the rise of national self-confidence fuelled anti-Semitic feelings among various Christian writers. Aware of such intense loathing, a number of Jews separated themselves from the Jewish community and sought to gain acceptance in Christian society by becoming a Jewish–Christian Protestant sect.

Chapter 12 explores the impact of the Enlightenment on Jewry at the beginning of the nineteenth century. In France the summoning of a Great Sanhedrin paved the way for the improvement of Jewish life. The spirit of emancipation encouraged Jewish activists such as Israel

Jacobson to adapt Jewish practices to contemporary circumstances. However, these adaptations to the Jewish heritage unintentionally undermined confidence in Jewish values and intensified Christian hostility to Judaism. In Russia the aim of emancipation was to bring about the assimilation of the Jewish population, a policy based on centuries-old Christian hatred of the Jewish nation. In response to such attempts throughout Europe to modernize Jewish life, Orthodox Jewish writers expressed dismay, whereas Jewish reformers welcomed the erosion of medieval patterns of Jewish existence. Within gentile circles, liberals campaigned for the improvement of Jewish life, while reactionaries feared the consequences of such a policy. By the end of the century, Christian mobs throughout the continent once again attacked Jewish communities, thereby illustrating that Christian anti-Semitism had not disappeared despite the well-intentioned actions of Christian as well as Jewish progressives.

Chapter 13 relates the frustrated attempts of Jewish apologists to improve the condition of the Jewish community. In England Benjamin Disraeli advocated the granting of civil rights to Jewry. Such attempts, however, evoked a hostile response from critics who attacked Jewry in terms reminiscent of previous Christian centuries. In France the Damascus Affair, in which Jews were accused of the ancient crime of ritual murder, concluded peacefully; none the less this medieval Christian charge inspired widespread hostility to Jewry. In addition, the Christian myth of the Wandering Jew pervaded French literature of the period. At the same time the advocates of German racism were critical of Jewry and Judaism – this animosity reached its climax in the ferocious Jew-hatred of Richard Wagner.

Chapter 14 surveys further outbreaks of Christian anti-Semitism in the nineteenth century. In Germany the denigration of the Jews in racist publications led to the creation of political parties which promoted anti-Jewish attitudes. Simultaneously the conclusions of Christian biblical scholars tended to undermine the traditional Jewish understanding of revelation. In France similar anti-Jewish views were expressed by a wide variety of writers and provided the background of the Dreyfus Affair. Witnessing this outburst of anti-Jewish feeling, the Jewish writer Theodor Herzl championed the cause of Zionism. Only by creating a Jewish state, he believed, could the problem of anti-Semitism be overcome. During this epoch the persecution of Jews in Russia also provoked many Jews to emigrate to other lands; others believed they could overcome this hostility through revolutionary programmes. Provoked by this agitation and disturbed by the publication of anti-Jewish texts, the authorities became persuaded that Jewry sought to gain world domination.

As Chapter 15 explains, in the years leading up to World War I Jews became scapegoats for the problems afflicting European society. In Germany numerous Christian polemicists protested against the malevolent influence of Jewish attitudes. In Russia during the war years Christian anti-Semites accused Jews of espionage and of collaborating with the enemy. With the onset of the Russian revolution, Jews were also charged with fermenting revolutionary activities. Subsequently a series of forgeries were published associating Jews with the revolutionary movement. In Britain writers also vilified the Jewish people, and the publication of the *Protocols of the Elders of Zion* reinforced the myth of an international Jewish conspiracy. Similarly, in the United States a number of Christian writers attacked Jews for their involvement in the revolutionary movement. French hatred of Jews was also animated by the conviction that Jewry sought to dominate world affairs.

As Chapter 16 demonstrates, the anti-Jewish sentiments of the war years crystallized in Adolf Hitler's conception of the Jewish people. According to Hitler, the Jews are an evil race seeking world domination: his vitriolic denunciation of Jewry echoed the sentiments of Christian writers down the centuries. On the basis of such attitudes, Jews were subject to various forms of persecution under Nazi rule, culminating in *Kristallnacht*, during which numerous Jewish buildings were destroyed. Eventually the Nazis constructed death centres in which millions of Jews lost their lives. During these war years most Christians, including those in positions of authority, refused to help the Jewish community. And once the war ended, the Vatican and others close to it aided a number of war criminals to escape from the allies.

Chapter 17 examines the development of anti-Semitism in the post-Holocaust world. In Germany little guilt was expressed for the horrors of the war. Instead most Germans continued to harbour anti-Semitic attitudes. Similar attitudes were manifest in Austria, and in Britain ultra-right groups have advanced the theory of a world-wide Jewish conspiracy. In the United States anti-Semitism has also been expressed in recent years, particularly within the Black community. French antipathy toward the Jews has also resulted in the denunciation of Zionism, and attacks have been made on Jewish property. Poland too has witnessed the resurgence of anti-Semitism in recent years. In Russia as well anti-Semitism has been manifest. Such outbursts of Jew-hatred have not been fuelled by theological anti-Judaism, yet the stereotypes, myths and language of traditional Christian anti-Semitism have served as the vocabulary of this most recent onslaught on the Jewish community.

For twenty centuries, then, Christian anti-Semitism has served either directly or indirectly as a fundamental cause of Judeophobia. In the ancient, medieval, and early modern period, hostility toward the Jews was explicitly Christian in origin. In modern times this legacy of Christian anti-Semitism provided the background and language of Jew-hatred even when it has lacked an overt religious content. Yet in recent decades, as Chapter 18 explains, the Church has become increasingly aware of this bloody history and has sought to overcome Christian antipathy toward Judaism and the Jewish nation. Church bodies have formulated numerous decrees denouncing anti-Semitism, and positive encounter with Jews has been encouraged. Pioneering scholars have also reformulated Christological doctrine and modified the traditional understanding of God's covenants; in addition, many Christians today have modified the idea of Christian mission. There are thus positive signs of hope as the second millenium draws to a close, despite the heritage of twenty centuries of Christian hatred of Judaism and the Jewish people.

CHAPTER ONE

The Greco-Roman World

The story of Christian anti-Semitism begins in the Greco-Roman world. Living among pagans, Jews and Judaism were subject to discrimination and persecution. Where Greek power was dominant, the typical view was that anything non-Greek was barbaric. The Jewish tradition was thus regarded with contempt. None the less it was only when Christianity emerged in the first century AD that Jews came to be viewed as contemptible and demonic. In its advocacy of anti-Jewish attitudes, the Church drew upon Hellenistic ideas that had penetrated into the Jewish faith. For a number of Jews the Torah was interpreted in allegorical terms, and such a conception was transformed by Christianity into a justification for separating religious meaning from ritual observance. Revival movements in the ancient Jewish world – the disciples of which believed themselves to be the true Israel – also provided a source for the Christian conviction that the Jewish faith constituted the fulfilment of biblical teaching. Further, Gnosticism which grew out of the attempt to harmonize Hellenistic thought with the Jewish tradition, added to the Christian denigration of the God of the Old Testament. Finally, the Pharisaic spiritualization and universalization of Judaism intensified the Christian determination that the good news of the New Testament should be spread to all people. Christianity thus utilized features inherent in the Judaism of the Hellenistic and Roman period to shape its own identity and distance itself from the faith from which it had originated.

Pagan Anti-Judaism

The development of Christian anti-Semitism took place in a pagan environment. During the Hellenistic period Jews did not occupy specific economic positions which aroused envy, nor were they subject to racial persecution. Rather the Greeks and Romans objected to the Jews on social grounds, and such hostility gave rise to a general polemic among classical writers such as Cicero.

In Egypt the Jewish community was especially numerous, and many Jews were used as middlemen between rulers and the general population. In this context Egyptian intellectuals utilized the biblical account of the Exodus to vilify the Jews who lived in their midst. According to Scripture, the ancient Egyptians perished on account of Pharaoh's reluctance to release the Israelites; the plagues were the result of actions of the Jewish God. Such antagonism led to anti-Jewish riots in Alexandria as well as a tradition of anti-Jewish propaganda in Egyptian literature.

This invective took the form of counter-myths to the Exodus. According to these stories, the Jewish nation had been a diseased population who married slaves; their flight from Egypt was due to the Egyptians themselves who wished to rid themselves of these lepers. The observance of the Sabbath was viewed within this tradition as a result of the disease-ridden condition of the Jewish populace: the Israelites could travel for only six days at a time because they were so unwell. Such accounts were produced in the third century BC by the Egyptian priest Manetho, and were subsequently repeated by such Hellenistic historians as Cheremona and Lysimachus of Alexandria and Apollonius Molon and Pompeius of Trogus.

In line with such animosity on the part of the Egyptians, Hellenistic society generally reacted against Jewish exclusivity and Jewish particularism. Because of their observances, Jews lived apart from their neighbours and generally refused to assimilate Greek customs. They regarded the gods of the Greeks as false, and their culture as unclean. As a result, the Jewish community and the pagan population lived in constant tension. Nevertheless Jews were protected by Rome. Although they were not frequently granted citizenship, they were allowed to live according to their traditions. Another factor which tended to mitigate against Greco-Roman antipathy was the fact that Jewish thought in Palestine and the diaspora borrowed a number of features from Hellenism. Such conditions helped to defuse what otherwise might have been an explosive socio-religious situation.

In response to the hostility expressed by non-Jews against Jews, a number of Jewish apologists argued that Greek philosophers such as Plato had learned about philosophy from Moses. Judaism, these writers maintained, contained a higher and purer religious system than that found among the Greeks and Romans, and attempts were made by the Jewish community to convert gentiles to the true faith. In the Greco-Roman period Judaism became missionary in outlook and attempted to establish itself as a universal religion. Proselytes were to be considered as enjoying the same status as born-Jews, and numerous "God-fearers" (sympathizers to Judaism) were attracted to the synagogue. As far as non-Jews were concerned, the Noachian laws (laws given to Noah) were seen to provide a basis for the acceptance of the righteous of all nations into the World-to-Come.

In time the Jewish population living under Roman domination in Palestine rebelled: the first revolt took place from AD 66 to 73, and the second lasted from AD 133 to 136. As a consequence, Jewry came to be viewed with suspicion and distaste. Yet these wars did not provoke widespread persecution. The Romans simply desired to provide a social framework which would place each ethnic group – including the Jews – into a suitable administrative relationship with Roman authorities. Although the Temple was destroyed and Jerusalem devastated by Roman armies, the Roman government wished to co-operate with the Jewish populace which resided in Palestine. Despite this accommodating attitude to foreign peoples most Romans viewed Jewish ways as superstitious, and customs such as circumcision, the dietary laws and Sabbath observances were regarded with disdain. Jewish law, however, was viewed as legitimate, and both Roman and Jewish leaders worked together to establish a basis for co-existence.

What aspects of this pagan view of Judaism were taken over by the Church? Since Christians subscribed to the biblical account of the Exodus from Egypt, the anti-Exodus polemic found in Egyptian literature had no effect. Similarly, because Christians shared the Jewish condemnation of polytheism and paganism, they could not absorb the Greco-Roman antipathy to the Jewish faith: Christians, as well as Jews, were intolerant of the religious convictions and practices of those among whom they lived. None the less it may well be that the repulsion felt by the Greeks toward circumcision influenced the Church, and the attitude of the Church Fathers to Jewish ritual may also reflect traditional pagan antipathy.

Pagan anti-Semitism thus provided the seedbed for the evolution of Christian anti-Jewish sentiment. Yet Greco-Roman attitudes were balanced by Roman pragmatism. It was only later, with the development of Christian theology, that religious hatred became a central feature of the ancient world. Pagans regarded the Jewish community with aversion and puzzlement; Christians, however, conceived of Jewry as spiritually contemptible and demonic. As rival faiths, Judaism and Christianity entered into conflict, and the history of their interaction is a tale of human suffering and tragedy.

The Spiritualization of the Torah

Despite the antagonism that existed between Jews and pagans in the ancient world, there were a number of Jewish thinkers who absorbed various elements of Hellenistic culture. By translating Hellenism into Jewish terms, these writers attempted to reconcile the Jewish tradition with Greek thought in order to present Judaism as a universalistic faith. Paradoxically, this quest in the Greco-Roman period provided the basis for Christianity's eventual spiritualization of Scripture and its consequent antithetical attitude to rabbinic Judaism.

The Hellenistic interpretation of the Hebrew Scriptures was most eloquently formulated in the writings of the Jewish philosopher Philo (first century BC to first century AD). According to Philo, God's creative power was initially manifest as the *Logos* or Word of God, a concept which unified the biblical Word of God with the Platonic concepts of the Ideal World and the Divine Mind. The immanent expression of the *Logos* was Natural Law which rules the cosmos and expresses itself in all things. Within this context the Torah should be understood as universal in scope. None the less the Torah is a special revelation to God's chosen people, whose mission is to serve as a light to the nations: Israel's task is to draw all people to a recognition of God's universal truth. The Torah is thus an expression of the universal path that all humanity seeks, but which is possessed solely in its fullest manifestation by the Jews. Such ideas paved the way for the Christian conception of Christ and the *Logos* and the doctrine of the incarnation of God on earth.

Such a universalistic conception of Scripture led to the allegorization of particularistic commandments in the Torah. The Sabbath, for example, was understood not as the day on which God rested from creation, but rather as the day on which the *Logos* emanated from God and served as the basis for the pattern of creation. For this reason this

4

day was dedicated to the pursuit of spiritual wisdom. Similarly, ritual food laws were seen in allegorical terms – they were conceived as designed to signal God's characteristics of mercy and cleanliness as opposed to violence and bloodthirstiness: only animals which exhibit the first kind of characteristics were permitted for food whereas those which possess the second type were forbidden. Again, circumcision was viewed as an allegory of cutting away illegitimate pleasures as well as the sin of pride.

Institutions such as the Temple, priesthood and sacrifice were also viewed symbolically. For Philo all aspects of the Temple served as an allegory of the cosmos. Its colours and furniture relect earth, air, fire and water; the sacrifices and libations symbolize fruits and animals; and the candles the heavenly spheres. Relying on Platonic categories, Philo envisaged the cosmos as a shadow of the higher spiritual realm of the Divine *Logos* whose spiritual domain is the sanctuary of God. Within this context the High Priest represents God's *Logos* which mediates in the Temple of the Universe as well as the temple of the human soul. Such a concept of the *Logos* as the cosmic High Priest was eventually transformed by New Testament writers and given Christological significance.

The purpose of such spiritualization and universalization of Jewish concepts was to invest Jewish ritual with mystical significance. In this quest the letter of the Law was not to be disregarded. Through his interpretation of Jewish law and institutions Philo sought to establish an intrinsic link between inner and outer meaning. It is impossible, he wrote, to dispose of outward observance and none the less experience the inner meaning of the Law. It is precisely the physical prescriptions in the Torah which express the spiritual significance of God's revelation. Philo's allegorical interpretation was designed to illustrate that God's decrees are the expressions of a universal spiritual faith.

Despite Philo's holistic vision of the Torah, the Church Fathers utilized his spiritualizing tendency to draw a distinction between the spirit and the letter of the law. For Christians it is possible to observe a universal Law of Nature without taking into account the concrete injunctions contained in the Bible. For these early Christians, Jewish law was abrogated by the coming of the Messiah; true sacrifice was to be understood as the sacrifice of the heart through prayer and penitence; and authentic incense as that which ascends to Heaven through heartfelt prayer. Hellenistic Judaism therefore unintentionally paved the way for a parting of the ways between traditional Jewish thought and the Christian faith. This theological rift was the inadvertent result of the Jewish attempt to harmonize tradition and religious teaching with what they perceived to be the truths of secular culture. Instead of achieving their aim, they provided a justification for the separation of religious significance from ritual practice. This had unforseen tragic consequences for the Jewish people when Christianity became the ascendant faith of the ancient world.

Revival Movements in the Greco-Roman World

During the second century BC Jewish traditionalists reacted against the Hellenizing influences initiated by the Seleucid ruler, Antiochus Epiphanes. These pietists (*Hasidim*) urged the nation to return to ancient ways and uphold the Torah against any external threats. Subsequently a number of sectarian groups carried on this tradition, and as apocalpytic expectations gained a hold on Jewish consciousness, messianic longing was expressed in the literature of the period. Many Jews anxiously awaited the coming of the Messiah who would bring about an era of redemption and reconciliation. Under God's domination, it was believed, the reign of evil powers would come to an end and those who belonged to the true Israel would be saved.

In anticipation of these cataclysmic events, various Palestinian sects considered themselves to be the true heirs of the covenant. The Samaritans, for example, regarded themselves as the inheritors of the original promise made to Israel. Situated on Mount Gerizim, they rigorously followed Pentateuchal law, rejecting the interpretation of Scripture expounded by official Judaism. Lacking any of the later writings of the Hebrew Bible, they viewed Moses as the sole prophet of Israel who would return as a messianic figure and bring about the restoration of the nation. Believing themselves to be the true keepers of the Torah and the sanctuary of the Exodus, they maintained that all Israel would eventually return to their form of belief and participate in the new age that would follow the advent of the Messiah. Another sect of this period was the *Nazaraioi* living in Jordan, who practised an ascetic way of life. Abstaining from meat as well as Temple sacrifice, they kept the Sabbath, circumcision and other Jewish practices. Like the Samaritans, they saw themselves as representing the true Judaism of patriarchal times.

The Essenes constituted a third sect in Greco-Roman times, claiming to possess the true Zadokite priesthood as well as the correct calendar for festivals. In opposition to the Temple cult in Jerusalem, these individuals adopted eschatological doctrines concerning Davidic and Aaronic Messiahs who would undertake kingly and priestly functions in a reconstituted Israel. Further, they looked to the coming of a Mosaic prophet who would serve as a forerunner to these messianic personages. Critical of official Judaism, they envisaged the present as an era of darkness presided over by the powers of Belial.

A fourth major group of the Hellenistic Jewish world were the Pharisees, who in all likelihood were descended from the *Hasidim* of the Maccabean period (second century BC). Like the Essenes, they desired to attain perfection by separating from their co-religionists so as strictly to observe Jewish law. It was their aim to set a high standard for religious observance; congregating in the synagogue, they strove to lead the nation back to true Torah Judaism. According to Pharisaic doctrine, they were the true inheritors of the ancient Israel and the promise of messianic fulfilment.

In their different ways these different sects set out to call the people to a total dedication to God's covenant. In their view the Jewish people had gone astray, and a conversion of the heart was required to restore the community to its previous situation. In proclaiming their message, these groups proposed a new interpretation of Israel, no longer based on birth but rather on conversion and personal commitment. Among a number of these sects, those who were persuaded of the truth of this vision were to pass through proselyte baptism in the same manner as gentiles who converted to Judaism.

The essential characteristic of these sectarian movements was their conviction that the true Israel must be distinguished from those who had abandoned their divinely sanctioned purpose: Jews who were loyal to the tradition constituted a spiritual community who, having undergone conversion of the heart, would eventually triumph against the forces of darkness that were assembled against them. In the final apocalyptic battle, they would prevail. Official Judaism on the other hand was seen as no longer part of the covenant – those Jews were like the gentiles. Filled with messianic longing, the sectarians regarded themselves as living in the last days, awaiting their vindication in the apocalyptic climax of human history.

It was in such a milieu that Christianity developed as a sectarian messianic Jewish movement. Drawing on Jewish apocalyptic imagery, the early Christians believed that their Teacher of Righteousness was the long-awaited Messiah. Vindicated by God through his resurrection, Jesus was thought to have ascended to Heaven where he sits on the right hand of the Father. According to Christianity, it is through Jesus' ministry and death that all peoples can attain forgiveness and salvation. Sectarian Judaism of the Greco-Roman period thus paved the way for the Christian conception of the apocalyptic transformation of world history inaugurated by God's Anointed One.

In common with other groups at this time, the early Christians believed themselves to be the true Israel in opposition to official Judaism, and such a conception provided the basis for the subsequent repudiation of Judaism and the vilification of the Jews. The absolute claims made by the Church about Jesus' redemption as promised in the Scriptures were set alongside Jewish blindness and hard-heartedness. Jewish existence was thereby negated as an abiding historical reality, and the Jewish faith was seen as a stage on the way to Christianity rather than as an authentic religious experience with its own inherent validity. In this way Jewish sectarianism inadvertently provided a foundation for the eventual repudiation of traditional Judaism through the Christian proclamation of the good news of Christ's redemption.

The Impact of Gnosticism

As we have seen, a number of Jewish thinkers in the diaspora attempted to assimilate Hellenistic patterns of thought to the Jewish tradition. Such a quest led to the development of gnostic doctrines in a variety of sects. Drawing on the symbolism of Greek philosophy, Oriental religions, and the Hebrew Scriptures, these gnostic groups shared a number of beliefs. The Supreme Divine Being, they argued, must be distinguished from the demiurge who is responsible for creation and involved in the material world. Subscribing to a form of dualism, the members of these sects argued that the world is ruled by two opposing heavenly powers, generally viewed as male and female.

The Supreme First Principle was conceived among these gnostics as an all-good Deity, whereas the Creator-Demiurge was regarded as a fallen and imperfect being. According to some Christian gnostics (such as Marcion), the first principle was identified with the New Testament "God of Love", whereas the secondary Creator-God was equated with Old Testament law which was understood as evil. In opposition to Genesis 1:31 ("And God saw everything that he had made, and behold, it was very good"), the gnostics believed that the universe is the result of a primordial fall from pure being. In addition, they maintained that the soul was created to be in exile in a lower, evil world into which it had fallen; the only hope of return was through secret knowledge (*gnosis*). Some sects also believed that liberation from the material world could only occur through antinomian attitudes and practices.

Within Judaism at the end of the Second Temple period, gnostic ideas were to be found in the teachings of such sectarian groups as the Essenes. Common both to Gnosticism and the Dead Sea Scrolls is the view of esoteric knowledge as a redemptive factor which can enable select individuals to bridge the abyss separating the human from the divine. Thus *The War Scrolls* teach that members of the sect are to be those "who hear the glorious voice and see the holy angels, men whose ears are opened and hear deep things . . ." The literature of the sect also adopted a dualistic perspective in its conception of a schism between the principle of God (light) and the principle of evil (darkness). Each has its own host of spirits and angels.

Such ideas which emerged within Judaism and spread beyond the Jewish world, constitute a third source of anti-Judaism in ancient society. Although dualistic theories were firmly rejected by Christian orthodoxy in the second century AD, the earliest Christians in Alexandria as well as in the Palestinian Church were Gnostic-Essenic in orientation, and this type of Christianity eventually penetrated into Western Christendom. By the fourth century AD it had become the dominant form of Christian spirituality despite the biblical affirmation of the goodness of creation. In this way Hellenistic Jewish thought inadvertently planted in Christian soil the seeds of doctrines which would later be used to denigrate the God of the Hebrew Scriptures, the Jewish legal tradition, and the Jewish adulation of the created order.

Pharisaism and the Spiritualization of Judaism

The revolution initiated by the Pharisees began two centuries before the destruction of Jerusalem and the Second Temple. According to Pharisaic doctrine, the Oral Torah was part of God's revelation to Moses on Mount Sinai. By promulgating laws based on the 613 commandments contained in the Pentateuch, this scholarly class provided a means of emancipating the Jewish people from a system of Judaism based around the priesthood, the Temple, and a national homeland. The oral tradition served as a mechanism for coping with the changed circumstances and fortunes of the Jewish people in exile. As codified in the *Mishnah* (second century AD), the Oral Law adapted customs to the needs of daily life.

The new formulation of the Jewish faith in Hellenistic and Roman times embraced Greek thought in a variety of ways. The Pharisees translated their concept of the Jewish nation into a form which Jews could transport with them no matter what system served as the dominant political order of their country of residence. Pharisaic Judaism also embraced the idea of a spiritual Jew whose life was regulated in accordance with the Covenant. Such a notion transcended ethnic descent and gave rise to the concept of the true Israel: those whose lives were structured by divine law. The obligation to serve God in this way was incumbent upon all born-Jews, but it also became a viable option for gentiles. In this light, conversion to Judaism became a possibility as never before. Those who chose the Jewish faith were to be regarded as the home-born, and the synagogue served as a meeting place for all observant Jews. Thus Pharisaism opened the way to missionary activities and a universalization of the faith. Further, linked to this stance was the Pharisaic conviction that righteous pagans who keep the Noachian commandments (a form of natural law) could be saved. According to the rabbis, it is not only Jews who have a place in the World-to-Come, but all righteous gentiles.

Pharisaism also adopted an historical stance which emancipated the Jew from an involvement with tribe and homeland. Just as a Jew could live a viable Jewish life without a land, political autonomy, or the Temple, so he was not to be overly concerned with the particular details of history. What was of vital importance was the spiritual significance of past events rather than their specific details. For this

reason, Jewish exegetes were at liberty to engage in midrashic speculation about incidents recorded in Scripture in order to extract the
meaning of the past for the present.

Regarding messianism, the Pharisees preserved central apocalyptic
doctrines: the resurrection of the dead, and belief in the hereafter. Yet
these ideas were formulated in terms of obedience to the Law. Following
the messianic age, those who had led righteous lives governed by the
Torah would enter Heaven (*Gan Eden*) whereas those who had violated
God's decrees would be confined to Hell (*Gehinnom*). Such an eschatological vision enabled the Jewish community to remain hopeful of future
glory amidst the tribulations of history and the loss of a Jewish homeland.

As far as God's presence was concerned, the Pharisees maintained
that after the destruction of the Temple, the *Shekinah* (God's presence)
followed his people into exile. This means that God ceased to be
localized in the Temple; instead he became available wherever Jews
resided. In this context, the Pharisees believed that the exile itself was
due to Israel's disobedience; what was required from the nation was
adherence to the Torah. As a result of their waywardness, God had
driven the people from their ancient homeland. In anticipation of this
disaster the Pharisees relocated their centre to Jamnia outside
Jerusalem, where scholars met after AD 70 to continue the tradition of
oral interpretation of the Law.

The destruction of Jerusalem and the Temple thus became for the
Pharisees the opportunity to initiate a spiritualizing and universalizing
transformation of the Jewish faith. Although overwhelmed by the
decimation of the country, they nevertheless created a framework for
Jewish survival in the diaspora. This revolution provided Judaism with a
constitution independent of the previous apparatus of a national faith,
and through this reformulation the people were freed from previous
institutions and political boundaries, becoming a universal people with a
transportable heritage. Paradoxically it was by adopting this very concept
of universalism and spiritualization that Christians were also encouraged to seek converts from among Jews and gentiles. With the dissolu-
tion of the nation, the Christian community claimed for itself the role of
being a light to the nations; as the true Israel, it saw itself as the authentic
inheritor of the biblical tradition. For the Church, Judaism was an
obsolete faith rejected by God because of its rejection of Christ, and it
was Christianity which had now become the spiritual fulfilment of the
Hebrew Scriptures.

CHAPTER TWO

Anti-Judaism in the New Testament

With the emergence of the Christian community, anti-Jewish sentiment in the Greco-Roman world intensified. The early Church
believed itself to be the authentic heir to the promises given by God in
Scripture: Jesus' messiahship ushered in a new era in which the true
Israel would become a light to the nations. Such a vision of the
Christian community evoked hostility against the Jewish people, who
were regarded as apostate and unrepentant. This animosity was fuelled
by the Gospel writers who described Jesus attacking the leaders of the
nation, whom he accused of hypocrisy and iniquity. The Church taught
that what is now required is circumcision of the heart rather than
obedience to the Law – Christians are to remain faithful not to the
Torah but to Christ. In proclaiming this Christian message Paul
emphasized that the Hebrew people had been rejected by God, and the
new covenant had taken the place of the old. In the Epistle to the
Hebrews this antithesis between the Jewish people and the Christian
community is heightened – Christ is conceived as the true eternal
Temple in opposition to the earthly and temporal cult of Jerusalem.
Such a contrast is also to be found in the Fourth Gospel, which
differentiates between the fulfilled spiritual universe of Christianity
and a fallen world of darkness represented by the Jews. The New
Testament thus laid the foundation for the theological negation of
Judaism and the vilification of the Jewish people.

The True Israel

In the Synoptic Gospels many of Jesus' utterances reflect current
Jewish teaching. His views on divorce, for example, were in accord with
the school of Shammai; his concept of the Sabbath being made for man
rather than man for the Sabbath was current in Pharisaic circles; his

emphasis on the centrality of intention as opposed to external forms was also a familiar theme. Nevertheless important differences existed between Jesus' ministry and that of Pharisaic teachers and scholars. Jesus' concern for righteousness was linked to the advent of the messianic era. Convinced of the imminent coming of God's reign, Jesus called for repentance in the light of the coming Kingdom. Inclusion in this realm was ultimately dependent on how individuals responded to Christ's words.

According to the Gospel tradition, Jesus viewed himself as the Messiah; thus when he entered Jerusalem prior to his crucifixion he believed his proclamation of the Kingdom would usher in a new era of human history. Yet rather than triumph in glory, Jesus was killed like a common criminal. For his disciples this event served as the ultimate test of faith. Rather than abandon hope, they trusted in their Lord who appeared to them as the risen Christ. Initially active in their midst, he eventually ascended to Heaven to be with the Father until the end of time.

How were the disciples to make sense of Jesus' suffering and death? The Scriptures, they believed, provided confirmation of Jesus' role as the dying Messiah. In particular, these early Christians looked to the Suffering Servant passages in Isaiah which spoke of a rejected servant of the Lord whose pain and death made atonement possible for all Israel. In these passages, this figure is described as "despised and rejected by men; a man of sorrows, and acquainted with grief; and as one from whom men hide their faces, he was despised, and we esteemed him not. Surely he has borne our griefs and carried our sorrows; yet we esteemed him stricken, smitten by God and afflicted. But he was wounded for our transgressions, he was bruised for our iniquities; upon him was the chastisement that made us whole, and with his stripes we are healed" (Isaiah 53:3–6). Before his death Jesus linked his destiny to this prophecy, and his disciples joined this vision with the Psalmist's depiction of the suffering and glory of the Messiah in Psalm 22, his prayer for deliverance in Psalm 69, and his reign over the whole earth in Psalm 18. Again Psalm 110 provided a basis for their belief that the Messianic King was to sit at God's right hand until his enemies were vanquished: "The Lord says to my lord: 'Sit at my right hand, till I make your enemies your footstool.'"

In their understanding of Jesus' mission, Daniel 7 provided the image of a glorious figure who would appear with God on Judgement

Day. "Behold, with the clouds of heaven there came one like a son of man . . . to him was given dominion and glory and kingdom, that all peoples, nations, and languages should serve him" (Daniel 7:13–14). All these biblical passages were viewed as predicting a future Messiah who would be rejected, suffer, die, be resurrected, and reign in glory at God's right hand until the Day of Judgement (Mark 12:35–37; Matthew 22:41–45; Acts 2:34–35).

According to the early Christians it was the Jewish leaders who were the enemies referred to in the Psalms – they were the ones who led the suffering prophet to his agonizing death. Jesus was the Son of Man of whom it was written that he would be rejected and suffer. This was done by the official leadership of the nation. Until the time when God would disclose himself to all people, salvation was reserved for those who recognized Christ. It would be these individuals whom God would redeem in the last days. Jesus was thus in the words of Psalm 118 "the stone whom the builders rejected", but had "become the head of the corner". As Isaiah declared, he was the stone that would "become a rock of stumbling to both houses of Israel" (Isaiah 8:14). Yet the same stone is a sure foundation of his people (Isaiah 28:16). Using the prophecy of Daniel, Jesus is seen as the stone who will disperse God's enemies on the last day and become "a great mountain which will fill the entire earth" (Daniel 2:34–35).

The Church, rather than the official leadership of Judaism, was understood to possess the true interpretation of Scripture, and Christians were thereby heirs of biblical prophecy. Armed with the good news, Jesus' disciples set out to spread Jesus' messianic mission to Israel. Yet the nation as a whole refused to listen; only a few were drawn into the new community of Christian believers. Unable to read the signs of the times, the Jewish people did not pay heed to Jesus' message of repentance – this was the faithless, hard-hearted Israel who is unable to understand. Paradoxically, however, it was the unrighteous of the nation who would enter into the Kingdom of God because of their trust in Christ: "Truly I say to you, the tax collectors and the harlots go into the Kingdom of God before you" (Matthew 21:31).

Thus Christianity in its earliest stages constituted a Jewish messianic sect which claimed to be the true Israel over against an apostate nation. Demanding conversion of the heart, it castigated official Judaism, accusing it of sinfulness and treachery. Matthew referred to these unbelievers as hypocrites, blind fools and serpents. In contrast to these unbelievers, who would be uprooted and thrown into the fire, the Church was seen as the true plant of God: "I am the vine, you are the branches. He who abides in me, and I in him, he it is that bears much fruit, for apart from me you can do nothing. If a man does not abide in me, he is cast forth as a branch and withers; and the branches are gathered, thrown into the fire and burned (John 15:5–6). Such a view of the Church – in opposition to the official leaders of the nation – was a starting point for the tragic history of Christian anti-Jewish vilification and attack.

Jesus and the Leaders of the Nation

Although New Testament scholars have been anxious to point out that the conflicts between Jesus and the leaders of the nation were in all likelihood interpolated into the Gospels by later Christians for polemical purposes, these confrontations reflect early Christian antipathy to the teachers of the Law. Linking himself to the prophetic tradition, Jesus was portrayed as the conscience of Israel. Just as the ancient prophets condemned the leaders of the people, Jesus attacked the Scribes and Pharisees for their iniquity. Jesus believed that these individuals made a mockery of God's law. Thus he declared: "Beware of the Scribes who like to go about in long robes, and to have salutations in the market places and the best seats in the synagogues and the place of honour at feasts, who devour widow's houses and for a pretence make long prayers" (Mark 12:38–40)

Like the Scribes, the Pharisees were also accused of betraying God's purposes. "For the sake of your tradition," Jesus pronounced concerning them, "you have made void the word of God. You hypocrites! Well did Isaiah prophesy of you when he said: 'This people honours me with their lips, but their heart is far from me; in vain do they worship me, teaching as doctrines the precepts of men'" (Matthew 15:6–9). Again, in true prophetic fashion Jesus reproached the Pharisees for their rejection of God's moral commandments: "But woe to you Pharisees! for you tithe mint and rue and every herb, and neglect justice and the love of God; these you ought to have done, without neglecting the others" (Luke 11:42).

Throughout the Gospels, Jesus is portrayed as rejecting moribund, ritualized religious practices. For this reason he renounced the Pharisaic interpretation of scriptural law. Thus, for example, Jesus defended his disciples for plucking grain on the Sabbath (Matthew 12:1–8). The Pharisees were unconcerned as to whether Jesus' disciples were hungry; their only interest was that the Sabbath law not be violated. Jesus replied to their rebuke by stressing the one-sidedness of their interpretation. He reminded them that David transgressed the law that reserved the eating of the loaves of offering to priests. Furthermore, on the Sabbath the Temple priests performed their function without being accused of breaking the Sabbath. If they could do this, he argued, why cannot his disciples do the same in the new Temple, which is Jesus himself. Jesus' aim was to show that his disciples' action could be defended by an appeal to biblical narrative and tradition. For Jesus, love must take precedence over law, even over the Sabbath. The error of the Pharisees was to believe that they were the only correct interpreters of the will of God.

A further encounter between Jesus and the Pharisees is said to have occurred because of the presence of a paralytic in the synagogue on the Sabbath (Matthew 12:9–14). Jesus was not dissuaded by the Pharisees' questioning and replied: "What man of you, if he has one sheep and it falls into a pit on the Sabbath, will not lay hold of it and lift it out? Of how much more value is a man than a sheep!" (Matthew 12:11–12). In another confrontation in Matthew Jesus pointed out that an act of compassion and love must take precedence over any legalistic prescription: Jesus healed a blind and dumb demoniac. When the Pharisees saw this, they said, "It is only by Be-elzebul, the prince of demons, that this man casts out demons" (Matthew 12:24). In response Jesus argued that their conclusion was contradictory: "Every kingdom divided against itself is laid waste, and no city or house divided against itself will stand; and if Satan casts out Satan, he is divided against himself; how then will his kingdom stand?" (Matthew 12:25–26). Jesus' central concern here was to relieve human pain. The Pharisees, however, did not share this desire.

In a different passage in Matthew (Matthew 15), Jesus further emphasized the iniquity of the leaders of the people. Jesus was in Galilee when he was approached by the Scribes and Pharisees from Jerusalem. "Why do your disciples transgress the tradition of the elders?" they inquired. "For they do not wash their hands when they eat." In his reply Jesus exposed them as transgressors of God's will and went on to explain that religious impurity is located in the moral rather than the ritual sphere:

Not what goes into the mouth defiles a man, but what comes out of the mouth, this defiles a man . . . Do you not see that whatever goes into the mouth passes into the stomach, and so passes on? But what comes out of the mouth proceeds from the heart, and this defiles a man. For out of the heart come evil thoughts, murder, adultery, fornication, theft, false witness, slander. These are what defile a man; but to eat with unwashed hands does not defile a man (Matthew 15:11, 17–20).

Again, a speech of Jesus recounted in Matthew (reminiscent of the denunciations made by the prophets of Israel) summarized his condemnation of the hypocrisy and iniquity of the leaders of the people:

The Scribes and Pharisees sit on Moses' seat; so practise and observe whatever they tell you, but not what they do; for they preach, but do not practise. They bind heavy burdens, hard to bear, and lay them on men's shoulders; but they themselves will not move them with their finger . . . Woe to you Scribes and Pharisees, hypocrites! for you are like whitewashed tombs, which outwardly appear beautiful, but within they are full of dead men's bones and all uncleanness (Matthew 23:1–4, 27).

Such prophetic condemnation of hypocrisy and iniquity was based on the Christian conviction that the leaders of the nation had directed the people away from God's true intention for them. Jesus is said to have attacked those who claimed to hold the keys to the Kingdom but refused entrance to others: "Woe to you lawyers!" he declared, "for you have taken away the key of knowledge; you did not enter yourselves, and you hindered those who were entering" (Luke 11:52). This challenge to the false religion of Israel became a rallying cry for Christians, and Jesus' denunciation of the leaders of the people served to justify the Christian denunciation of both the Jews and the Jewish faith through the centuries.

The Abrogation of the Law

In Acts 7 Stephen declared that from the time of Moses, the people of Israel had turned from worshipping God; for this reason the covenant originally designed for the nation had been withheld until Jesus' coming. Mosaic law thus never represented God's true intention, since what God had wished to give the people had been nullified by their disobedience. The true covenant was now made available through a new Mosaic prophet. Further, Stephen argued that God does not dwell in the Jerusalem Temple, but rather fills the cosmos: "Yet the Most High does not dwell in houses made with hands; as the prophet says, 'Heaven is my throne, and earth my footstool. What house will you build for me, says the Lord, or what is the place of my rest?'" (Acts 7:48–49).

Although the early Church did contain a number of conservative Jews who insisted that all converts be fully observant proselytes to Judaism, Hellenizers in sympathy with Stephen maintained that salvation was no longer dependent on the observance of Jewish ritual and moral commandments – rather it is found solely through faith in Jesus Christ, the Prophet-King-Son of Man. Only his followers constitute God's chosen people: all others are outside the true covenant. The Church alone possesses the correct interpretation of Scripture. According to this view, salvation now exists as the fulfilment of Scripture as predicted by the prophets. Christianity is thus not a new patch put on an old garment, or a new wine poured into old bottles, but needs a new garment and a new wine (Luke 5:36–39).

On the basis of this understanding of law and salvation, the Church endeavoured to spread the gospel beyond the Jewish community – the Christian message was for all who had ears to hear. By the second decade of the Church's mission, it was accepted that God was carving out a new people from among the gentiles. Since the Jews steadfastly continued to remain faithful to the old covenant, God had rejected them and had created a new Israel. This idea is expressed in the New Testament by frequent contrasts between unbelieving Jews and believing gentiles. Thus the Jewish leaders are depicted as rejecting and killing Jesus, whereas the first believer was a Roman centurion (Mark 15:39). The Good Samaritan is contrasted with the faithless Jew (Luke 10:33). The gentiles will come from all places to sit at the Messianic banquet while the sons of the Kingdom will be cast into outer darkness: "I tell you, many will come from east and west and sit with Abraham, Isaac, and Jacob in the kingdom of heaven, while the sons of the kingdom will be thrown into the outer darkness" (Matthew 8:11–12).

The parable of the wedding feast (Matthew 22:1–14; Luke 14:16–24) highlights God's rejection of the Jewish people. When the guests who were invited (the observant Jews) refuse to come, the king's (God's) messengers go out a second and third time to gather the rabble (the unrighteous and the gentiles). This parable illustrates that unrepentant Israel is rejected, whereas the gentiles who were originally outside the covenant are now the true Israel. For Matthew, those who were initially invited were not simply too busy as in Luke; they "seized the servants, treated them shamefully and killed them" (Matthew 22:6). In response the king was angry, destroyed those murderers, and burned their city (Matthew 22:7). In addition, once the wedding hall was filled with guests, the king threw out a man who had no wedding garment (Matthew 22:11). In this parable Matthew emphasizes that God will punish the Jewish people for their lack of repentance and draw into the covenant gentiles as long as they are faithful.

The belief that apostate Israel not only rejected the gospel but also sought to kill God's messengers is frequently stressed in Scripture. The Synoptic Gospels minimize the responsibility of the Romans for Christ's death; instead the elders, the chief priests and the Scribes play a dominant role. Similarly, blame for the deaths of Jesus' disciples such as Stephen and James is attributed to the Jewish religious authorities. This idea serves as the basis of the parable of the vineyard (Mark 12:1–12; Matthew 21:33–46; Luke 20:9–19). Here the vineyard owner (God) puts his vineyard (Israel) in the hands of tenants (the Jews), and at times sends his servants (the prophets) to gather his share of the fruit. Yet the tenants attack and kill them. Eventually the owner sends his son, but he is also killed so that the tenants can take squatters' rights. Yet since they are the owner's tenants, the owner will come and destroy them, and give the vineyard to others.

In the Gospel of Matthew the belief that the Jews murdered the prophets evoked hatred and vituperation against official Judaism: "Woe to you, scribes and Pharisees, hypocrites! for you build the tombs of the prophets and adorn the monuments of the righteous, saying, 'If we had lived in the days of our fathers, we would not have taken part with them in shedding the blood of the prophets.' Thus you witness against yourselves that you are sons of those who murdered the prophets. Fill up, then, the measure of your fathers. You serpents, you brood of vipers, how are you to escape being sentenced to hell?" (Matthew 23:29–33). Such accusations illustrate that by the second decade of its mission, the Church had come to believe that the Jews had been repudiated by God. In their place the gentiles had become the true community of Israel, and those who had entered the covenant were no longer under an obligation to keep the Law.

Paul's Mission to the New Israel

For Paul there is no distinction between the circumcised and the uncircumcised: both Jews and gentiles are in the same situation before God. According to Paul, as traditionally interpreted (although this interpretation is now being questioned), the Torah is identical in content with natural law; in this respect both Jews and gentiles know God's will and are equally sinful. Yet since the Jew possesses God's revelation, he is aware of his inadequacies, and in his fallen state he witnesses to the power of sin. Thus Paul declared: "The name of God is blasphemed among the gentiles because of you" (Romans 2:24).

Since Jews and gentiles belong to fallen humanity as represented by the Old Adam, salvation can only come through a new covenant based on Christ. Through the coming of the Messiah human beings can attain a transformed nature that provides for spiritual authenticity. This transformation brings to an end all presumptions of special rights and privileges. Thus confidence in such practices as the food laws, festivals, new moons and Sabbaths must be set aside: "Therefore let no one pass judgement on you in questions of food and drink or with regard to a festival or a new moon or a Sabbath. These are only a shadow of what is to come; but the substance belongs to Christ (Colossians 2:16–17).

For Paul, what is required instead is the circumcision of the heart. This is possible, he believed, only through the power of Christ which does away with the Old Adam. Obedience is not possible under the Mosaic covenant, only through a new covenant involving baptism. Through baptism it is possible to put off the body of flesh, and be raised with Christ (Colossians 2:11–12). Only this new covenant can provide the power to become a living law when God's commands are written on tablets of the human heart (2 Corinthians 3:3).

The distinction between the two types of circumcision is explained further in Paul's discussion of Abraham's children. While Abraham was uncircumcised, God gave him the promise of salvation; thus Abraham is the father of those who attempt to achieve righteousness through faith rather than the Law. In this light he is the father of spiritual Israel, descended by faith in the promises given to him rather than through physical lineage. It is Christ, then, who is his true heir: "Abraham 'believed God, and it was reckoned to him as righteousness.' So you see that it is men of faith who are the sons of Abraham" (Galatians 3:6–7).

Again, in Paul's exegesis of the revelation of the Law on Mount Sinai, the Torah was referred to as the "dispensation of death" – a pale shadow of the dispensation of life available through Christ. Commenting on Exodus 34:29–30, Paul maintained that Moses' veiling his face when teaching the Law demonstrated that the Law expressed the hardening of Israel's heart under the old covenant. The Torah was under the power of unbelief (the veil) which separated us from the glory of God. It is only when an individual turns to the Lord that the veil is removed (2 Corinthians 3:7–18).

For Paul, all who take on the yoke of the Law put themselves under the power of the curse. Christ, however, has freed his followers from such a state through his crucifixion. By hanging on a tree, he took the curse of the Law upon himself. In accordance with the scriptural dictum: "For a hanged man is accursed by God" (Deuteronomy 21:23), "Christ redeemed us from the curse of the law, having become a curse for us – for it is written, 'Cursed be every one who hangs on a tree' – that in Christ Jesus the blessing of Abraham might come upon the gentiles, that we might receive the promise of the Spirit through faith" (Galatians 3:13–14).

In his teaching Paul maintained that the reign of the Torah is synonymous with the domination of demonic powers. Under Jewish law, the people were subject to the elemental spirits of the universe, but through Jesus' death and resurrection, they are free sons of God in Christ. Thus in Galatians Paul urges the community not to return to their former state: "Formerly, when you did not know God, you were in bondage to beings that by nature are no gods; but now that you have come to know God, or rather to be known by God, how can you turn back again to the weak and beggarly elemental spirits, whose slaves you want to be once more?" (Galatians 4:8–10).

In his presentation of the two covenants in Galatians, Paul offers an allegorical interpretation of the two wives of Abraham. Hagar and her offspring symbolize the era of slavery, whereas Sarah and her children belong to the period of freedom. The followers of Christ are the children of Sarah, but those who adhere to the Mosaic covenant are seen as sons and daughters of Hagar. For Paul, Hagar and her children represent Mount Sinai while those who believe in Christ are part of spiritual Jerusalem: "We, brethren, like Isaac," he writes, "are children of promise ... Cast out the slave and her son; for the son of the slave shall not inherit with the son of the free woman" (Galatians 4:28, 30).

The Church then has not simply superseded Judaism; rather the two faiths stand in opposition. Judaism belongs to the realm of fallen Adam, but Christianity fulfils the divine promises recorded in Scripture. Those who are part of the Mosaic covenant will be cast out, but the children of the new covenant will find salvation in Christ. Paul's polemic against the Jews is thus a rejection of the Jewish tradition. The Mosaic covenant belongs to an apostate people – but God's true covenant was given before the revelation on Mount Sinai and is fulfilled with the advent of the Messianic age. Only those who belong to this spiritual community will inherit the divine promises vouchsafed in Scripture.

In Romans 9–11 Paul contends that the true Israel is this spiritual community; it is the Israel of the promise as opposed to the Israel based on lineal descent. Only a remnant from among the Jews are intended for salvation (these individuals are represented by the Jewish Christians), and there is a divine purpose to be found in the reluctance of the Jewish community to accept Jesus as Christ. They have been hardened by God so that the gentiles can be gathered in. But as soon as this ingathering occurs, God will turn their hearts and Christ will return to complete the work of salvation. The eventual conversion of the Jews is thus envisaged by Paul as the final event in the eschatological unfolding of God's plan for humankind.

Anti-Jewish Antitheses in Hebrews and the Gospel of John

In Hebrews the contrast between the new and old covenant is intensified. The new covenant transcends the old – it contains the true inner meaning of what is anticipated in the Mosaic covenant. Here Judaism is understood as mutable in opposition to the Christian message which is eternal. In presenting this view the author of Hebrews argued that the Son of God is superior to the angels who revealed the old covenant. The Christian revelation however was spoken directly by Christ: "In these last days he (God) has spoken to us by a Son, whom he appointed the heir of all things, through whom he created the world' (Hebrews 1:2).

The Torah is thus only a portent of what is to come. All the great personages of the Hebrew Scripture (Abel, Enoch, Noah, Abraham, Sarah, Isaac, Jacob, Joseph, Moses, Joshua, Rehab, the Judges, and the Prophets) testified to the coming of Christ. These figures lived in anticipation of God's promises. "All these, though well attested by their faith, did not receive what was promised, since God had foreseen something better for us, that apart from us they should not be made perfect" (Hebrews 11:39–40). Furthermore, since the ancient Israelites rebelled against Moses, they were not allowed to gain true rest. Such a promise was not to be found in the land of Canaan, but in the Kingdom of God. It is into this eschatological rest that the true people of God shall proceed, whereas the rebellious people of the old covenant will be refused entry: "And to whom did he swear that they should never enter his rest, but to those who were disobedient? So we see that they were unable to enter because of unbelief" (Hebrews 3:18–19).

As far as the Temple cult is concerned, the author argues that Melchizedek represents the true type of eternal priest of Christ in opposition to the Levirite priesthood who are mortal. Cultic sacrifices in the Temple provided no permanent forgiveness, whereas the forgiveness of sins offered through Christ's sacrifice is once and for all: "He has no need, like those high priests, to offer sacrifices daily, first for his own sins and then for those of the people; he did this once for all when he offered up himself" (Hebrews 7:27). The reign of Temple sacrifice thus belongs to the temporal sphere which is passing away – its sanctuary was only a copy of the heavenly sanctuary. As the eternal high priest, Christ provides a means of reconciliation, and it is into the inner tent of the heavenly sanctuary that he is leading his true people.

In the Fourth Gospel such a repudiation of Judaism crystallized into an antithesis between a fulfilled spiritual universe of Christ as opposed to a fallen world of darkness represented by the Jews. Jesus is the spiritual Temple in contrast to the Jewish Temple which will be destroyed (John 2:13–22); he is the spiritual water of eternal life rather than the physical water of Jacob's well (John 4:6–15); he is the bread of truth in contrast to the manna of the wilderness that did not last (John 6:41–58). Only through him is access provided to the Father.

Thus only those who know Christ can know God, and apart from the knowledge of Christ, there is no knowledge of God: "I am the way, and the truth, and the life; no one comes to the Father but by me" (John 14:6). Unlike the faithful, the Jews are unbelievers who see and yet fail to believe. They are therefore the incarnation of the false principle of the fallen world. Belonging to alienated existence, their reaction to the Son of God is to plan his murder. They are not of God, but of the devil:

> You are of your father, the devil, and your will is to do your father's desires. He was a murderer from the beginning, and has nothing to do with the truth, because there is no truth in him. When he lies, he speaks according to his own nature, for he is a liar and the father of lies . . . The reason why you do not hear them (God's revealed words in Jesus) is because you are not of God (John 8:44, 47).

According to the Fourth Gospel, Jesus is God's I Am, identified as the one true path to the Father, whose integrity is contrasted with the Jews' murderousness. Because of Jesus' claims, the Jews sought to kill him, and when they turned him over to Pilate they asserted that he must die because he ha blasphemed against God: "When the chief priests and the officers saw him, they cried out: 'Crucify him, crucify him! . . . We have a law, and by that law he ought to die, because he has made himself the Son of God" (John 19:6–7). In this presentation Pilate refused to crucify Jesus under Roman law, and handed him over to the Jews. It is thus the Jewish, rather than the Roman authorities, who are held responsible for his death. In John chapter 15 the writer asserts that as Jesus is in the Father, and the Father is in him, so his disciples abide in Jesus and Jesus in them. The Jews on the other hand represent the demonic order: as they sought to kill Jesus, so they will seek to do the same to all his disciples who manifest his presence in the world. Not surprisingly, such a diatribe against the Jews and the Jewish faith has served as a basis for Christian persecution of the Jews through the centuries.

CHAPTER THREE

The Church Fathers and Jewish Hatred

Following New Testament teaching, the Church Fathers developed an *Adversos Judaeos* tradition which vilified the Jews. According to these writers, just as Jews were guilty in the past of indecency, so they have continued to be a lawless and dissolute people. For this reason all future promises apply solely to the Church. Appealing to Scripture, the Fathers attempted to demonstrate that the conflict between the Church and the Synagogue was prefigured in Scripture. Separated from the Christian message of salvation, the Jews have been rejected and are subject to God's wrath. It is the Christian community (rather than the Jews) who constitute the elect. This is the culmination of the messianic vision of the ingathering of all people to Zion. The Christian faith, as the religion of the Roman Empire, serves as the vehicle for bringing God's redemption to humanity, but the Jews are to suffer rejection and misery because of their unwillingness to accept Jesus as the Messiah. Destined to wander in exile, they find no peace. Jewish law has thus been superseded through Christ's death, and it is now the Christian faith alone which offers salvation to the world.

The Iniquity of the Jews

The New Testament served as the basis for the Patristic *Adversos Judaeos* tradition that flourished from the second to the sixth century. This literary form embraced treatises, sermons, discourses and other Christian writings which sought to demonstrate that the Jews had been rejected by God. Such anti-Jewish sentiment was based on the claim that the Jews had refused to accept Christ. According to the Church Fathers this was not a single act of apostasy; rather the Jews have always been an apostate nation. The Patriarchs, as ancestors of the Church, were virtuous but with the Egyptian sojourn the Hebrews engaged in various types of evil activity. The purpose of the Mosaic Law was to curb such depravity. Thus all the crimes forbidden in the Torah mirror the Israelites' lifestyle. In his writings John Chrysostom asserted that Jews in Egypt built a brothel there, made love with the barbarians and worshipped foreign gods.

After the Israelites had escaped from Egyptian captivity, they assumed their idolatrous ways in the desert. According to the Fathers of the early Church, the Hebrews' worship of the golden calf was typical of Jewish idolatry. Thus Prudentius wrote in *Apotheosis* that such worship was due to the deafness of the Jews to God's word. By giving over their earrings to fashion a golden idol, they had impaired their hearing: "Have these truths soaked into the ears of the Jews? . . . All the trappings have vanished from their ears and gone to fashion a cast head of Baal, robbing their ears of the honour."

Once in the Promised Land, the nation continued such idolatrous behaviour. In the words of Tertullian in *An Answer to the Jews*; "According to the divine Scriptures the people of the Jews quite forsook God and did degrading service to idols and, abandoning the Divinity, surrendered to images . . . In later times, in which the kings were governing them, they did again worship golden kine and graves and enslave themselves to Baal." In the fourth century, Ephrem in *Rhythm Against the Jews* accused the Jews of idolatry, contending that the persecution of Christ was prefigured in previous times:

> What is thine iniquity, O Daughter of Jacob, that thy chastisement is so severe? Thou hast dishonoured the King and the King's Son; thou shameless one and harlot! The King was dishonoured in the wilderness and the King's Son in Jerusalem. The Father was exchanged for the calf and for sundry similitudes, and the Son was exchanged for a thief and a blood-shedder. And the Spirit of the Lord they did vex among strange nations. The Trinity that was old she despised and behaved herself madly, and loved vain gods and devils and fortunes and images.

In Patristic sources the Jews were also accused of blaspheming against God's nature, resisting his spirit, and engaging in sensual practices. Chrysostom in *Eight Orations Against the Jews* linked such sensuality with the rejection of God: "As an animal when it has been fattened by getting all it wants to eat, gets stubborn and hard to manage, so it was with the Jewish people. Reduced by gluttony and drunkenness to a state of utter depravity, they frisked about and would not accept Christ's yoke." In contrast with Christian asceticism, Jews indulged the vices of the flesh. For Ephrem the synagogue was a harlot – she was cast off because "she was wanton between the legs". In Aphrahat's *Demonstrations Against the Jews* Jerusalem was equated with Sodom and Gomorrah. John Damascene declared in *On the Sabbath, Against the Jews* that the Sabbath was given to the Jews because of their grossness and propensity for material things. In addition a number of polemicists asserted that the Jews were guilty of infanticide. Thus Chrysostom portrayed the ancient Israelites as debauchers and idolators who sacrificed their sons and daughters to demons and even ate their own children. Such a conception of the Jews justified God's rejection of the Hebrew nation. In the third century Hippolytus in *Expository Treatise Against the Jews* summarized their fall from divine grace:

> Why was the Temple made desolate? Was it on account of the ancient fabrication of the calf? Or was it on account of the idolatry of the people? Was it for the blood of the prophets? Was it for the adultery and fornication of Israel? By no means, for in all these transgressions they always found pardon open to them. But it was because they killed the son of their Benefactor, for He is coeternal with the Father.

The previous crimes which characterized the ancient Hebrews were said to have continued to the present day. Just as the Jews were responsible in past times, so they were equally guilty of iniquity in contemporary circumstances. In his sermons Chrysostom emphasized that the Jews continued to be a lawless and dissolute race, destined to evoke God's wrath. With venom he depicted the Jewish community of his own age:

> The synagogue is not only a whorehouse and a theatre; it is also a den of thieves and a haunt of wild animals . . . not the cave of a wild animal merely, but of an unclean wild animal . . . The Jews have no conception of things at all, but living for the lower nature, all agog for the here and now, no better disposed than pigs or goats, they live by the rule of

debauchery and inordinate gluttony. Only one thing they understand: to gorge themselves and to get drunk.

For Chrysostom and other writers of this period the Jews were not human beings – they were demons incarnate, an apostate and immoral nation who have been cast off by God into utter darkness.

The Jews and the Future Church

According to the early Church, prophetic denunciations in the Bible against iniquity applied to the Jewish people, whereas all future promises related to the Church. Given such an interpretation, Scripture contains a catalogue of Jewish wickedness. In his *Tract Against the Jews* Augustine maintained that the Jewish people are incapable of understanding the true nature of the Bible: they believe the divine promises apply to the Jewish nation. But, Augustine asserted, the Jews are in fact the enemies of God. Accordingly, when the prophets declared that God has cut off the House of Israel, such pronouncements referred to the Jews. But when Israel was described in positive terms, these statements applied to the Christian Church.

Thus both the apostate Jews and the universal Church were anticipated in the Hebrew Scriptures. Those who are righteous belong to the Christian community, while the Jews are the enemies referred to in the Psalms and the Suffering Servant passages in Isaiah. In formulating this view, Christian exegetes viewed the account of Jacob and Esau as prefiguring these two religious groups. Genesis records that "When her (Rebekah's) days to be delivered were fulfilled, behold, there were twins in her womb . . . and two peoples, born of you, shall be divided; the one shall be stronger than the other, the elder shall serve the younger" (Genesis 25:23–24). Here "the elder" refers to the Jews who would serve "the younger", namely the Church.

In *Contra Judaeos*, Maximinus formulated a series of similar sibling rivalries which prefigure the Jewish/Christian conflict. Heading this list was Cain who symbolizes the Jews, whereas Abel (who was killed by his brother) represents Christ. Similarly Tertullian argued that God rejected the bloody sacrifices of the Law (the Jewish sacrificial system) while accepting spiritual worship of the Church. In Aphrahat's writings the statement in John 8:44, "Your father was a murderer from the beginning", was identified with Cain. Ephrem also identified the Jews with Cain: "Today the glory has passed from the people of Israel and they stand among the nations ashamed as Cain was, at the unnatural deed." In the fourth century, Prudentius maintained that the Jew was the murderous brother who now wanders the face of the earth: "From place to place the homeless Jew wanders in ever-shifting exile, since the time when he was torn from the abode of his fathers and has been suffering the penalty for murder and having stained his hands with the blood of Christ whom he denied, paying the price of sin."

This antithesis was also applied to the two wives of Abraham (Sarah and Hagar) as well as Jacob's two wives (Rachel and Leah). As we have seen, Paul viewed the children of Sarah as the true Christian Israel whereas he believed the Jews were the children of the slave woman. Following this interpretation, Augustine argued that the Jews are a carnal people as against the Christians who are spiritual. Hagar was the fallen Jerusalem, bound in servitude to Sarah's offspring who belonged to the heavenly realm. A parallel analogy was drawn by Cyprian in his *Three Books of Testimonies Against the Jews*: "Also Jacob received two wives: the elder Leah, with weak eyes, a type of the Synagogue; the younger, the beautiful Rachel, the type of the Church, who also remained long barren and afterwards brought forth Joseph, who was himself a type of Christ."

According to patristic tradition the Church is the bride of God whereas Israel has been a harlot: she had been given a bill of divorce and sent away. In his *Rhythm Against the Jews*, Ephrem presented a figurative description of this divorce:

> She despised the voice of the prophets and the preaching of the Apostles ... He wrote and delivered to her the divorcement as being rejected and polluted. He took the veil from her head and from her eyes also chastity. He stripped her of her ornaments and doubled back and lifted up her covering. He took her necklace from her neck and took away her bracelets and her armlets and as an adulteress and a harlot he drove her out and sent her forth from his chamber.

Similarly Aphrahat's, referring to Hosea's preaching in Hosea 2:2 ("For she is not my wife, and I am not her husband – that she put away her harlotry from her face, and her adultery from between her breasts"), declared: "Israel has played the whore, and Judah has committed adultery. And the people which is of the peoples (the Christian community) is the holy and faithful people, which has gone down and adhered to the Lord." Such imagery emphasized that God's promises applied not to the Jews but to the future Church. Divorced from the message of forgiveness and hope, the Jews have been rejected and subjected to God's wrath.

Divine Election

In explaining the election of the gentiles, the early Church argued that the Christian community has taken the place of the Jews. This was not conceived simply as a substitution; rather the new Israel was understood as implicit in Scripture. The prophets had insisted that the election of the Jewish nation was only provisional – the covenant has been inherited and fulfilled by those who accepted Jesus as the Messiah. In the past, biblical heroes and prophets prepared the way for this event, but from the beginning the Jewish people continually refused to accept God. Christians on the other hand, constituted a believing community.

In presenting this view, the Church Fathers appealed to the Pauline doctrine that the true sons of Abraham are those who are justified by faith. The descendants of Abraham are thus not the Jews, but the gentiles. In the words of Isaac of Antioch in *Homilies Against the Jews*, the uncircumcised gentiles have taken the place of Israel. Circumcision has ceased to be the mark of election. Instead, figuratively speaking, circumcision was a "seal" on a bag which has been kept for the true inheritors of this treasure. Neither the seal nor the bag now serve any purpose, and the Jews have become the possessors only of an empty container:

> Abraham was stamped like a vessel because of the treasure that was in him. And the seal continued in your generations because of the treasure that was in you (the Jews) until now. Now . . . the treasure has come forth . . . In you it was in custody and was safeguarded, and it was preserved under the stamp. To me it was given for use. Therefore I do not circumcise myself like you . . . O nation. You were the guardians of the riches that were preserved for the generations (the gentile

Church) ... Its rightful owners have taken the trust and you are concerned with the regulations. Unseemly are the seals ... when the garments on which they were are worn out. They were trampled and fell and were cut off.

As in the New Testament, patristic sources interpreted the texts describing Israel as a light to the nations as prophecies about the gentile Church. Conversely Scriptural passages concerning sinful Israel were understood as demonstrating her rejection. The Psalms for example promised the rule of a Davidic king over the nations – these texts were presumed to refer to Christ. The nations to be conquered and converted are gentiles. Such texts as Psalm 2:7–8 ("Thou art my son, this day I have begotten thee; ask of me and I will give the nations as thy inheritance") were read as God's decree to Christ that he would inherit the gentile Church. Prophetic texts concerning God's faithful people were also understood as referring to the gentile Church: "Many and strong peoples shall adhere to the Lord" (Zechariah 2:11); "Those who are not my people I shall call my people" (Hosea 2:23).

Following the New Testament, the Fathers maintained that the election of the gentiles is the culmination of the messianic vision of the ingathering of the nations to Zion. According to Ephrem, the good news of Christ's redemption shall flow from Zion: "I shall open my gates with joy and the hosts of the gentiles shall enter into thee and become in thee an elect people, and the Lord shall reign over Zion and many peoples shall come and worship me in Jerusalem." The Jews, however, despaired because of this rejection: "Then Zion spoke, weeping distractedly. The Lord hath left me because I have provoked him, and God hath forgotten me; yes, he hath rejected me."

Once the Church became the religion of the Roman Empire, the concept of divine election was understood in political terms. The Roman Empire came to be identified with the reign of the Davidic Messiah. Thus Chrysostom identified Christendom with Christ's dominion over the world. Everywhere paganism was overcome by the Church, and this victory was envisaged as Christ's defeat of the demons. With all humanity united in Christ, brotherhood and peace held sway. The same combination of messianism and Roman imperialism was found in Eusebius' *Oration on Constantine*:

As knowledge of the one God and the one way of religion and salvation, even the doctrine of Christ, was made known to all mankind; so at the self same period, the entire dominion of the Roman Empire being vested in a single sovereign, profound peace reigned throughout the world. And thus by the express appointment of the same God, two roots of blessing, the Roman Empire and the doctrine of Christian piety, sprang up together for the benefit of men.

In contrast with this vision of the universal Church, the Jewish dispersion was seen as the result of divine wrath. Jewish suffering in the diaspora was due to God's anger against the Jews. Persecuted Christians on the other hand were viewed as God's beloved servants. They were to be loved because they suffered for Christ, but Christians were to despise those who rejected Christ and brought about his death. In the words of Chrysostom: "The martyrs especially hate the Jews, for the reason that they love so deeply the one who, by them, was crucified. The Jews said, 'His blood be on us and on our children' while the martyrs shed their own blood for him whom they destroyed."

Jewish Rejection and Exile

According to Patristic tradition, the Jewish people were destined to suffer numerous calamities. Because of their refusal to accept Jesus as the Messiah, they were cast out and despised. In his *Demonstrations of the Gospel*, Eusebius wrote that because of the Jews' impiety, their kingdom was utterly destroyed, the Torah abrogated, and their ancient worship uprooted. Their royal metropolis, he wrote, was burned with fire, their holy altar consumed with flames and desolation, their city inhabited no longer by its old possessors. In this process the Jews were dispersed among the gentiles throughout the whole world with "never a hope of any cessation of evil or breathing space from troubles." The Jews were thus misguided in continuing to observe Jewish law since the Temple, the priesthood, and the sacrificial system have been eliminated.

For the Christian community on the other hand, non-cultic worship was regarded as the culmination of the spiritual development predicted by Malachi: "Oh, that there were one among you who would shut the doors, that you might not kindle fire upon my altar in vain! I have no pleasure in you, says the Lord of hosts, and I will not accept an offering from your hand" (Malachi 1:10). Identifying Judaism with the cult, the Church saw the destruction of the Temple as a sign of God's disfavour. The Jewish nation had become exiled, and the observance of ancient festivals in the diaspora was viewed by Christians as a violation of God's law. In light of this teaching, Chrysostom vilified the synagogue – to go there was no better than visiting a brothel, a robber's den, or any indecent place:

> For if their place of worship was a den of robbers in those days, when what pertains to their way of life still prevailed, if a person should call it a brothel today, or a criminals' hangout, or a resort of demons, or a citadel of the Devil, or the ruin of souls, or a cliff and a pit of complete destruction, or any other name whatever, he would speak more kindly than the place deserves.

In their writings the Church Fathers utilized the Book of Daniel to demonstrate that the Jews were to endure various captivities. Both the Egyptian and Babylonian captivities were limited in time, but there will be no future liberation from the exile of the Jews after their refusal to accept Christ – no Messiah will deliver them from their wandering. As Hippolytus explained in *Expository Treatise Against the Jews*:

> For now that the true light has arisen, ye wander as in the night and stumble on places with no roads and fall headlong, as having forsaken the way that says, "I am the Way". Furthermore hear this yet more serious word: "And their back do thou bend down always." That means, in order that they may be slaves to the nations, not four hundred and thirty years, as in Egypt, or seventy years, as in Babylonia, but bend them to servitude, he says, always.

Chrysostom argued that the Jews will be crucified throughout history because they crucified Christ: "It is because you killed Christ. It is because you stretched out your hand against the Lord. It is because you shed the precious blood, that there is now no restoration, no mercy any more, and no defence . . . This is why you are being punished worse now than in the past." Again, in *Demonstrations of the Gospel*, Eusebius contended that the rejection of the Jews was due to their own hard-heartedness:

Therefore the Jews, because they rejected the Prophet and did not harken to his holy words, have suffered extreme ruin, according to his prediction. For they neither received the Law of Christ of the New Covenant, nor were they able to keep the commands of Moses without some breach of his Law, and so they feel under the curse of Moses, in not being able to carry out what was ordained by him; being exiled from their mother city, which was destroyed, where alone it was allowed to celebrate Mosaic worship.

According to some writers, circumcision was given to the Jews as a sign of Cain. Thus Justin Martyr wrote in *Dialogue with Trypho* that "Circumcision according to the flesh, which is from Abraham, was given for a sign, that you alone may suffer that which you now justly suffer, and that your land may be desolate and your cities burned with fire, and that strangers may eat your fruit in your presence and not one of you may go up to Jerusalem." As wandering figures – homeless and reviled by God and man – the Jews lack any means of salvation. Jewish misery thus bears testimony to God's wrath which has fallen upon those who refuse to accept Christ. The only hope for this reprobate people is to recognize that the Christian community constitutes the true Israel and become members of the Church. In this regard Augustine argued (following Paul's teaching in Romans 9–11) that Jews must repent the error of their ways and embrace the true faith; it is only by becoming followers of Christ that they can be saved.

The Fulfilment of the Law

According to the Church Fathers, Jewish law and the Temple cult are intrinsically unworthy and have become obsolete in the light of Christ's redemption. Christians are thus under no obligation to keep the biblical prescriptions. In his Epistle, Diognetus emphasized that Jewish practices have no efficacy:

> As for those who think that they can offer him sacrifices with blood and fat and holocausts . . . they differ in nothing, so it seems to me, from those who show the same devotion to deaf idols . . . Is it not ridiculous to boast of a mutilation of the flesh as a sign of the chosen people, as though they were particularly loved by God? . . . I have said enough to show you

how the Christians are right in keeping away from the plain silliness and error, the fussiness and vaunting of the Jews.

In patristic sources the concept of a pre-Mosaic religion plays a significant role. According to Eusebius, during the pre-Mosaic era human beings were naturally virtuous. The Patriarchs were thus not Jews, but simply members of the human race who were virtuous without being bound by legal restrictions. In place of a code of law, they were motivated by the law of conscience – that which is universal in scope. This spiritual religion has now become available to all peoples through Christ. It is not a new covenant, but rather the restoration of the original religion of the Patriarchal period. Within this framework the Ten Commandments should be understood as the basic law of God, whereas Mosaic legislation is temporary, given only to the Jewish nation.

Legislation in the Pentateuch was therefore designed for an intermediate period – from Moses to Christ – and is of an inferior status than Patriarchal faith. Its purpose is punitive rather than redemptive, and was intended to elevate the Jews from the state of moral decay into which they had fallen in Egypt. In the words of Chrysostom: "And this is what God did. He saw the Jews raving mad, choking themselves in their lust for sacrifices, and ready if they didn't get them to desert to idolatry ... then it was that he permitted sacrifices." Similarly the Sabbath was instituted to restrain the Jews' lust for material gain. Further, circumcision was prescribed to separate the Jews from those who practised idolatry.

Jewish law has thus been superseded by a new dispensation. Christians are the true keepers of God's law of inward obedience. In place of Moses, Christ is the new lawgiver. By following scriptural legislation the Jewish community misconstrued God's intention, acted against his will, and have become a lawless nation. Christians, on the other hand, are liberated from the Law's outward practices and are able to interpret its inner meaning. Through their repentance, they have circumcised the heart. According to Isaac of Antioch, Joshua's stone knives, by which God commanded him to circumcise the people of Israel a second time, signify the circumcision of Jesus – this symbolizes a circumcision of the heart of Christians rather than the flesh. Dietary laws are likewise dealt with. They were initially given to Israel to restrain them from gluttony, but their real meaning is internal.

Similarly cultic observances were seen as irrelevant. In support of this view, the Church cited numerous prophetic utterances condemning formal worship: "I hate, I despise your feasts, and I take no delight in your solemn assemblies" (Amos 5:21); "What to me is the multitude of your sacrifices? says the Lord; I have enough of burnt offerings . . . Incense is an abomination to me. I cannot endure your new moons and Sabbaths and assemblies" (Isaiah 1:11–13). Temple sacrifice thus does not fulfil God's will, and the destruction of the Temple confirmed this judgement. As Chrysostom explained: "After permitting them to offer sacrifices, he allowed them to do so nowhere else in the world except in Jerusalem. Then after they had offered sacrifices for a short time, he destroyed the city. God intended by demolishing the city to lead the Jews away from the practice in spite of themselves."

What is now required is the sacrifice of the heart. Christian spiritual worship thus supersedes cultic observance. The true faith is the spiritual Temple of the Holy Spirit found in each believer and also within the body of the Church. As far as the priesthood is concerned, the priests of Christ are superior to the Aaronite priests, and the Eucharist is identified with the spiritual worship of bread and wine offered by Melchizedek. As Chrysostom explained, the priests of Melchizedek have now taken the place of those who officiated in the Temple: "'If perfection had been attainable through the Levitical priesthood . . . what further need would there have been for another priest to arise after the order of Melchizedek (Hebrews 7:11) rather than the one after the order of Aaron?' It is clear from this that the former priesthood had come to an end and a different one, very much better and more sublime, had been introduced in its place."

In expounding this interpretation of the Christian supersession of Judaism, the Fathers stressed that they possessed the correct understanding of Scripture. The Jews, however, are blind to its true meaning. They are incapable of seeing the Christological implications of God's Word. This is due in part to Jewish literalism, for Jews are incapable of discerning the inner meaning of Scripture. In the words of Irenaeus (second century): "Therefore the Jews departed from God, in not receiving his Word, but imagining that they could know the Father apart by himself, without the Word, that is, without the Son; they being ignorant of that God who spake in human shape to Abraham and again to Moses."

Christ is the incarnation of God's Word – it is he whom the Jews have never known, since they have preferred the exegesis of the Scribes and Pharisees to the direct word of the Bible. Rabbinic hermeneutics thus constitutes the veil over the Scriptural text; it induces blindness and leads the Jews astray. According to Augustine, the Jews are a carnal people and belong on a lower level of existence. Jewish teachings and customs are thus useless; they belong to Israel after the flesh in opposition to spiritual Israel, the Church: all that is Jewish has been set aside now that Christ has come.

CHAPTER FOUR

Medieval Persecutions, Ritual Murder and the Talmud

The tradition of anti-Semitism created by the Fathers of the Church continued into the Middle Ages. During the centuries of the Crusades Jews were massacred throughout western Europe. Although some Christian leaders condemned such barbarism, the masses continued to attack those who stubbornly clung to the Jewish faith. Christian hostility was further intensified by a number of charges levelled against the Jewish population. Repeatedly Jews were accused of murdering Christian children to incorporate their blood into unleavened bread for Passover; such allegations of ritual murder spread from country to country and many Jews were victimized for supposedly committing such atrocious acts. Jews were also accused of blaspheming the Christian faith in their sacred literature, and as a consequence copies of the Talmud were burned. In addition, the Jewish population was blamed for causing the Black Plague by poisoning wells. Those who perished in the Christian onslaught as a result of these allegations prayed for vengeance. In faithfulness to God, these martyrs went to their deaths confident that Christians would suffer eternal torment for their sins.

Western Jewry in the Middle Ages

The Byzantine tradition of anti-Semitism, which was established by the Fathers of the Church, laid the foundation for future anti-Jewish hostility in the Christian West. Little is known about Jewish–Christian relations in the Roman period, but in later centuries Church Councils promulgated decrees governing relations with the Jewish community. In the fifth and sixth centuries the Church issued legislation (as contained in the *Codex Theodosianus* and the Justinian Code) which denied Jews numerous rights. Repeatedly Church officials warned against the pernicious influence of the Jewish population, and at times attempted to convert them by force.

In the ninth century Archbishop Agobard of Lyons wrote a number of anti-Jewish epistles in which he expressed alarm about Christian contact with those of the Jewish faith. "No matter how kindly we treat them," he stated "we do not succeed in drawing them to the purity of our spiritual faith. On the contrary, several among us, willingly sharing with them the food of the body, have also allowed themselves to be seduced by their spiritual nourishment . . . Labourers and peasants are inveigled into such a sea of errors that they regard the Jews as the only people of God, so that only among them is to be found the observance of a pure religion and of a faith far more certain than our own." In consequence, Agobard formulated a series of remedies to protect Christians from Jews and Judaism. His successor Amolon reiterated these restrictions: "I have twice publicly asked that our faithful draw aside from them, that no Christian serve them either in the cities or in the villages, letting them perform their labour with the help of their pagan slaves; I have also forbidden the eating of their food and the drinking of their liquors."

Shortly after the year 1000, rumours began to circulate in Christian lands about the "Prince of Babylon" who had brought about the destruction of the Holy Sepulchre in Jerusalem and the persecution of Christians at the instigation of the Jews. In response, princes, bishops and townsfolk sought revenge against the Jewish population, and attacks took place in Rouen, Orléans, Limoges, Mainz and elsewhere. Jews were converted by force or massacred. At the end of the eleventh century, Pope Urban II preached the First Crusade at the Council of Clermont-Ferrand. As Christian knights, monks and commoners set out on their holy mission, they took revenge on Jewish infidels living in Christian lands.

In the Rhine valley, where Jewish communities were probably the most numerous in Europe, the most horrendous massacres took place. As bands led by French and German lords swept through the Rhineland, Jews were mercilessly slaughtered. A first massacre took place at Speyer on 3 May 1096; when news of this event reached Worms the Jewish community took refuge in their own homes and in the palace of the Bishop. Yet there was no way they could escape slaughter and death. These terrible events were recorded by the Jewish chronicler Solomon bar Simeon. "The terror fell upon those who were living in the episcopal palace," he wrote. "The foe killed them even as the others, putting them to the sword." None the less a number of these Jews sought to kill themselves as martyrs rather than be put to death by the Christians:

> They fulfilled the words of the prophet: "The mothers are laid upon their children, and fathers fell upon their sons." This one killed his brother, that one his parents, his wife, and his children; the betrothed killed each other, even as the mothers killed the children. All accepted with a full heart the Divine verdict ... The enemies stripped them naked and dragged them off, granting quarter to none, save those few who accepted baptism.

Several days later the Jews of Mainz were attacked and attempted to defend themselves. The Christian chronicler Albert of Aix described these horrific events:

> Having broken the locks and knocked in the doors, they seized and killed seven hundred who vainly sought to defend themselves against forces far superior to their own; the women were also massacred, and the young children, whatever their sex, were put to the sword. The Jews, seeing the Christians rise as enemies against them and their children, with no respect for the weakness of age, took arms in turn against their co-religionists, against their wives, their children, their mothers, and their sisters, and massacred their own. A horrible thing to tell of – the mothers seized the sword, cut the throats of the children at their breast, choosing to destroy themselves with their own hands rather than to succumb to the blows of the uncircumcised.

Although bishops and noblemen protected the Jews in various cities where they were under threat, Jewish communities throughout Europe were besieged and thousands of Jews lost their lives in this onslaught. Despite these massacres, European Jewry was able to resume their former existence in the following decades. However in 1146 Pope Eugenius III and St Bernard of Clairvaux preached a new Crusade which was accompanied by anti-Jewish sentiment. Incidents took place in Cologne, Speyer, Mainz and Würzburg in Germany, and in Carentan, Ramerupt, and Sully in France. Later in the twelfth century the Third Crusade led to massacres in London, York, Norwich,

Stamford and Lynn. Twenty years afterwards, during the Albigensian Crusade, persecutions took place in the Midi. In 1236, when a further Crusade was preached, massacres also took place in western France, England, and Spain as depicted by the Benedictine Dom Lobineau:

> There were few lords who in the first fervour of the preaching did not find the Cross light to bear; but to many it became a burden thereafter. To remedy this discomfort, they were permitted to renounce the vow they had made to serve against the Infidel ... The greatest and the first expedition of these crusaders was to massacre the Jews, who were not the cause of the evils which the Saracens were inflicting upon the Christians in the East.

In the next century such fanaticism led to uprisings in the abortive Crusade of 1309 in Cologne, the Low Countries, and Brabant; this was followed by the Shepherds' Crusade in the Midi in 1320 as well as outbreaks in Bordeaux, Toulouse, Albi, and Spain.

Persecution and Christian Opinion

A number of chroniclers of the eleventh century mentioned these massacres of the Jews by crusading Christians. An annalist from Würzburg described such events with detachment: "An enormous host coming from all regions and all nations, went in arms unto Jerusalem and obliged the Jews to be baptized, massacring by thousands those who refused. Near Mainz 1,014 Jews, men, women, and children, were slaughtered, and the greatest part of the city burned." Other chroniclers expressed their approval of such actions. In the words of the monk Bernhold, "While the Crusaders awaited their reply without, the Jews (of Worms), tempted by the Devil and under the rule of their own obduracy, killed themselves in the apartments of the bishop." Again the Chronicler Fruitolf contemptuously reported: "In the villages they traversed, the latter (the Crusaders) killed or forced baptism upon what remained of those impious Jews, who are truly enemies which the Church tolerates in its bosom. Of these there were a certain number that returned to Judaism, even as dogs to their own vomit."

Despite such reactions, there were some Christian leaders who condemned this barbarism. Thus the monk Hugon wrote: "It may, forsooth, appear wonderful that in a single day but one massacre animated by the same mystical fervour can have taken place in numerous places." Yet, he continued, "this occurred despite the fact that the clergy was hostile to it and despite the sentences of excommunication by many ecclesiastics and the threats of numerous princes." In an anonymous Saxon chronicle, the author referred to the Crusaders who devastated Jewry as the enemies of mankind. "They lost no time," he wrote, "sowing tares among the wheat, raising up false prophets, mingling untrue brothers and licentious women with the army of Christ. By their hypocrisy, by their lies, by their impious corruptions, they caused dissension in the army of the Lord . . . They decided to avenge Christ upon the pagans and the Jews. This is why they killed 900 Jews in the city of Mainz without sparing the women and children . . . Indeed, it was pitiful to see the great and many heaps of bodies that were carried out of the city of Mainz on carts."

Although Christian opinion was divided about the massacres of the Jewish population, these events tended to inflame public hostility and led to the deterioration of the status of Jews in medieval Europe. Such a situation was reflected in inspirational religious works of this period in which Jews were vilified. For example in one text, Jews are presented in the most negative terms:

> More bestial than naked beasts
> Are all Jews, without a doubt . . .
> Many hate them, as do I
> And God hates them, as well I wist,
> And everyone must hate them indeed.

A number of these literary works condemn Judaism and advocate conversion to Christianity. Thus in *Desputoison de la Sinagogue et de Sainte Église*, a Jew describes his desire to convert:

> Our foolish hope was in vain,
> And expectation has deceived us,
> Waiting for one who has not come,
> But Messiah has come: I shall be baptized
> And renounce my wicked sect.

The Crusades and their aftermath thus brought into focus Christian contempt for the Jews who stubbornly clung to their ancestral faith. These were the villainous figures of the New Testament, the people castigated by the Church Fathers. Their only salvation was to turn from their foolish ways and embrace the true faith – either willingly or through force.

Ritual Murder

Although the early Church did not accuse the Jewish community of committing murder for magical purposes, in the twelfth century this accusation appeared in various places. In its final form Jews were charged with murdering Christian children to incorporate their blood in the preparation of unleavened bread for the Passover. The first case of such ritual murder took place in 1144 in Norwich, England. The body of a young apprentice was discovered on the evening of Good Friday in a wood; it was rumoured that he had been killed by Jews in imitation of Christ's passion. According to tradition, this murder had been planned by a meeting of rabbis which took place at Narbonne. Although the Church authorities attempted to protect the Jewish population, riots took place and a leading Jewish figure was killed by a knight who was his debtor. This case eventually gave rise to a local cult, and the relics of the murdered child (St William) became the goal of pilgrimage. The next case occurred in Würzburg in 1147, during the Second Crusade, when the body of a Christian was found and Jews of the city were blamed for his death.

Three years later a different allegation appeared: Jews were censured for profaning the Host. Thus Jean d'Outremeuse, the chronicler of Liége, alleged that

> in this year, it happened at Cologne that the son of a converted Jew went on Easter day to church, in order to receive the body of God, along with the others; he took it into his mouth and quickly bore it to his house; but when he returned from the church, he grew afraid and in his distress made a hole in the earth and buried the Host within it; but a priest came along, opened the hole, and in it found the shape of a child, which he intended to bear to the church; but there came from the sky a great light, the child was raised out of the priest's hands and borne up to heaven.

Although accusations of ritual murder were infrequent at first, several cases took place in England at the end of the twelfth century, and subsequently the allegation spread to the continent. In 1171 at Blois, thirty-eight Jews were burned at the stake; in 1191 the number reached a hundred at Bray-sur-Seine. This was followed in the next century by numerous cases, and eventually the Emperor Frederick II convened a group of dignitaries to determine the truth of this allegation. When the nobles and clergy were unable to reach a conclusion, he turned to converted Jews for an answer. Converts from the cities of the empire travelled to his court and pronounced that there was nothing in the Hebrew Scriptures or the Talmud to support the claim that the Jews used blood for ritual purposes. On the contrary, Jewish law forbids such an act. As a result of this investigation, the Emperor attempted to acquit the Jews of this charge, and in 1247 Innocent IV promulgated a bull related to this issue.

> Although the Holy Scriptures enjoin the Jews: "Thou shalt not kill" and forbid them to touch any dead body at Passover, they are wrongly accused of partaking of the heart of a murdered child at the Passover, with the charge that this is prescribed by their laws, since the truth is completely the opposite. Whenever a corpse is found somewhere, it is to the Jews that the murder is wickedly imputed. They are persecuted on the pretext of such fables or of others quite similar.

Despite such a pronouncement, accusations of ritual murder and the profanation of the Host continued to circulate. In 1272 another Papal Bull was promulgated to stem the tide of hostility. According to this Bull (of Gregory X), Christians fabricate false charges against Jews to provoke hatred and violence.

> It happens sometimes that Christians lose their children and that the enemies of the Jews accuse them of having kidnapped and killed these children in order to offer sacrifices with their heart and blood, and it also happens that the parents themselves, or other Christians who are enemies to the Jews, hide the children and attack the Jews, demanding of them, as ransom, a certain sum of money, on the entirely false pretext that these children had been kidnapped and killed by the Jews.

Although such Papal decrees were designed to protect Jews from attack, Christians actively pursued the Jewish population. In Brussels, for example, Jews were accused of profaning the Host in 1370. In consequence twenty Jews were burned at the stake, two commemorative chapels were constructed in the next century, and a religious festival was instituted in the capital. Similarly Jews were accused of ritual murder at Trent in the Tyrol in 1473 – nine Jews were tortured, confessed to killing a boy, and executed. Subsequently several trials for ritual murder took place in Austria and Italy, followed by expulsions and *autos-da-fé*.

Jews during this period were thus victimized for atrocious acts even though Church authorities decreed that these charges were groundless. By libelling the Jews in this manner, the Jewish community was portrayed as sadistic, thirsting for Christian blood. Such allegations inflamed the hatred of the Christian masses, encouraged Jews to be seen as cruel murderers, and persuaded gentiles to view them as subhuman beings. Not surprisingly the Nazis revived this myth in the twentieth century in their quest to illustrate that the Jewish population was a cancerous growth on the healthy body of the Aryan race.

The Badge and the Talmud

In 1215, the Fourth Lateran Council promulgated a series of decrees affecting the Jewish community. Nearly 1,500 Churchmen from throughout the Christian world endorsed the decisions taken by Pope Innocent III. Regarding Jewish clothing, the Council stated:

> In the countries where Christians do not distinguish themselves from Jews ... it is decreed that henceforth Jews of both sexes will be distinguished from other peoples by their garments, as moreover has been prescribed unto them by Moses. They will not show themselves in public during Holy Week, for some among them on these days wear their finest garments and mock the Christians clad in mourning. Trespassers will be duly punished by the secular powers, in order that they no longer dare flout Christ in the presence of Christians.

The enforcement of such provisions differed from country to country. In France a circular badge of yellow cloth was worn. From the thirteenth to the fourteenth centuries, twelve Councils and nine Royal Decrees insisted on the strict observance of this law. In 1361, when

King John the Good recalled the Jews to France after their exile, he ordered them to wear an insignia which was half red and half white. In Germany a particular type of hat was worn rather, than a badge of clothing; texts from the fourteenth and fifteenth centuries refer to this hat as red and yellow, but in the following centuries a badge took its place. In Poland Jews were required to wear a pointed green hat, whereas in England stripes of cloth were sewn across the chest, often in the shape of Tablets of Law. In Spain and Italy an insignia was worn. These various distinguishing marks impressed on the minds of gentiles the differences between Christians and Jews, encouraging Jews to be regarded as a different species from ordinary humans.

During this period the newly instituted Inquisition, under the control of the Dominicans, was charged with the responsibility of eliminating all heretical views. The Dominicans were anxious to uproot all heresies, and they took an active interest in Jewish doctrine. At the beginning of the thirteenth century, these protectors of Church orthodoxy were disturbed that Aristotelian concepts had penetrated into European thought through Arabic and Jewish translations. In 1210 and 1215 the Church condemned Aristotle's *Physics* and *Metaphysics*, and in 1228 Pope Gregory IX forbade contact with Greek philosophy. In the Jewish world similar hostility was levelled toward Aristotelianism, and Maimonides' *Guide for the Perplexed* (based on Aristotelian ideas) was burned. Such antipathy to philosophical speculation provoked two rabbis (Solomon ben Abraham and Jonah Gerondi) to unite forces with the Dominicans of Montpellier. Addressing the Church authorities, they asked: "Why do you pay no attention to our heretics and our atheists corrupted by the doctrine of Moses of Egypt (Moses Maimonides), author of impious works? Since you are uprooting your heresies, uproot ours as well, and order the burning of the wicked books."

As a result of such entreaties, the Inquisition took an interest in Jewish sources, particularly the Talmud. An apostate of Judaism, Nicholas Donin (who had become a Dominican brother of la Rochelle) travelled to Rome to inform Pope Gregory IX that the Talmud contains blasphemies against the Christian faith. As a consequence the Pope urged the kings of France, England, Castile and Aragon to investigate this claim. In France, Louis IX initiated such an investigation, and throughout the country copies of the Talmud were confiscated. In 1240 a public debate was held in Paris between Eudes de Châteauroux (the Chancellor of the Sorbonne) and Nicholas Donin, representing Christianity, and Yehiel of Paris and Moses of Coucy on the Jewish side. Among the questions posed were: Did Simeon ben Yohai declare that the best of the *goyim* should be seized? Is it true that a *goy* who rests on the Sabbath or studies the law should be killed? Does the Talmud state that Jesus was an illegitimate child and that he will be condemned in Hell? In response, Jewish scholars countered such queries with quotations from Jewish sources, endeavouring to show that Judaism espouses a tolerant attitude toward Christians and Christianity. Yet as a result of this disputation, the Talmud was condemned and burned. Without success the Jewish community attempted to rehabilitate the Talmud – in 1248 a second commission (headed by the Dominican Albert the Great), confirmed the verdict of the first debate, arousing further animosity toward the Jewish population. Such anti-Jewish sentiment is reflected in *minnesingers* of the period such as Konrad von Würzburg:

> Woe to the cowardly Jews, deaf and wicked,
> Who have no care to save themselves from the sufferings of hell.
> The Talmud has corrupted them and made them lose their honour.
> It would be well to forbid their heretical Talmud,
> A false and ignoble book.

Again, an anonymous poet declared:

> They have fallen so low,
> For Gamaliel has taught them
> The heretical Talmud
> Whose false sayings
> Conceal from them the true faith.

In France the *Desputoison de la Sinagogue et de Sainte Église* echoed the events of 1240. In this work the author represented Jews as poisoners of the body and the mind. Thus in these centuries Christians continued to persecute the Jews for imagined crimes against Christianity. Isolated from the gentile masses, they were regarded with contempt, hostility, and fear.

The Black Plague and the Jewish Response

From 1347 to 1350 the Black Plague destroyed one third of Europe's population. According to Boccaccio's account:

> In the cities, men fell sick by thousands, and lacking care and aid, almost all died. In the morning their bodies were found at the doors of the houses where they had expired during the night . . . It reached the point where no further account was taken of a dying man than is today taken of the merest cattle. Nor were the villages spared. Lacking the succour of a physician, without the aid of any servant, the poor and wretched farmers perished with their families by day, by night, on their farms, in their isolated houses, on the roads, and even in their fields. Then they abandoned their customs, even as the city dwellers: they no longer took any concern for their affairs nor for themselves; all, expecting to die from one day to the next, thought neither of working nor of putting by the fruits of their past labours, but sought rather to consume what they had before them.

This catastrophe was the last in the chain of events affecting the Jewish community. According to medieval scholars, the plague was due to an unfavourable conjunction of the planets as well as the pollution of the air and poisoning of the waters. For ordinary persons, however, it was seen as a divine punishment, or the act of Satan who was in league with the Jews. In Savoy, Jacob Pascal of Toledo was accused of distributing deadly drugs to co-religionists in Chambéry. As a result of this charge, Jews were arrested at Thonon, Chillon and Le Châtelard, and confessed under torture. From Savoy the legend spread to Switzerland, where various executions took place. None the less, in Germany princes and magistrates attempted to protect the Jewish population, and in 1348 Pope Clement VI issued a bull which called into question this allegation. Despite this intervention, Germans continued to massacre Jews in Colmar, Worms, Oppenheim, Frankfurt, Erfurt, Cologne and Hanover. Jews were also attacked for religious reasons. Bands of flagellants wandered throughout Germany and France, mortifying themselves in order to avert God's wrath. Such exhibitions frequently culminated in the massacre of the Jewish population. As the chronicler Jean d'Outremeuse explained:

The good cities were full of these Flagellants, and the streets as well . . . they began to forget the service and ritual of the Holy Church, and maintained in their folly and their presumption that their rites and their songs were finer and more worthy than the ceremonies of the priests and clerics . . . In the time when these Flagellants went among the countries . . . it was commonly said and certainly believed that this epidemic came from the Jews, and that the Jews had cast great poisons in the wells and springs throughout the world, in order to sow the plague and poison Christendom; which was why great and small alike had great choler against the Jews, who were everywhere taken where they could be held, and put to death and burned in all the regions where the Flagellants came and went.

In Germany it was widely believed that the Jews were immune to the plague. None the less some chroniclers maintained that such an explanation was unlikely. Thus the chronicler Conrad von Megenberg reported:

In many wells, bags filled with poison were found, and a countless number of Jews were massacred in the Rhineland, in Franconia, and in all the German countries. In truth, I do not know whether certain Jews had done this. Had it been thus, assuredly the evil would have been worse. But I know, on the other hand, that no German city had so many Jews as Vienna, and so many of them there succumbed to the plague that they were obliged to enlarge their cemetery greatly and to buy two more buildings. They would have been very stupid to poison themselves.

Throughout Germany most major Jewish communities were destroyed by the plague; indeed the German Jewish population was so decimated by this disaster that in subsequent years a number of cities such as Speyer invited Jews to live in their midst with promises of protection and security. Slowly Jewish communities were reconstituted and Jewish life began anew.

The massacres of this period and those of previous centuries traumatized Jewish communities. Some of their reactions were incorporated into the Jewish liturgy; others served as the basis of religious chants (*selihot* and *kinot*). In various chronicles of these centuries Jewish animosity was expressed in the most vehement terms. Solomon bar Simeon for example declared:

The pope of sinful Rome rose up and urged all the peoples of Edom to believe in the Christ crucified: to unite in order to Jerusalem and conquer the city so that the strayed might return to the site of their shame, to the tomb of him whom they have chosen as their God . . . Let the bones of Emico, the persecutor of the Jews be ground in a mill of fire! . . . O God of vengeance, O Lord God of vengeance, appear! It is for thee that we have let ourselves be slaughtered every day. Return sevenfold the wrongs of neighbours so that they may curse you! Before our very eyes let the nations be punished for the blood of thy servants that they have shed.

In addition, numerous literary works of this period exhorted God to mete out divine justice. Thus in a poem about the martyrdom of Isaac (chatelain of Troyes) and his family who were tried for ritual murder, the author appealed to God for justice:

> Sinners have come for Isaac Cohen,
> He must abjure, or perish.
> He says: "What do you want of me? For God I will die.
> As priest, I will offer him the sacrifice of my body."
> "You cannot escape, we hold you fast.
> Become a Christian," but he swift replies: "No.
> For the dogs, I would not leave God nor his name!"
> Then Haim was called, the master of Brinon,
> And another *kadosh* was led forth;
> Then they thrust him into a slow fire
> And with good heart he prayed to God often and low,
> Gently suffering his pain in the name of the living God.
> God of vengeance, jealous God, avenge us on our foes!
> From awaiting your vengeance, the day seems long to us.

Those who perished in the Christian onslaught and remained faithful to their ancestral faith were regarded as hallowing God's name. In their heroism and faithfulness, these victims cried out to God for revenge. Hatred and faithfulness were thus mixed together in the blood and tears of those who perished in these terrible centuries of suffering.

CHAPTER FIVE

The Demonic Image of the Jew

During the Middle Ages the Jewish community was detested, and the stereotype of the demonic Jew became part of Western culture. Repeatedly during this period Jews were accused of possessing attributes of both the Devil and witches. As the personification of evil, they were relegated to a sub-species of the human race. Jews were also viewed as magicians *par excellence*, able to work magic against the Christian community; this belief served as the basis for the charge that the Jewish population desecrated the Host and committed acts of ritual murder. Yet while it is true that Jews did engage in magical practices, they were excluded from non-Jewish circles of sorcerers and witches, and Jewish magic was dependent on the power of good rather than the demonic realm. Thus Christian allegations of this period were based on ignorance and fear. None the less, the masses attacked Jews in their pursuit of the demons, and in this Christian onslaught thousands of innocent victims lost their lives.

The Vile Jew

In Germany, France, Italy and England, Jews were detested throughout the Middle Ages, and anti-Semitism served as a central theme of Christian literary and artistic compositions. A fourteenth-century French satire, for example, depicts a Parisian Jew falling into a public latrine. When other Jews attempted to help him, he decreed: "I beg you not to pull me out now, for today is the Sabbath. Wait until tomorrow so as not to violate our law." Some Christians overheard this conversation and reported the situation to King Louis. The king then ordered his men to keep the Jews from removing this individual from the latrine. "He has observed the Sabbath", the king proclaimed. "He will observe our Lord's Day as well." However, when they came to rescue him on Monday, the Jew had died.

After the Black Plague there were few Jews left in the Low Countries, but numerous works were written about Jewish life. Some referred to the charge of ritual murder:

> The Jews, wicked and cruel as dogs,
> Brutally seized the child
> Threw him down and trampled him . . .
> Swiftly stripped him bare
> And once he was naked
> The filthy Jews, stinking dogs,
> Inflicted several wounds
> With daggers and knives . . .

Although no Jews remained in England after the expulsion of 1290, anti-Jewish polemics were repeatedly produced. Thus in about 1255 a story of ritual murder appeared and during the following century gave rise to twenty-one different versions of the ballad entitled "Sir Hugh or the Jew's Daughter". In the latter half of the fourteenth century Geoffrey Chaucer incorporated this theme in his *Prioress's Tale*:

> Ther was in Asyne, in a greet citee,
> Amonges Christene folk, a Jewerye . . .
> And as the child gan forby for to pace,
> This cursed Jew hym hente, and heeld hym faste.
> And kitte his throte, and in a pit hym caste.
> I seye that in a wardrobe they hym threwe
> Where as thise Jewes purgen hire entraille.
> O cursed folk of Herodes al newe! . . .
> O yonge Hugh of Lyncoln, slayn also
> With cursed Jewes, as it is notable,
> For it is but a litel while ago,
> Praye eke for us . . .

In Italy the theme of the pound of flesh connected with a merciless creditor was transformed into a tale about a Jewish woman in *Il Pecorone* by Ser Giovanni Fiorentino.

These motifs were also found in religious drama of the period. In scenes from the New Testament Jews were portrayed in the most heinous fashion, and numerous epithets were used to characterize them: "false Jews", "false thieves", "false miscreants", "wicked and felonious Jews", "perverse Jews", "disloyal Jews", "false swine". The Jewish people were thus presented as vile and treacherous, and sadism became a central feature of the stage: torture, crucifixion and rape were repeatedly enacted to a believing audience. A number of German miracle plays of this period dealing with the Assumption of the Virgin, for example, contain a final scene in which Titus destroys Jerusalem to avenge the Divine Mother. In other plays contemporary events were presented in equally inflammatory terms. Thus in *Mistère de la saincte hostie*, a Jewish usurer forces a Christian debtor to give him a piece of the Host which he wishes to defile. "Desire seized me to crucify it, cast it into the fire and persecute it, and against the ground to trample, boil, beat, and stone it", he declared. Yet no matter what he does, the Host bleeds but remains intact. Witnessing this event, the Jew's wife and family denounce him and request baptism. The Jew, too, says he wishes to embrace the Christian faith when the provost comes for him. But the provost is not fooled and the Jew is burned. As he dies he calls for the devil to carry him away:

> O Devil, I feel I am burning
> Devils, devils burn and flame
> I flare and flame in every limb
> I perish now in fire and flame
> My body, mind and soul
> Burn now and fiercely consume
> Devils come speedily
> And carry me off from this ordeal.

The Devil and the Jews

From the time of the early Church, Christian theologians were preoccupied with demonology, and the Christian masses subscribed to primitive superstitions about the Devil, witches, and wizards. In the Middle Ages, scholastics were anxious to explain the role of the Devil in the terrestial and celestial spheres. According to Thomas Aquinas, demons could assume carnal form. Although they are incapable of procreation, they can introduce into a woman the seed of a man which they had received – the children procreated in this way were not in fact descendants of demons, but were indirectly spawned by them.

In the next century, the Dominicans engaged in speculation about the demonic realm. During this period the heretical doctrine of Catharism maintained that Satan rules the earth, and it was believed to be a great sin to commune with him. In 1320 Pope John XXII issued the bull *Super illius specula* against false Christians who "sacrifice to demons and worship them, produce or procure images, rings, flasks, mirrors, and still other things to which they attach the demons by their magic arts, gaining answers from them, seeking their aid in order to carry out their wicked designs, submitting to the most shameful servitude for the most shameful things."

Under the next Pope (Benedict XII), trials for witchcraft took place in Toulouse in 1335. Two years later the Inquisitor Nidder produced a detailed description of wizards and their activities. After the Black Plague, the Devil's associates were hunted down, and witch burnings became increasingly familiar events. In seeking out the guilty, the Inquisitors insisted on obtaining the victim's confession, and torture was invariably used to obtain the necessary evidence. In 1404 the Holy Office proclaimed that it had burned over 30,000 witches.

In the fifteenth century, witch-hunting flourished in Savoy, Switzerland and Germany. According to Pope Innocent VIII the Teutonic territories were filled with agents of the Devil. The German inquisitors Sprenger and Institoris published a treatise, *Malleus Malficarum*, and Satan's assistants were rounded up throughout the land. During this period the Devil was conceived as an individualized personality who roamed the earth, searching for innocent victims. Possessing horns, talons, a tail, and a goat's beard, he was black in colour and exuded a strong odour. The Devil was ubiquitous, working evil, sowing hatred, pronouncing spells, and possessing individuals. His chief agent was the witch, a woman of impurity and deceit.

In line with much popular Church teaching about the Jews through the centuries, the Jewish population was perceived as possessing the attributes of both the Devil and witches. Depicted as possessing horns, tails, and the beard of a goat, they were accused of producing a terrible odour (*foetor judaïcus*). Although able to perform magical feats, Jews were viewed as suffering from malignant diseases which only Christian blood could cure. Born misshapen, they were seen as haemorrhoidal, and men as well as women were afflicted with menses. Such themes are reflected in the accusation of ritual murder made against the Jewish community in Trnava at the end of the fifteenth century:

> Firstly, the traditions of their ancestors tell them that the blood of a Christian is an excellent means to cure the wound produced by circumcision. Secondly, they see that this blood permits them to prepare a dish that wakens mutual love. Thirdly, suffering from menstruation, both men and women alike, they have noted that the blood of a Christian constitutes an excellent remedy. Fourthly, they are obliged, by virtue of an ancient and secret commandment, to offer yearly sacrifice with Christian blood.

Thus in the Middle Ages Jews were viewed as the personification of evil. Dabbling in the occult, they were associated with devils and demons. At times they were depicted as the Devil himself; alternatively, they were seen as intermediaries between the Devil and innocent human beings. Given such diabolical attributes, it is not surprising that the Jewish people were relegated to a sub-species of humanity, and as a result butchered without remorse or guilt. As the vermin of the earth, they were a contagion in the body of Europe.

The Jew as Sorcerer

In the medieval period, Christians regarded the Jew as the magician *par excellence*. Since Satan was the ultimate source of magic, Jews were seen as his earthly agents. Repeatedly the masses attacked Jewish communities because of their conviction that Jews worked magical practices against Christians. A typical example was the assault upon Jews in England which was initiated by an incident that occurred in September 1189, at the coronation of Richard I. On this occasion a Jewish delegation which had brought gifts and pledges of allegiance to the new king were driven from the palace, accused of casting enchantments on the king, and set upon by the crowds. This onslaught was followed by numerous attacks on Jewish communities throughout the country.

The central feature of this suspicion of magical practice applied to the entire people – every Jewish act was construed as a diabolical device for working magic against gentiles. Thus at the beginning of the thirteenth century in Paris, the custom of casting earth behind one after a funeral brought a charge of sorcery. Again, the practice of washing hands on returning from the cemetery aroused similar suspicions. Because of these charges, some rabbis found it necessary to suspend a number of Jewish practices. In this atmosphere of suspicion the *mezuzah* was also viewed as an object of dread; because of the fear of Christian retribution Jews in the Rhineland were forced to cover them, for in the words of a thirteenth-century writer, "the Christians out of malice and to annoy us, stick knives into the *mezuzah* openings and cut up the parchment." Yet despite such acts, some Christian officials actually used the *mezuzah* for magical purposes. Thus at the end of the fourteenth century the Bishop of Salzburg asked a Jew to give him a *mezuzah* to fix to the gate of his castle.

In the medical field Jewish doctors were seen as agents of magic, and were frequently called upon by Christians to perform miracles, despite Church prohibitions reiterated by Popes and Synods. According to tradition, demons were frequently responsible for disease, and medicine was therefore viewed as an effective means of curing the ill. Paradoxically, when his ministrations proved successful, the Jewish physician was seen as a magician to be respected and feared, but if the patient died, the doctor was accused of murder. This charge was linked to the general belief that Jews sought to poison the Christian community. Physicians in particular were charged with this crime, but Jews in general were regarded as adept at this art. So widespread was the belief that Jews poisoned gentiles, that in 1550 when the Polish king Sigismund Augustus demanded of Ivan IV that he allow Lithuanian Jews into Russia for business purposes, Ivan replied: "It is not convenient to allow Jews to come with their goods to Russia, since many evils result from them. For they import poisonous herbs into our realms." Similarly Luther wrote: "If they (the Jews) could kill us all, they would gladly do so, aye, and often do it, especially those who profess to be physicians. They know all that is known about medicine in Germany; they can give poison to a man of which he will die in an hour, or in ten or twenty years; they thoroughly understand this art." Not surprisingly, such attitudes provoked the massacre of thousands of Jews in the fourteenth century for poisoning wells during the Black Death.

Another charge levelled against the Jewish population was that they engaged in acts of sorcery in connection with the Eucharist. Given the belief in transubstantiation, the mutilation of the Host was viewed as a most heinous crime: according to numerous accounts Jews attacked the Host in various ways. In addition some reports related that Jews fashioned an image of Christ from wax and through their magic art transmitted various tortures through this image to both Jesus and his followers. Such sympathetic magic was allegedly also used to inflict suffering on Church leaders. Thus in 1066 the Jews of Trèves were accused of having made a wax image of Bishop Eberhard; it was alleged that this object was baptized by a priest (whom the Jews bribed) and burned on the Sabbath – as a result, the bishop became ill and died.

The ritual murder accusation was also linked with Jewish sorcery. In the medieval period a wide range of occult remedies specified the use of human flesh, blood, entrails, hands and fingers; menstrual blood in particular was seen as especially efficacious. In this light the allegation that Jews used Christian blood for magical purposes was readily understandable. One of the earliest medieval references to this practice was made by Thomas of Cantimpre in the thirteenth century, in which he attributed the need for Christian blood to the Jewish affliction of haemorrhage which could only be cured by the application of this fluid. In 1235 the Jews of Fulda were charged with killing five children and confessed that they did so in order to obtain blood for the purposes of healing. Again, Matthew Paris's account of the crucifixion of Hugh of Lincoln by Jews in 1255 recounts that their intention was to use the boy's bowels for divination. Further, at the beginning of the fifteenth century the city Council of Freiburg requested the expulsion of the Jews from the city because they believed that the Jewish community periodically murdered a Christian child to prolong their lives. From these examples it is clear that the suspicion of magic lay behind the accusation of ritual murder – the notion of using blood for Passover *matzot* was a later refinement of this charge.

In the Middle Ages, gentiles who were brought before the Inquisition confessed to a wide range of magical practices: the adoration of Satan, the desecration of the Host and other consecrated objects, the sacrifice of infants, cannibalism, the use of human ingredients in salves and potions, the creation of wax images baptized in their names, and the crime of poisoning. This catalogue of offences determined the character of the charges made against the Jewish population. As a strange and mysterious people with whom the majority of Christians had little contact, it is not surprising that the Jewish nation was generally regarded as guilty of the most nefarious diabolical rites against humanity.

The Truth behind the Myth

Although the legend of the Jew as sorcerer was a Christian creation, Jews did engage in magical practices in the Middle Ages. Beginning in the gaonic period, in the sixth century AD, Jewish magic drew on mystical and Gnostic sources. Those who practised this art were acquainted with methods of inducing disease and death, arousing and killing passion, and employing demons for divinatory purposes. Among Jews – as among Christians – there was a widespread belief that sorcerers could alter their shapes and roam the woods in the form of wolves, hares, donkeys or cats, and transform victims into animals. It was also believed that a magician could project his soul to distant places and then return to his body.

The concept of the witch is also found in Jewish literature. In thirteenth-century sources they are depicted as having dishevelled hair, flying at night, and feeding on the blood and flesh of infants and adults. They are accompanied by demons who assume the forms of animals to carry out their designs. Thus Manahem Ziyuni, in his commentary on the Bible written in 1430, declared:

> There are men and women who possess demonic attributes; they smear their bodies with a secret oil . . . and instantly fly off like the eagle over seas and rivers and forests and brooks, but they must return home before sunrise; their flight follows a predefined course from which they cannot deviate. Anyone who trespasses upon their meeting place is likely to suffer grave harm . . . They transform themselves into various animals and into cats.

Again, Menasseh ben Israel believed that witches could change their form, because Satan "fashions around their bodies the simulated forms of animals . . . the proof lies in the fact that when the paws of a pseudo-wolf are amputated the witch or magician appears minus hands and feet." Generally it was believed that such demonic figures were not Jewish; yet in some instances Jewish witches were depicted as engaging in such activities.

Despite the Jewish interest in magic, Jews were excluded from the gentile fraternity of sorcerers and witches. The witch-cults blasphemed various Church rites in their own ritual: such observance would have little meaning for Jews. Further, demonic practices of this period were based on a worship of Satan, whereas Jewish magic functioned within the context of the Jewish faith which excluded any association with God's arch-enemy. The central principle of medieval Jewish magic was its reliance on the power of good, which was invoked by calling upon the names of God and his angels. It was rooted in the Jewish tradition and exhibited none of the anti-Church elements hunted down by the Inquisition. Thus Jewish magicians were on the whole God-fearing, pious individuals, who observed the tenets of the Jewish faith. Within the ranks of Jewish wonder-workers were scholarly men who had a thorough training in Hebrew and Aramaic and an understanding of rabbinic literature; such knowledge enabled them to invoke God's names so as to effect magical cures. Jewish women, too, served as folk-magicians, healers of wounds, and preparers of love-potions.

According to tradition, demons and angels populate the world, and through their intermediacy the powers of magic can be brought into operation. The particular role of angels is to serve as God's emissaries; demons, on the other hand, can be influenced by the powers of a magician. One of the most common features of medieval Jewish magic was the incantation of names. This act comprised several ingredients: an appeal to ancient masters of magic, citations from or allusions to biblical passages, the invocation of angels, the emanation of holy names, and a specific request or command. A familiar characteristic of this process was to do things in reverse; thus biblical quotations were often recited both forward and backward, and mystical names reversed. One type of incantation was especially suited to dispelling demons – its effect derived from its form rather than content, such as the Talmudic spell against the demon Shabriri:

> Shabriri
> briri
> riri
> iri
> ri

In theory the demon shrank and finally vanished as he heard his name decreasing letter by letter. Again, a charm directed against a fever demon, quoted by Eleazar of Worms is: "Ochnotinos, chnotinos, notinos, otinos, tinos, inos, nos, os."

During the Middle Ages Jews also utilized sympathetic magic, yet it appears not to have been used either to harm or to kill an enemy. Rather it was commonly applied to force thieves to return stolen objects: the image of a suspected thief was drawn on a wall, and nails were struck into the image so that he would confess. Another use of such a procedure was to arouse passion. In a fifteenth-century work in Hebrew and Yiddish the following instructions were given:

> Take virgin wax and make a female figure, with the sex organs clearly delineated, and with the features of the person you have in mind . . . Then bury the figure and cover it carefully so that its limbs are not broken, and leave it thus for twenty-four hours. Then bury it under the leaves, being careful that no one witnesses your acts, and cover it with a stone so that it does not break. When you disinter it, dip it carefully in water three times, so that it is washed clean, one in the name of Michael, again in the name of Gabriel, and the third time in the name of Raphael, and immerse it in some urine. Then dry it, and when you wish to arouse passion in her, pierce the heart of the image with a new needle, in that spot where it will cause most pain.

One of the most popular magical devices was the amulet, which was either worn on the body or attached to objects and animals. Jewish amulets were of two types: written texts, or objects such as herbs, foxes' tails, and stones. A Talmudic amulet which was widely used in the Middle Ages was the 'preserving stone' which was believed to prevent miscarriage. A man born with a caul was counselled to wear it at all times as a protection against demons. Towards the end of the Middle Ages it became common to hang a piece of the *Aphikomen* (part of the unleavened bread used at the Passover *seder*) in a home or carry it in a pouch to protect one against evil spirits. Again, a metal plate inscribed with the letter "*heh*" (a sign of the Tetragramaton) was a common amulet. Written amulets were also widely favoured.

> An effective amulet, tested and tried, against the evil eye and evil spirits, for grace, against imprisonment and the sword, for intelligence, to be

able to instruct people in Torah, against all sorts of disease and reverses, and against loss of property . . . Protect him in all his two hundred and forty-eight organs against imprisonment and against the two-edged sword. Help him, deliver him, save him, rescue him from evil men and evil speech, and from a harsh litigant, whether he be Jew or Gentile. Humble and bring low those who rise against him to do him evil by deed or speech, by counsel or by thought . . .

These few examples illustrate the pervasiveness of Jewish magic and superstition among Jewry in the medieval period. Influenced by current cultural and social patterns, Jews formulated their own magical procedures based on biblical and Talmudic precedent. Yet although the practice of sorcery was an important aspect of Jewish folklore, Christian allegations about Jewish magic were misinformed and mistaken. Jews were neither the Devil nor his agents; their preoccupation with sorcery was induced by the desire to protect themselves from ill-fortune. To view Jews as dark and ominous figures with evil designs on the Christian population is to misconstrue their preoccupation with the occult.

Persecution of the Demons

Motivated by the belief in the demonic power of the Jewish people, a number of clergymen encouraged the persecution of the Jews. Thus the preaching friar and miracle worker Vincent Ferrer travelled throughout Spain and France attempting to convert the teachers. As the leader of bands of flagellants, he entered synagogues and demanded of worshippers that they accept the Cross. In Toledo, for example, he burst into the synagogue, expelled the congregation and renamed the place the Church of the Immaculate Virgin. This scourge of the Jews also persecuted Jewish communities in Saragossa, Valencia and Tortosa. Another tormentor was the Inquisitor, John of Capistrano. In Italy and Germany he preached about death, Hell, punishment, and the Anti-Christ. Leading a campaign against the Jewish population, he threatened princes who protected local Jewish communities with the wrath of God. From 1453 to 1454 he initiated a series of trials for ritual murder which resulted in a number of *autos-da-fé*.

Even individuals of a gentler disposition hated Jews with equal ferocity. Thus Bernardino of Siena, the founder of the sect of the Holy Name of Jesus, believed that the Jews were conspiring against Christians through usury, while Jewish doctors sought to undermine their health. His successor, Bernardino of Feltre, was equally hostile about Jewish practices: "They bleed the poor to death and grow fat on their substance," he declared, "and I who live on the bread of the poor, shall I then be mute as a dog before outraged charity? Dogs bark to protect those who feed them, and I, who am fed by the poor, shall I see them robbed of what belongs to them and keep silent? Dogs bark for their masters; shall I not bark for Christ?"

In the activities of the Jews the Devil's hand was seen at work: the Jew-Devil stalked Europe, seeking Christians as his prey. Accused of sorcery, Jewish doctors in particular were seen as agents of the demonic realm. Viewed as evil magicians, they were condemned by the Church. Thus in the thirteenth century the Council of Béziers forbade Christians from resorting to the care of Jews, and this prohibition was repeated by the Councils of Albi, Vienne, and the University of Paris. According to legend, Charles the Bald, Hugh Capet, and the Emperor Charlemagne were poisoned by Jewish physicians, and the Vienna Faculty of Medicine pronounced that the private code of Jewish physicians required them to kill one patient in ten. Thus both Jewish doctors and usurers were seen as united in a common quest to rob Christians of their money and their health. The Jew in the Middle Ages was therefore understood as the demonic counterpart of the Christian saints, and in the mythology of the age Jews came to represent all that is evil and impure.

In the light of this conception of the Jew-Devil, the Jews were depicted in medieval chronicles as predators who sought to destroy the entire social life of the communities where they lived. Hated by gentiles, Jewish communities turned inwards and formed their own closed worlds. Yet despite such isolation, they were not able to protect themselves from the Christian onslaught, and when faced with a choice between death or conversion many went to their deaths as martyrs. During the years of the Black Plague it was reported that they "went to die dancing and singing, as gay as if they were on their way to a wedding: and would not convert, neither father nor mother for their children . . . and when they saw the burning fire, women and children leapt into it singing the while." In some cases Jews committed collective suicide rather than die at the hands of the uncircumcised. Those who met their deaths in this way were assured of the reward of eternal life. Suffering in this life was thus diminished by the promise of heavenly reward. In this light Rabbi Meir of Rothenburg's words of counsel express the devotion of an entire people: "Whosoever has taken the firm decision to remain loyal to his faith and to die, if he must, a martyr, does not feel the sufferings of torture. Whether he be stoned or burnt, buried alive or hanged, he remains without feeling, no moan escapes from his lips."

Some Jews, however, were unable to sustain such heroism, and converted under the threat of death. Yet subsequently they wished to return to their ancestral faith. For these apostates, there still remained hope. In the words of the fifteenth-century Talmudist, Israel Isserlein:

> We must remember that he who returns to Judaism imposes upon himself a continual penitence, for he turns his back upon the advantages and felicities from which he benefited as a Christian, and assumes the sufferings and persecutions which the Jew needs must endure. He did not have to bear this burden while he was a Christian, and in truth his fault is expiated when he assumes it of his own free will, with the sole purpose of again becoming a member of the Jewish community.

This period of Jewish suffering was marked at the end of the Middle Ages by the transformation of Jewish quarters into ghettos where gates were locked at night. Behind the ghetto walls, the Jewish people withdrew into themselves, ever fearful of their Christian neighbours. Accused of sorcery and black magic, the Jew-Devil was thus imprisoned from the surrounding world – as a result the Jewish pollution of Christendom was restrained, and the demonic dark force of evil turned in on itself.

CHAPTER SIX

Post-Medieval Anti-Semitism in France, England and Germany

Although the Jewish community was expelled from France in the fourteenth century, negative images of Jews continued to play a role in French culture. Catechisms, lives of Jesus, and canticles portrayed the Jewish people as tools of Satan. In addition, tracts abounded which denounced the Jews in terms reminiscent of the Middle Ages. In England, Jews were similarly vilified even though the Jewish nation was expelled in 1290. German Jews were also detested – such hostility was most powerfully expressed in Martin Luther's *Against the Jews and Their Lies*. Such publications were followed by a wide range of tracts which denigrated Judaism and the Jewish people. Thus despite the existence of powerful court Jews throughout Germany, the Jewish masses lived simple lives and endured considerable hardship during this period.

French Jewry in the Post-Medieval Period

The expulsions from France in the fourteenth century evicted Jews from most of the territories of France until the eighteenth century. None the less, at the beginning of the sixteenth century colonies of Marranos existed in Bayonne, Rouen, Nantes and Bordeaux. These former Jews professed Christianity and had generally lost an identification with their former faith. Yet despite the disappearance of practising Jews from French life, the Jewish problem continued as a persistent factor in society. Stereotypes of Jews occupied the imagination. Jews were viewed as usurers, seeking to gain money by sharp dealings, and Judas was associated in the public mind with a traitor and betrayer.

No doubt, as Christians grew up they learned to distinguish between good and evil and were informed of the strange people in their midst who were guilty of the greatest crime against humanity: the death of Christ. At parish schools the catechism was taught in which Jews were presented as villainous figures. Thus the catechism of Abbé Fleury asked:

> Did Jesus have enemies? – Yes, the carnal Jews. – To what point did the hatred of Jesus' enemies go? – To the point of causing his death. – Who was it who promised to hand him over? – Judas Iscariot. · Why was this city (Jerusalem) treated in this way? – For having caused the death of Jesus. – What became of the Jews? – They were reduced to servitude and scattered throughout the world. – What has become of them since? – They are still in the same state. – For how long? – For seventeen hundred years.

Judas and the Jews were seen as interchangeable, and the Jewish people were presented as the tools of Satan. In the lives of Jesus and the saints, as well as in the accounts of pilgrimages, the Jewish population was presented in the most horrific fashion. Thus in a fifteenth-century life of Jesus, his suffering is portrayed as the result of Jewish animosity:

> Some insulted him; others, with the backs of their hands, struck his noble and gentle mouth; others spit into his face (for it was the custom of the Jews to spit in the faces of those whom they cast out from among themselves); others tore out his beard or pulled at his hair, and thus trampled under their accursed feet the Lord of the angels . . . And still spitting into his noble countenance, they struck his head with a stick, so that the thorns of his crown sank into his forehead . . . Pilate commanded that in this shameful and inhuman state he be led before all the Jewish people, who had remained outside in order not to sully themselves on the day of the Sabbath. But these accursed sons of the Devil all cried out with one voice: "Take him away, take him away, crucify him."

Stories about the desecration of the Host and ritual murder were also current during this period, and in some texts the Jewish people were vilified because of their inhuman character: "a monstrous people, having neither hearth nor home, without a country and of all countries; once the most fortunate in the world; now the evil spirit and the detestation of the world: wretched, scorned by all, having become, in their wretchedness, by a curse, the mockery of even the most moderate."

Some writers stressed that the Jews are to be punished for their iniquity: "Death in sin, death with sin, death even, as it often happens, by sin – that, my dear listeners, is what frightens me and what must frighten you even as it does me. That is God's most terrible weapon in the arsenal of his wrath; that is what the Son of God threatens the Jews with today." Such hatred of the Jews was inflamed by canticles, such as that composed in the seventeenth century by Grignon de Montfort, which was based on a medieval mystery of the Passion. Its bloody imagery inevitably evoked bitter animosity toward the race that in Christian eyes tortured and killed the Saviour of humanity.

Jesus flagellated

Jesus sees a dreadful death
Coming upon him threateningly:
To be victorious
He must as well be omnipotent

(Refrain)

I am the guilty one
but Jesus is innocent.
Ah! Wretched am I –
I say it moaning.
The furious executioners
Like ravening wolves
Bruise his face,
Tear his garments.

(Refrain)

He is covered with wounds,
His blood flows in rivulets.
Overwhelmed with bruises,
His flesh falls in strips.

(Refrain)

Jesus Crowned with thorns

Into his sacred hands are put
For sceptre, a frail reed.

Everyone mocks him
Saying: Ha! How fine!
It is for us, O sinners.
That he endures these pains.
He is crowned with thorns.
With blows of a stick;
Everyone makes faces at him
Shrieking like a demon.

(Refrain)

This cruel crown
Pierces his skull.
The brain oozes out
With blood and sweat.

(Refrain)

Jesus Crucified

This insolent rabble
Again tears everything from him;
His poor blood robe
Sticks everywhere to his skin.
It is for us, O sinners,
That he endures these pains.
While the fiercest
Prepare everything for his death
Some of the greediest
Draw lots for his clothes.

(Refrain)

O cruel savagery! His limbs are broken,
His flesh is all bruised,
His nerves laid bare.

(Refrain)

Jesus Dead and Buried

O abominable sinners,
It is done, Jesus is dead.
We are all guilty.
What is our fate to be?
It is for us, O sinners,
That he died in such pain.

The French Vilification of the Jews

Despite such anti-Jewish propaganda, there was no French anti-Jewish upheaval during the period of the Reformation. This was due in part to the fact that the Protestants became the target of Catholic contempt and hostility. Nevertheless, in the seventeenth century, an incident connected with the Guild of Fripiers (old clothes dealers) gave rise to an intense anti-Semitic outburst. When the Guild was on guard duty, they passed near the Church of St Eustache. A young bystander, John Bourgeois, mockingly cried out: "There go the gentlemen from the synagogue." In response the men of the Guild attacked him. Subsequently, a complaint was lodged against the Fripiers. One of the Guild was arrested, and in reaction the young man was set upon by the Fripiers, tormented, and killed.

For several years political pamphlets discussed this incident, believing the Fripiers to be of Jewish descent. Initially, prose tracts were published, such as *A monitory letter published by all the parishes of the City of Paris against the Jews of the Synagogue: A simple and true account of the cruel murder and horrible massacre committed on 26 August 1652:* and *A scrutiny of the life of the Jews, of their religion, trade and associations*. One tract decreed that "there is no one who does not know that the Jews are the opprobrium of all nations and have been so for sixteen hundred years and more . . . Their customs show their malediction no less than their bondage. There is no one who does not know that they have no other profession in life than usury, and that their false witnesses and their infamous practices have sown corruption the world over."

Other tracts contained denunciations of the Jews in verse:

> Infamous murders,
> Detestable nation,
> Abhorred by men,
> Everywhere rejected,
> Must you today
> Renew the effort
> Of your horrid cruelties
> Which put to death
> The God by whom we live?

In another tract the Jews were presented as detested and accursed villains:

> Demons escaped from hell,
> Race of the Jews, detestable men,
> More accursed than Lucifer
> And more wicked than all the devils.
> Cruel tigers, begone,
> Unworthy as you are to live among us.
> When you thirst so for blood
> You must fear the punishment
> With which the Holy Inquisition
> Will chastise your parricides.
> Untie the hands and feet
> Of a citizen put to the torture.
> Would you make of him
> The image of an *Ecce Homo*
> Subject to insult and outrage?

Other verses suggest remedies for the Jewish problem – Jews should be expelled or identified by wearing a specific insignia:

> Cast out from our walls
> People of such evil ways.
> Or, by the king's command,
> Make them wear a sign
> That distinguishes them from Christians
> And sets them among the dogs.

Another text proposes that they should be hung:

> Let them be seen, hands and feet
> Bound, those of their horde
> Following the footsteps closely
> Of him whom they laid low
> By a death all too cruel.
> Let them be seen on the scaffold
> With no favour, grace or pardon.

Another alternative is that the Jews should be castrated so that the nation cease to continue:

> I believe it is more fitting
> That the steel arrange matters differently.

And that there be removed from them entirely
That member which in them is already imperfect.
In order that in punishment of their vice
They may survive their torment
And that according to our just desires
Their name here on earth perish with them.

Such texts illustrate the intense antipathy against the Jews. Even though a number of French humanists of this period advocated a more tolerant policy, prejudice was rampant and anti-Jewish sentiment incorporated previous Christian stereotypes of Judaism and the Jewish people.

Agitation against the Jews in England and Germany

In 1290 the Jewish community was expelled from England; none the less, there is evidence that non-baptized Jews entered London illegally in the fourteenth and fifteenth centuries. In 1498 Henry VII took a solemn oath not to allow Jews into his dominions – this was later observed by his successors. In 1540 a Marrano colony existed in London, but it was dispersed two years later. In the sixteenth century Henry VIII consulted Italian rabbis when he wished to divorce Catherine of Aragon who had previously married his elder brother, the Prince of Wales. The king hoped that scriptural teaching concerning Levirate marriage might allow him to obtain a divorce. This episode led to an interest in Hebrew studies in England, and several Jewish converts from the continent served as teachers of Christians.

At the beginning of the seventeenth century a number of Puritans converted to Judaism: others insisted that Jews be allowed to settle again in England. After the monarchy was overthrown and Oliver Cromwell acceded to power the issue became more pressing, particularly since a small ex-Marrano colony had been established in London. Anxious that the Jews be permitted to resettle in England, a Dutch rabbi, Manesseh ben Israel, undertook a mission to Cromwell. A special commission consisting of clerics and representatives of the City of London was appointed to study the proposal. Although Cromwell was well-disposed to the idea, there was great consternation and alarm. Thus the propagandist William Prynne wrote:

As I kept on my way . . . in Lincolns Inne Fields, passing by seven or eight maimed Soldiers on Stilts, who begged me: I heard them say aloud one to another, "We must now all turn Jews, and there will be nothing left for the poor." And not far from them another company of poor people, just at Lincolns Inne back gate, cried aloud to each other: "They are all turned Devils already, and now we must all turn Jews." Which unexpected concurrent providences and Speeches, made such an impression on my Spirit, that before I could take my rest that night, I perused most of the passages in our *English Histories* concerning the Jews' carriage in England, with some of their misdemeanours in other parts, to refresh my memory.

After considerable agitation, Cromwell closed the debate and the situation remained as before: Jews were not officially permitted to resettle. None the less, the Marrano colony in London was allowed to increase its numbers and construct a synagogue.

As in England, Jews in post-medieval Germany were detested and vilified. In 1477 a burgher, Peter Schwartz, explained why they were persecuted throughout the land:

The Jews have been punished severely from time to time. But they do not suffer innocently; they suffer because of their wickedness, because they cheat people and ruin whole countries by their usury and secret murders, as everyone knows. That is why they are so persecuted, and not innocently. There is no people more wicked, more cunning, more avaricious, more impudent, more troublesome, more venomous, more wrathful, more deceptive, and more ignominious.

The scholar Johann Reuchlin offered a more traditional explanation: "Every day, they outrage, blaspheme, and sully God, in the person of his Son, the true Messiah Jesus Christ. They call him a sinner, a sorcerer, a criminal. They treat the sainted Virgin Mary as a witch and a fury. They call the apostles and disciples heretics. They regard us Christians as stupid pagans."

In 1516 a converted Jew, Johannes Pfefferkorn, published a pamphlet, *Der Judenspiegel*, which denounced the Talmud. Advocating the suppression of Jewish books, he obtained from Emperor Maximilian the consent to seize and destroy all copies of the Talmud. In response, Reuchlin defended Jewish sources, and attempted to demonstrate that the Talmud and kabbalistic sources confirm the truths of Christianity. This conflict erupted into a widespread debate between Christian humanists and others, and all European men of letters sided with Reuchlin. Yet paradoxically their condemnation of Pfefferkorn was couched in anti-Semitic terms. Thus one of Reuchlin's supporters, Ulrich von Hutten, declared that "Germany could not have produced such a monster (Pfefferkorn). His parents are Jews, and he remains such, even if he has plunged his unworthy body into the baptism of Christ." Again, Erasmus wrote: "Pfefferkorn is revealed to be a true Jew . . . He appears quite typical of his race. His ancestors attacked Christ only, whereas he has attacked many worthy and eminent men. He could render no better service to his co-religionists than by betraying Christendom, hypocritically claiming to have become a Christian . . . This half-Jew has done more harm to Christendom than all the Jews together."

Martin Luther's Diatribe

Initially, Martin Luther condemned the persecution of the Jews and advocated a tolerant policy towards them. Concerning the controversy between Reuchlin and Pfefferkorn, he criticized the confiscation of the Talmud and rabbinic literature. In his pamphlet, *That Christ was Born a Jew*, he adopted a sympathetic stance toward the Jewish faith. Yet when his early missionary efforts failed to win the Jewish people to Christ, he grew hostile and in 1542 he published his pamphlet *Against the Jews and their Lies*. In this work Luther attacked both Judaism and the Jewish people. "The Jews", he wrote, "being foreigners should possess nothing, and what they do possess should be ours. For they do not work, and we do not give them presents. None the less, they keep our money and our goods and have become our masters in our own country and in the Dispersion. When a thief steals ten guelders, he is hanged; but when a Jew steals ten barrels of gold through his usury, he is prouder than the Lord himself!"

According to Luther, the Jews are an unwanted pestilence, repeatedly expelled by those among whom they live:

No one wants them. The countryside and the roads are open to them; they may return to their country when they wish; we shall gladly give them presents to get rid of them, for they are a heavy burden on us, a scourge, a pestilence and misfortune for our country. This is proved by the fact that they have often been expelled by force: from France, where they had a downy nest; recently from Spain, their chosen roost, and even this year from Bohemia, where in Prague they had another cherished nest; finally, in my own lifetime, from Ratisbon, Magdeburg, and from many other places.

Repeating the charges of previous centuries, he portrayed the Jewish people as demoniac in nature:

Know, O adored Christ, and make no mistake, that aside from the Devil, you have no enemy more venomous, more desperate, more bitter, than a true Jew who truly seeks to be a Jew. Now whoever wishes to accept venomous serpents, desperate enemies of the Lord, and to honour them to let himself be robbed, pillaged, corrupted, and cursed by them, need only turn to the Jews.

What is to be done with this foreign element? Luther proposed a number of remedies:

First, their synagogues should be set on fire, and whatever does not burn up should be covered or spread over with dirt so that no one may ever be able to see a cinder or stone of it. And this ought to be done for the honour of God and of Christianity in order that God may see that we are Christians, and that we have not wittingly tolerated or approved of such public lying, cursing and blaspheming of his Son and his Christians . . . Secondly, their homes should likewise be broken down and destroyed. For they perpetrate the same things there that they do in their synagogues . . . Thirdly, they should be deprived of their prayerbooks and Talmuds in which such idolatry, lies, cursing and blasphemy are taught. Fourthly, their rabbis must be forbidden under threat of death to teach any more . . . Fifthly, passport and travelling privileges should be absolutely forbidden to the Jews . . . Sixthly, they ought to be stopped from usury . . . Seventhly, let the young and strong Jews and Jewesses be given the flail, the axe, the hoe, the spade, the distaff, and spindle, and let them earn their bread by the sweat of their noses . . . To sum up, dear princes and nobles who have Jews in your domains, if this advice of mine does not suit you, then find a better one so that you may all be free of this insufferable devilish burden – the Jews.

In a pamphlet published several months later, *Schem Hamephoras*, Luther attacked the Jews for their unwillingness to convert to the true faith. "It is as easy to convert a Jew as to convert the Devil," he wrote. "A Jew, a Jewish heart, are hard as stone, as iron, as the Devil himself. In short, they are children of the Devil, condemned to the flames of Hell." Luther insisted that his vituperation against this despicable nation was justified:

> Perhaps some merciful and holy soul among us Christians will be of the opinion that I am too rough with these poor and pitiable Jews, mocking and deriding them. O Lord, I am much too feeble to mock such Devils. I would do so, but they are much stronger than I am in raillery, and they have a God who is a past master in this art; he is called the Devil and the wicked spirit.

Speculating why Jews are so skilful, Luther mockingly declared:

> I cannot understand how they manage to be so skilful, unless I think that when Judas Iscariot hanged himself, his guts burst and emptied. Perhaps the Jews sent their servants with plates of silver and pots of gold to gather up Judas' piss with the other treasures, and then they ate and drank his offal, and thereby acquired eyes so piercing that they discover in the Scriptures commentaries that neither Matthew nor Isaiah himself found there, not to mention the rest of us cursed goyim.

More seriously, he argued that the Jews are in league with the Devil:

> I cannot understand it except by admitting that they have transformed God into the Devil, or rather into a servant of the Devil, accomplishing all the evil the Devil desires, corrupting unhappy souls, and raging against himself. In short, the Jews are worse than the devils. O God, my beloved father and creator, have pity on me who, in self-defence, must speak so scandalously of thy divine and eternal Majesty, against thy wicked enemies, the devils and the Jews.

Such savage sentiments were rooted in centuries of Christian anti-Semitism; four centuries after Luther they were invoked by those who endorsed Hitler's final solution to the Jewish problem.

After Luther

In the face of anti-Jewish sentiment, in the sixteenth century Yosel of Rosheim attempted to protect the rights of his co-religionists and intercede with the government. He was successful in blocking the expulsion of Jewry from Hungary and Bohemia and convened a rabbinical synod which adopted a code of commercial ethics. With regard to this policy, he declared: "I shall cause this programme to be observed if the authorities do what is necessary to let us live in peace; to put an end to the expulsions, to permit us to move about, and to curtail their bloody accusations. For we, too, are human beings, created by almighty God to live beside you on the earth."

In the seventeenth century, German Jewish communities pursued a traditional way of life, yet during this period the court Jew came to play a crucial role in state affairs. Each royal or princely court had its own Jewish auxiliary. Emperor Leopold, for example, summoned a Heidelberg Jew, Samuel Oppenheimer, to his court and assigned him the responsibility of provisioning his armies. A letter written by Oppenheimer to a dignitary of the court illustrates the range of his activities: "As long as I lived in Vienna," he wrote, "I provisioned almost every year, the two armies engaged against the French and the Turks, supplying flour, oats, horses, and money for recruits, as well as munitions, powder, lead, cannon, artillery, wagons, horses, and oxen." Throughout the country these court Jews administered finances, provisioned armies, raised money, provided textiles and precious stones to the court, began new industries, and initiated manufacturing enterprises.

In return for these services, royalty and nobles maintained social contact with those who regulated their affairs. In her memoirs, Glückel von Hameln described such social intercourse. At a marriage of court Jews with royalty in attendance she wrote:

> When the couple was standing under the canopy it appeared that, in the confusion, someone had forgotten to write the *ketubah*. What was to be done? All the nobles and the young princes were already there and ready to watch the ceremony. The rabbi then said that the groom must furnish a surety and promise to write the *ketubah* immediately after the marriage. And he read aloud the *ketubah* from a book. After the nuptial blessing, the nobles were led into the festive hall of Elias Cleve, hung with gilded leather. There was a great table in the centre, covered with the choicest delicacies. Thus the nobles were treated according to their rank.

Such court Jews stood at the pinnacle of the social scale, forming an élite class. Yet the vast majority of Jews continued to live simple lives and frequently endured considerable discrimination. In the municipality of Frankfurt, for example, Jews were forced to wear a distinctive insignia and were forbidden to linger in the streets, walk in pairs, use certain streets, or appear during Christian festivals. The city of Hamburg limited the number of guests that could attend a wedding banquet, the types of presents given, and the kinds of food served. In 1726 the Court of Vienna decreed that only the eldest son of a Jewish family could marry within the law – the other sons were to remain bachelors. This proscription was applied to Bohemia and Moravia, and later was adopted in Prussia, the Palatinate, and Alsace.

During this period the invention of printing made it possible to popularize numerous works on Judaism which denigrated Judaism and the Jewish nation. By the eighteenth century nearly a thousand texts were produced, including missionary tracts intended to convert the Jewish population, studies of Jewish customs, treatises dealing with the Jewish problem – some of which sounded anti-Jewish to Jewish readers. There were also polemical works such as *The Enemy of the Jews*; *The Scourge of the Jews*; *Jewish Practices, a Study of their Impious Life*; *A Brief Catalogue of the Horrible Jewish Blasphemies*; *The Inflamed Poison of the Dragons and the Furious Bile of the Serpents*; and *The Jewish Baths, in which is publicly shown the secret practices and Jewish knavishness, how they drink the blood of Christians, as well as their bitter sweat*. These works echo the Christian anti-Semitic attitudes prevalent in the Middle Ages.

At the beginning of the seventeenth century the Christian myth of the wandering Jew became prevalent – in 1602 *The Brief Account and Description of a Jew Named Ahasuerus* was published and translated into numerous European languages. According to this work, the wandering Jew witnessed the Crucifixion and was condemned by Jesus to wander until the time of the Last Judgement. In addition, a number of studies were produced which sought to illustrate anti-Christian blasphemies within Jewish sources. I. A. Eisenmenger's *Judaism Unmasked, a True and Accurate Report*, for example, maligned the Jews. After its publication the intervention of the Jewish community brought about its withdrawal, but a second edition was published in 1711. Yet despite such hostility, German Jewry was not subjected to any violent onslaught until modern times when the methodical elimination of the Jewish people became a central policy of the Third Reich.

CHAPTER SEVEN

Spanish Persecution and the Inquisition

Although Spanish Jewry flourished in the Middle Ages, by the fourteenth century Jews came to be regarded with suspicion and hostility. Measures were taken against the Jewish community, and in consequence many Jews embraced the Christian faith to escape attack. Such apostasy as well as the Christian onslaught on Jewry, led to the decline of the *aljamas* (Jewish communities), a trend which was resisted by Jewish leaders. During the fifteenth century the Church initiated a new form of persecution. Under Ferdinand and Isabella the Inquisition was established to purge *conversos* or New Christians – Jewish converts to Christianity as opposed to Old Christians of pure blood – who were suspected of practising Jewish customs. Tribunals were established throughout Spain which applied torture to extract confessions from the guilty – those who refused to confess were cast to the flames. Finally, at the end of the century, an Edict of Expulsion was enacted to rid the country of the Jewish race who had polluted the Christian population.

Jewish Persecution in Spain

Despite the fact that the Jewish community flourished in medieval Spain, by the fourteenth century anti-Jewish hostility spread across the Iberian Peninsula, leading to massacres in most Spanish villages. In 1321 the Jewish population was decimated by the Shepherds' Crusade, and two decades later Jews were accused of bringing about the Black Death. From 1355 to 1366, civil war was waged in Castile between the legitimate King Pedro the Cruel and his bastard brother Henry of Trastamara. The majority of Castilian Jews remained faithful to the legitimate king; in response Henry referred to his adversary as the "Judaized king" who was dominated by the Jews. In time it was

77

rumoured that this Judaized figure was in reality a Jew who had been substituted for Pedro at the time of his birth, and was thus more illegitimate than Henry himself. As the community became ravaged by war, the Jews were seen as the cause of the upheaval that was taking place.

After Henry's victory, the Cortes (legislature) met in Burgos and demanded that measures be taken against the Jews, and the Jewish question became a burning issue of the day. In 1371 the Cortes of Toro described the reason why the kingdom was suffering:

> Because of the great liberty and power accorded to the enemies of the faith, especially the Jews, in our whole kingdom, in the royal household as well as in the houses of the knights, the squires, and the nobles, and because of the high offices and the great honours which they enjoy, all Christians are forced to obey them and fear them and bow deeply to them, so that the councils of all the cities and of all places and all people are captives of the Jews and subjugated to them. Be it because of the honours which are accorded them in the royal household and in the houses of the great, be it because of the revenue and offices which they hold, for whatever reason, the Jews, evil and rash men, enemies of God and of all of Christianity, cause numerous evils and sow corruption with impunity, so that the greater part of our kingdom is tyrannized and ruined by the Jews, in contempt of the Christians and our Catholic faith.

What was to be done to remedy this situation? The Cortes of Toro demanded that there be no Jewish officials or tax-collectors; Jews should be required to wear a distinctive insignia; they should be prohibited from riding on horseback and dressing luxuriously; and all Jewish names should be changed if they were Christian in character. The degradation of the Jews during this period is reflected in numerous literary works. Chancellor Lopez de Ayala, for example, accused the Jews of being bloodsuckers in his satire, *Rimado de Palacios*:

> Here come the Jews all alike
> And present their detailed writings
> To drink the blood of the poor people
> Promising jewels and gifts to the courtiers.

In the latter half of the fourteenth century, anti-Jewish legislation was put into effect in Castile. Yet unlike Jews in other countries in Europe, the Jewish population did not turn inward behind ghetto walls. Instead many Jews looked to conversion to Christianity as a solution to their plight. Thus in 1380 a Cortes petition noted that numerous Jews and Jewesses who had turned to the true faith needed to be protected from their former co-religionists. In the same year Rabbi Shemtov Shaprut noted with anguish that "many of our co-religionists are abandoning our ranks and pursuing us with their arguments, trying to prove the truth of their faith to us with the aid of verses of the Holy Scripture and of the Talmud." Thus Christian persecution of the Jews in Spain led to apostasy rather than martyrdom: paradoxically such a step eventually gave rise to even greater hostility and bloodshed as the Inquisition sought to root out those backsliding Jews who ostensibly had adopted the Christian faith.

Attack on the Jews and the Decline of the Aljamas

By the end of the Middle Ages, Seville had become the richest city in Spain. From 1378 the archdeacon of Ecija, Ferrant Martinez, had been stirring up Christians against the Jewish population there. Although the king ordered him to refrain from such activity, he paid no attention. For twelve years he preached anti-Semitic sermons, encouraging Christians to expel Jews from the cities and demolish their synagogues. After the death of Juan I, king of Castile and Barroso, the Archbishop of Seville in 1390, Martinez, intensified his campaign against the Jews. On 6 June 1391 the Jewish section of Seville was attacked. The majority of the Jews were forced to convert, and the rest were killed. In the same month massacres of the Jews took place in most of the other Andalusian and Castilian cities, eventually reaching Aragon and Catalonia.

A number of rulers attempted to stop such riots, but their efforts were in vain. Throughout Spain mobs pillaged and murdered Jewry, believing they were doing God's will. Although some Jews remained loyal to their ancestral faith, many others – including rabbis –accepted baptism. How could the leaders of the community have so readily embraced Christianity? Speculating on this question Joshua Halorki (who himself later converted, adopting the name Jeronimo de Santa

Fé) discussed motives for such an act in his correspondence with the rabbi of Burgos, Solomon Halevi, who had become a Christian:

> Did you perchance lust after riches and honours? Or did the study of philosophy cause you to change so radically and to regard the proofs of faith as vanity and delusion, so that you therefore turned to things more apt to gratify the body and satisfy the intellect without fear and anxiety and apprehension? Or when you beheld the doom of our homeland, the multitude of afflictions that have recently befallen us, which ruined and destroyed us . . . did it then seem to you that the name of Israel would be remembered no more? Or perhaps the secrets of prophecy have been revealed to you and the principles of faith . . . and you saw that our fathers had inherited falsehood . . . and you chose what is true and established?

After such widespread conversions to Christianity, Spanish Jewry divided into opposing camps: traditionalists regarded Jewish apostates with horror – they were traitors who had abandoned their people. Converts, on the other hand, viewed their former co-religionists with disdain – religious Jews constituted a constant reproach to their new way of life. None the less familial ties bound both groups together, and converts continued to live in their previous residences and carry on their trades as before.

Yet in some cases the new Christians (*conversos*) became fervent persecutors of Jews. Thus in July 1392, Henry III wrote to the municipal authorities of Burgos: "The Jews of your *aljama* (community) have informed me that when they were attacked they left their homes in fear of death and took refuge in the houses of the best of you, where they live today in your safe custody, not daring to return to their houses in the *aljama*, for fear that certain Jews who now have become Christians will persecute them and do them much harm." In 1394, *conversos* in Perpignan incited hatred of the Jews and prevented them from returning to their homes. In some cases these converts turned over the assets of the Jewish community to the Church. In Jerez in 1391, for example, *conversos* donated the community's property to the Bursar of the Dominican monastery "because of the numerous benefits which we have received and receive daily from you, who inform us and instruct us in the Holy Catholic faith, ensuring the health of our souls." Similarly in Lerida the synagogue was turned into a church and dedicated to St Mary of the Miracle.

In the face of such apostasy the rabbi of Barcelona, Hasdai Crescas, attempted to rebuild Spanish Jewry with the support of the king and queen of Aragon. In 1393 he was granted authority to establish new *aljamas* in Barcelona and Valencia. In addition tax exemptions were granted to all Jews in the cities of Aragon, an amnesty was granted to those who had sought refuge abroad, and a new constitution was drafted to protect the rights of the Jewish population. Crescas himself wrote treatises attacking philosophical theology, which he believed had led the community astray, as well as anti-Christian tracts.

Despite such efforts to stem the tide of conversion, Spanish Jewry continued to decline. This was due in part to the missionary activities on the part of such preachers as Vincent Ferrer. In his sermons, which the Jews were forced to attend, he emphasized that Jesus and the Virgin Mary were Jews. In his view God did not want conversion by force; rather it should be obtained through persuasion. "The apostles", he wrote, "who conquered the world carried neither lance nor knife. The Christians should not kill the Jews with knives, but with their words." Throughout Aragon, Castile and Gascony, Ferrer preached against the Jews. In consequence mobs of Christians attempted to convert the Jewish population through all available means, despite his words of caution. In 1412 he succeeded in having the Statute of Velladolid passed, forbidding Jews to provide food for Christians, preface their names with the title "Don", change their place of residence, cut their hair, and shave their beards. In addition Jews were forced to wear simple clothing on which a distinctive badge was attached.

During this period Pope Benedict XIII summoned the Disputation of Tortosa in an effort to convert the Jews *en masse*. Christianity was championed by the apostate Joshua Halorki (or Jeronimo de Santa Fé) who was opposed by fourteen distinguished rabbis of Aragon. The point at issue was whether the Talmud supported the view that the Messiah had appeared in the person of Christ. The Disputation was attended by thousands of spectators, including numbers of Jews who at the close of each session confessed that they had been convinced by Halorki's arguments. From 1413 to 1414, three thousand Jews passed through the baptistries of Tortosa: in the annals of Jewish history this year is referred to as "the year of apostasy".

The Conversos

Despite the disintegration of the *aljamas*, Spanish Jewry enjoyed a period of calm at the beginning of the fifteenth century. In two bulls promulgated in 1421 and 1422, Pope Martin V decreed that forced baptism was not true baptism and condemned Jewish persecution. Under these more favourable conditions many of those who had converted to Christianity aspired to become full Jews again: this could be accomplished by moving to North Africa or Portugal. Yet this was not a solution open to all Jews, and those who remained in Spain baptized their children.

These Marranos kept apart from the Christian community; some were circumcised as adults. Such a return to Judaism was encouraged by the Fall of Constantinople to the Turks in 1453. This victory was seen by many Marranos as anticipating the fall of Edom and the deliverance of Israel. Thus in Valencia a group of Marranos, believing that the Messiah had just appeared on a mountain near the Bosphoros, sought to emigrate to Turkey. According to one of these converted Jews:

> The blind *goys* do not see that after we have been subject to them our God will now see to it that we dominate them. Our God has promised us that we will go to Turkey. We have heard that the Anti-Christ is coming; they say that the Turk is he, that he will destroy the Christian churches and will turn them into stables for the beasts and that he will bring honour and reverence to the Jews and the synagogues.

The practice of Judaism among the Marrano community was invariably adulterated as they sought to live Jewish lives in secret. Haunted by a sense of guilt, their prayers echoed such remorse:

> Lord, I have failed Thee by my meanness and my unworthiness, ruled by my evilness and by my treason in spite of myself. Thou, who hast visited me in true justice and hast cherished me like a son, see how I have fallen in a tribulation so great and so perilous, from which I cannot arise or escape. Knowing my guilt, I turn to Thee, Lord, repentant, sighing and weeping, as a son turns to his father, begging Thy holy mercy for forgiveness, that Thou mayest raise me from the great torment and the great tribulation into which I have fallen.

In order to free themselves from Christian allegiance, a number of Marranos attempted to de-Christianize themselves by following bizarre practices – fastening a crucifix to their buttocks, or destroying statues of Jesus. Others rationalized their duplicity. Thus the statesman and jurist Pedro de la Caballería answered a Jewish scholar, who asked him how he could justify becoming a Christian, by pointing out the advantages of his new way of life: "Imbecile", he said, "with the Jewish Torah what more could I have ever been than a rabbi? Now, thanks to the 'little hanged one' I have been given all sorts of honours. I am in command of the whole city of Saragossa, and I make it tremble. What is there to keep me from fasting at Yom Kippur and observing your holidays if I feel like it? When I was a Jew, I did not dare observe the Sabbath and now I do anything I want."

Not all *conversos*, however, sought to live such a double life; many became fervent Christians. Thus Fernán Pérez de Guzmán testified:

> I am going to put forward certain reasons to counter the opinion of those who, without distinction or difference, absolutely condemn that nation of New Christian converts of today, saying that they are not Christians and that their conversion was neither good nor useful . . . I believe that among them are people who are good and devoted, for the following reasons: first, I believe in the virtue of the holy baptismal water, which cannot be sprinkled and lavished without any result; second, I have known and I know good *conversos*, who of their own free will lead an austere life in the religious orders; third, I have seen them work and wear themselves out in the monasteries, reforming dissolute and corrupt orders, and others, such as the honourable bishop (Paulus de Sancta Maria), and his honourable son don Alfonso, Bishop of Burgos, who have produced writings of great utility for our holy faith.

Yet even the *conversos* who had become committed Christians were unable to escape their origins. Thus the poet Antonio de Montoro wrote to Queen Isabella at the time of her accession to the throne:

> I have said the Credo
> I have prayed to the pot of fat pork,
> I have heard Masses and I have prayed
> And still I have not been able to wipe out
> The lineaments of a *confeso*.

I have prayed with devotion
And I have counted the beads
But I have never been able to lose
The name of a common old Jew.

From the Christian side these Jewish apostates were despised because of their racial origins, despite the fact they had embraced the Church. The priest Andrés Bernáldez, for example, declared regarding their eating habits:

They never lose their Jewish way of eating, preparing their meat dishes with onions and garlic and cooking with oil, which they use in place of lard, so that they will not have to eat pork fat; and oil with meat is something which gives the breath a very bad odour; and their houses and their doorways smell very bad because of this way of cooking, and they themselves attribute their Jewish odour to these dishes.

Such hostility to Jewish converts was at times enshrined in official decrees. In 1449 the city officials of Toledo published a description of crimes committed by *conversos* and proclaimed:

We declare that all the said *conversos*, descendants of the perverse line of the Jews ... in reason of the above-mentioned heresies and other offences, insults, seditions, and crimes committed by them up to this time, should therefore be held as disgraceful, unfit, inept, and unworthy of holding any office and public and private benefit in said city or public notaries or as witnesses ... to have domain over Old Christians in the holy Catholic faith.

The Inquisition and the Marranos

Under King Ferdinand and Queen Isabella the Inquisition came into full force, seeking to purge *conversos* who were suspected of practising Jewish customs. In 1478 a papal bull was promulgated which established the Castilian Inquisition; four years later the first tribunal came into operation in Seville. Once the Inquisition was instituted, the tribunal requested that heretics give themselves up – this "Edict of Grace" lasted for thirty days. Those who came forward to admit that they observed Jewish rites were obliged to denounce all other

Judaizers. In compensation they were spared torture and imprisonment. Their sins were atoned for by flagellation, by wearing the *sambenito*, and by the confiscation of their belongings. In addition they were denied the right to hold office, practise a profession, or wear formal dress.

At the next stage of the Inquisitional process, Catholics were asked to name any suspects. An edict was promulgated which outlined various ways to recognize such individuals: Judaizers celebrated Jewish holidays, kept the dietary laws, consumed meat during Lent, omitted the phrase "Glory be to the Father, and to the Son, and to the Holy Ghost" at the end of psalms, cooked with oil, and so forth. Once suspects were identified, the Inquisitors sought to obtain a confession. To achieve this end torture was used, interspersed with kind words such as: "I pity you, when I see you so abused and with a lost soul . . . So do not assume the sin of others . . . admit the truth to me, for, as you see, I already know everything . . . In order that I may be able to pardon you and free you soon, tell me who led you to this error."

Individuals who confessed saved their lives – those who persisted in denying the accusations made against them were burned at the stake. In this quest to root out heresy, there were some who even praised the executions of innocent victims. Thus in the sixteenth century Francesco Pegna stated: "If an innocent is unjustly condemned, he has no reason to complain about the Church's sentence, which is based on sufficient proof, and what is hidden cannot be judged. If false witnesses have caused him to be condemned, he should accept the sentence with resignation, and rejoice in dying for truth." Although thousands of Jews died as martyrs, the majority of those who appeared before the Inquisition accepted reconciliation with the Church and were sentenced to imprisonment after undergoing various humiliations and having their property confiscated. In addition, their children and grandchildren were forbidden to wear gold or silver or hold public or ecclesiastical office.

The first tribunal was established in Seville where the majority of *conversos* attempted to placate the Inquisitors by manifestations of Christian dedication as well as offerings and gifts. The rich *converso* Mesa, for example, had the *quemadero* (the central place of atonement) decorated with statues of the prophets. None the less for seven years the Inquisition purged five thousand individuals who were punished and accepted reconciliation with the Church; seven hundred others were branded heretics and burned. In 1483, Tomas de Torquemada became Inquisitor for all of Spain, and tribunals were instituted in other provinces. In Aragon popular uprisings against the Inquisition took place; in Saragossa an attempt was made to assassinate the Inquisitor Pedro de Arbues. From 1486 to 1490 some 4,850 *conversos* were reconciled to the Church and fewer than two hundred burned.

Such zeal was defended by King Ferdinand even though he was aware of its economic implications. In response to the municipal authorities of Barcelona, who complained about the financial crisis the Inquisition had created, he answered: "Before consenting to the establishment of the Inquisition in the cities of our kingdom, we considered the harm this could cause craftsmen and commerce. But in our great zeal for our holy faith, we have placed the service of the Lord well above all our other interests, whatever they may be." Ironically, however, the Inquisition drove many *conversos* back to their ancestral faith – in their distress they appealed to the God of Abraham, Isaac and Jacob. Defying Christ and Christianity, they declared the *Shema* ("Hear, O Israel, the Lord our God, the Lord is One") as they met their death. Some Catholics were also so disillusioned by the Inquisition that they converted to Judaism.

Jews who had never undergone baptism were frequently caught up in the coils of the Inquisition. The Inquisitors imposed the duty of identifying Judaizing *conversos*, and charges were brought against those who attemped to convince baptized kinsmen to keep Jewish practices. In addition, those who promoted the return of *conversos* to Judaism were indicted. Jews were also accused of engaging with *conversos* in ritual murder. In 1490, six Jews and five *conversos* of La Guardia were charged with attempting to destroy Christendom through black magic. According to the accusation made against one of the accused (Yuce Franco):

His soul embittered and depraved, he went in good company with several others to crucify a Christian child on a Good Friday, in the same fashion, with the same animosity and cruelty as his forefathers had for our Saviour Jesus Christ, tearing his flesh, beating him and spitting in his face, covering him with wounds, crushing him with blows, and turning to ridicule our holy Faith ... He mixed its heart with a consecrated host. With this mixture, Yuce Franco and the others expected that the Christian religion would be overturned and destroyed, so that the Jews would possess all the property which belongs to the Catholics, that their race would grow and multiply while that of the faithful Christians would be extirpated forever.

After confessions were obtained, all the accused were burned.

Torture and Expulsion

Torture during the Inquisition was designed to extract confessions from the guilty. When this end was achieved the Inquisitors were satisfied. Yet paradoxically, the innocent suffered more than those who practised Judaism in secret. An example of such suffering is reflected in a report on Elvira del Campo who was accused of not eating pork and wearing clean clothes on the Sabbath:

She was carried to the torture chamber and told to tell the truth when she said that she had nothing to say. She was ordered to be stripped and again admonished, but was silent. When stripped, she said: "Señores, I have done all that is said of me and I bear false witness against myself, for I do not want to see myself in such trouble; please God, I have done nothing." She was told not to bring false testimony against herself but to tell the truth. The tying of the arms was commenced. She said, "I have told the truth; what have I to tell?" She was told to tell the truth and replied, "I have told the truth and have nothing to tell." One cord was applied to the arms and twisted, and she was admonished to tell the truth but said she had nothing to tell. Then she screamed and said, "I have done all they say."

The torture session then intensified, and according to rule more turns of the cord on the arm were applied.

Another turn was ordered. She cried: "Loosen me a little that I may remember what I have to tell, I don't know what I have done; I did not eat pork for it makes me sick; I have done everything; loosen me and I will tell the truth." Another turn of the cord was ordered . . . She was told to tell in detail truly what she did. She said: "What am I expected to tell? I did everything – loosen me for I don't remember what I have to tell – don't you see what a weak woman I am? Oh! Oh! my arms are breaking."

Once the sixteenth turn of the rope was administered, she was then ordered to be placed on the *potro* (rack).

> She said, "Señores, why will you not tell me what I have to say? Señor, put me on the ground – have I not said that I did it all?" She was told to tell it. She said, "I don't remember – take me away – I did what the witnesses say." She was told to tell in detail what the witnesses said. She said, "Señor, remind me of what I did not know – Señores, have mercy upon me – let me go for God's sake – they have no pity on me – I did it – take me from here and I will remember what I cannot here."
>
> She was told to state it, but replied, "I don't know how to say it – I have no memory – Lord, you are witness that if I knew how to say anything else I would say it. I know nothing more to say than that I did it and God knows it . . . The Law of which the witnesses speak – I don't remember what Law it was – cursed be the mother that bore me . . . Oh! Oh! they are killing me – if they would tell me what – Oh, Señores! Oh my heart!"

In Spain and later in Portugal the judicial sentence of the Inquisitors following such torture took place in public in the presence of dignitaries and crowds. These ceremonies, known as *autos da fé*, were accompanied by a sermon; the earliest took place in 1481, and they continued until the nineteenth century. The total of those who appeared to be charged numbered hundreds of thousands – over thirty thousand suffered the death penalty. The burning of heretics, however, did not take place during the *auto da fé* – those found guilty were handed over to the secular authorities who were responsible for their execution at the place of burning.

Such treatment of the Jewish population ended with expulsion. On 31 March 1492, Ferdinand and Isabella signed the Edict of Expulsion of the Jews of Spain:

> We have been informed by the Inquisitors, and by other persons, that the mingling of Jews with Christians leads to the worst evils. The Jews try their best to seduce the (New) Christians, and their children, bringing them books of Jewish prayers, telling them of the days of Jewish holidays, procuring unleavened bread for them at Passover, instructing them on the dietary prohibitions, and persuading them to follow the Law of Moses. In consequence, our holy Catholic faith is debased and humbled. We have thus arrived at the conclusion that the only efficacious means to put an end to these evils consists in the definitive breaking of all relations between Jews and Christians, and this can only be obtained by their expulsion from our kingdom.

CHAPTER EIGHT

The Dispersion of the Marranos

When the Inquisition intensified its efforts to root out Christian heresy
in Spain, Marranos fled to other countries for safety from their
Christian persecutors. Many sought refuge in Portugal, where they led
a Christian way of life while selectively observing Jewish practices.
Following Spanish precedent, the Portuguese Inquisition was established in 1536 and attempted to track down Marranos wherever they
lived. Other Marranos were driven to find homes in other lands. Both
Turkey and Salonica constituted Marrano refuges from Christian
oppression in the sixteenth century. Others went to Antwerp, Venice,
Ancona, and Bordeaux; in the next century Marranos settled in
Amsterdam, Hamburg, and London. Although in these centres
conversos returned to Judaism, they retained many of their former
cultural characteristics. During this period some Marranos gained
enormous political influence. The Duke of Naxos, for example,
became an important figure on the international scene, and sought to
create a homeland for the Jewish people. Others awaited the coming of
the Messiah to lead them back to Zion, and in the seventeenth century
numerous Marranos placed their hopes on the false Messiah
Shabbatai Tzevi. Some Marranos, however, like Baruch Spinoza,
broke away from traditional Judaism, and advanced heterodox religious views which unintentionally became the basis of further Christian
anti-Semitism in later centuries.

The Marranos of Portugal

Many Spanish Marranos who sought refuge from the Inquisition fled
to Portugal. These crypto-Jews, unlike their Spanish counterparts,
imitated the Christian way of life and complied with all Catholic rites
including attending mass and confession. None the less they selectively

observed various Jewish rituals and traditions such as Yom Kippur and the Fast of Esther. In addition, they found solace in Apocryphal texts, such as the Prayer of Esther which became a central prayer of the Marranos: "I whom you keep among the infidels, you know how much I hate their criminal feasts . . . this pomp to which I am condemned, this diadem in which I must appear. Alone and in secret I trample them under my feet."

Marrano insecurity frequently manifested itself in various messianic movements. In the early sixteenth century, for example, the adventurer David Reubeni presented himself to the court of Pope Clement VII as a representative of a Jewish kingdom of the East. The Pope referred him to the King of Portugal where he sailed in a ship flying a Jewish flag. Marranos there were jubilant; their frenzy led them to attack the inquisitorial prison of Badajoz. One of them, Diego Pires, became a Jew (taking the name Salomon Molcho) and joined Reubeni; together they travelled throughout Europe encouraging Messianic expectations. They were received by Charles V but finally were delivered to the Inquisition and burned at the stake.

The Inquisition was established in Portugal in 1536. Yet it was recognized that the New Christians constituted an important part of the population regardless of their religious beliefs and practices. Thus King John III informed the Pope that they greatly contributed to commerce and industry. They had served him well, he stated, and there was no reason to hate them. "How can one dare to require me to cut the throats of my own flock?" he asked.

Nevertheless the Inquisition operated with fervour, tracking down Marranos in cities, villages, forests and mountains. As in Spain, Jewish martyrs went to their deaths with bravery. Thus after burning twenty New Christians in 1542, the Inquisitor of Lisbon praised their courage: "Nothing astonished me so much as to see the Lord give such steadfastness to the weakness of flesh; children attended the burnings of their parents and wives those of their husbands and no one heard them cry out or weep. They said farewell and blessed them as if they were parting to meet again the next day."

During this onslaught a number of Marranos fled abroad, but many remained behind to practise Judaism in secret. However, among these individuals knowledge of Judaism seriously declined, such that in an *auto da fé* in 1705 an archbishop declared: "Miserable relics of Judaism! Unfortunate fragments of the synagogue! Last vestiges of

Judea! Scandal for the Catholics, laughingstock of the Jews themselves! . . . You are the laughingstock of the Jews because you do not
even know how to obey the law under which you live." Although the
distinction between New and Old Christians was eliminated at the
end of the eighteenth century, Marranism continued to survive.
Marranos continued to combine public Christian observances with
secret Jewish rites; as they continued to observe certain Jewish
holidays, they privately denied Christ whom they celebrated in
church.

The Dispersion of the Marranos

The expulsion of Jews from Spain in 1492 also drove thousands of
Jews from Spain into Barbary, Turkey and the few Christian
territories where they were allowed to settle. In the following two
centuries Marranos continued to find homes abroad. In most cases
these departures were facilitated through financial transactions, but in
other instances they were the result of clandestine emigration. Thus
in 1609–14 a number of Portuguese crypto- Jews and Spanish
conversos joined the Moriscos who had been expelled and crossed the
Pyrenees.

In Turkey the Marranos were well received, since efforts had been
made to attract them from the Iberian Peninsula ever since the
conquest of Constantinople. At that time Sultan Mohammed II
proclaimed: "Here, descendants of the Hebrews who live in my
country. Let each who desires it come to Constantinople, and let the
remnant of your people find asylum here." As a result many Jews fled
to Constantinople, and by the middle of the sixteenth century a
sizeable community had been established there. In the words of the
French ambassador d'Aramon: "Constantinople is inhabited principally by Turks, then by an infinite number of Jews, that is, Marranos
who were driven out of Spain, Portugal and Germany. They have
taught the Turks every handicraft, and the majority of the shops
belong to Jews." His contemporary Nicholas de Nicolay added:

> Among (the Jews) are very excellent workers in all arts and manufac-
> tures, especially the Marranos who have recently been banished and
> chased from Spain and Portugal. To the great detriment and shame of

Christianity, they have taught the Turks numerous inventions, artifices, and machines of war, such as how to make artillery, arquebuses, cannon powder, cannon balls, and other arms. Similarly, they have set up a printing shop, never before seen in these regions.

Salonica also constituted a Marrano refuge in the sixteenth century. The rabbis there encouraged them to become observant, yet among ordinary Jews they were often regarded with disapproval. Their ambiguous status led to considerable confusion: many Marranos did not know who they were and vascillated between Judaism and Christianity. There were even those who returned to Judaism, and then out of longing for Christianity embraced the Christian faith. Others adopted Islam and served in the military under the Sultan.

Marranos settled in new countries for a variety of reasons. Some went to places where they could live freely as Jews; others were attracted by commercial and economic advantages. Aware of the financial contributions these newcomers could make, a number of Christian governments granted them special privileges. Yet wherever they went the Marranos remained Spanish in character and used Castilian written in Latin characters or Hebrew script to communicate with one another or for publishing their writings.

Such communal identification led to a feeling of disdain for German or Polish Jews. Thus in a letter to Voltaire, who was critical of Jews and Judaism, Isaac de Pinto wrote:

M. Voltaire cannot be ignorant of the scrupulous exactness of the Portuguese and Spanish Jews not to intermix in marriage, alliance, or any other way, with the Jews of other nations . . . Their variance with their other brethren is such that if a Portuguese Jew in England or Holland married a German Jewess, he would of course lose all his prerogatives, be no longer reckoned a member of their synagogue, forfeit all civil and ecclesiastical preferments, be absolutely divorced from the body of the nation, and not even be buried with his Portuguese brethren. This is the cause of those distinctions and of that elevation of mind which is observed among them, and which even their brethren of other nations seem to acknowledge.

Social cohesion among the Marrano community meant that even when returning to Judaism, they retained their former cultural characteristics. According to de Pinto, "they do not wear beards, and do not affect any distinction in their clothing. Those who are well off pursue elegance and ostentation to the same extent as the other nations of Europe, from whom they differ only in religion." Such attitudes frequently led to criticism, such as that displayed by the preaching brother Labat who wrote of the Jews of Leghorn:

> They are free there, they do not wear any beard to distinguish them from the Christians. They are not confined to their neighbourhoods. They are rich; their business is extensive. Almost all have favours from the prince and they are protected to the point where it is proverbial in Tuscany that it would be better to beat the Grand Duke than a Jew. This only makes them all the more odious to everyone else. But they laugh at this, and I do not believe that there is any place in the world where they are more arrogant and more haughty.

Others, however, viewed these displaced Jews in a more favourable light. Commenting on the Jews of Venice, the English navigator Thomas Coryat wrote that they were

> such goodly and proper men, that I said to my selfe our English proverbe To looke like a Jewe (whereby is meant sometimes a weather beaten warp-faced fellow, sometimes a phrenticke and lunaticke person, sometimes one discontented) is not true. For indeed I noticed some of them to be most elegant and sweet featured persons ... I saw many Jewish women, whereof some were as beautiful as ever I saw, and so gorgeous in their apparel, jewels, chaines of gold, and rings adorned with precious stones, that some of our English Countesses do scarce exceed them.

The Marranos thus evoked differing responses from those among whom they lived. Spanish by origin, outwardly Christian, yet Jewish by inclination, they despised their co-religionists. Not surprisingly these contradictions frequently provoked profound crises of personal identity and loyalty.

The Marrano Duke of Naxos

The dispersion of the Marranos in the sixteenth century was dominated by the brothers Mendes. Francisco, living in Lisbon, and Diego Mendes in Antwerp, established a company which became the main spice importer for northern Europe. In addition to providing funds for kings, they transferred Marrano capital and property from Portugal to Flanders and then to Italy. After their death, Francisco's widow Beatrice de Luna headed the firm and was joined by her nephew Juan Micas. Knighted by Charles V, he was described by contemporaries as possessing a noble bearing and excellent manners: "He comported himself in humane and dignified fashion in all things . . . (he is a man who is) more fitting to be a Christian than a Jew." According to another, "there are few persons of account in Spain, Italy, or Flanders who are not personally acquainted with him."

After plans had been formulated for a marriage between Brianda de Luna, (the cousin and future wife of Juan Micas) and the favourite of Charles V, Francisco de Aragon, the Mendes family went to Venice and eventually to Constantinople where they were welcomed by the Sultan. There Juan Micas became Joseph Nasi and Beatrice de Luna became Gracia Nasi. In the capital Gracia Nasi devoted herself to pious works while Joseph became a powerful figure in Europe. Due to the Marrano network, he played a significant role in Ottoman foreign policy.

Introduced into the Ottoman court by the French ambassador to Rome, the Seigneur de Lansac, he became a fervent enemy of France due to a litigation concerning 150,000 ducats which he lent to Henry II in about 1549. According to French allegations, such a debt could be dispensed with if it were owed to a Marrano: "for the laws of the kingdom do not permit Jews such as the said Joseph Nasi to do business or traffic in anything; but they order that all their goods be confiscated." The logic of this position was that since Marranos deceived Christians by hiding their Jewish loyalty, they deserved to be deceived by the non-fulfilment of financial obligations. Eventually Joseph took revenge by persuading the Sultan to confiscate merchandise taken to the Levant under the French flag until the debt was paid.

The relationship between Joseph and the Crown of Spain was

equally complex. According to Philip II, Joseph was the instigator of an anti-Christian plot: He was "the one who contributes the most to the enterprises prejudicial to Christianity and who instigates them." Nevertheless, in 1570 Joseph asked Philip for safe conduct for himself and seventy others to return to Spain. He begged to be pardoned for practising Jewish law. It is unclear whether he was serious in this admission, or whether such a declaration was mere pretence. In any event, Joseph requested exemptions from custom duties for goods he wished to import. Philip inclined to agree to this petition, and it was the subject of secret Spanish dispatches, although in the end it did not take place.

In addition to his international activities, Joseph frequently acted as a protector of the Jewish people. When Pope Paul IV ordered twenty-five Marranos to be burned in 1556 in Ancona, Joseph and Gracia Nasi organized an international boycott of the port of Ancona. Earlier, during his stay in Italy, Joseph requested that Venice put an island at the disposal of homeless Marranos. In 1561 the Sultan granted him the city of Tiberias and surrounding lands to create a Jewish homeland, which he rebuilt despite the protestations of the apostolic legate in Palestine, Bonifazio di Ragusa, who inveighed against "the arrival of these vipers more deadly than those which haunt the ruins of the city". According to the French ambassador de Petremol, this enterprise was part of Joseph's plan to become king of the Jews. "Nasi", he wrote, has received permission from the Grand Signior . . . to build a city on the shore of the Lake of Tiberias wherein Jews only are to live. In fact, he proposes to begin his achievement here by this renewal, having the intention so far as one can judge of proclaiming himself king of the Jews. This is why he is demanding from France so insistently." The project was, however, unsuccessful due to the lack of Jewish enthusiasm for the creation of a Jewish polity. Few Jews came to settle in Tiberias. None the less, Joseph persisted in his plans to create a Jewish state. In 1566 the new sultan Selim II gave him the island of Naxos and made him Duke. In 1570 he encouraged Selim to declare war on Venice: the campaign began with the conquest of Cyprus over which Joseph hoped to rule as king. This plan never reached fruition, and in 1579 he died, rich but without having attained his political aspirations.

So great was Joseph's fame that he exerted a powerful influence on the Christian conception of the Jew in the years following his death. Through Christopher Marlowe's *Jew of Malta*, he contributed to the formulation of the character Shylock in William Shakespeare's *The Merchant of Venice*. In this play the villainous Venetian moneylender does business with Christians despite their antipathy to him. Protesting against their antagonism to him as a Jew, he declares: "I am a Jew. Hath not a Jew eyes ? Hath not a Jew hands, organs, dimensions, senses, affections, passions? . . . If you prick us, do we not bleed? If you tickle us, do we not laugh? If you poison us, do we not die? And if you wrong us, shall we not revenge?" The saga of Joseph Nasi, the all-too-human Marrano – Duke of Naxos and upholder of the Jews – symbolized the dual identity of the *conversos* in dispersion.

The Shabbatean Movement

The story of the Marrano dispersion was linked to the Jewish expectation of the coming of the Messiah in the seventeenth century. During this period Jewish believers, including many Marranos, believed the coming of the Messiah was near at hand. In this milieu the arrival of a self-proclaimed messianic king, Shabbatai Tzevi, brought about a transformation of Jewish life. Born in Smyrna into a Judeo-Spanish family, Shabbatai had received a traditional Jewish education and later engaged in the study of the Zohar. After leaving Smyrna in the 1650s he spent ten years in various cities in Greece as well as in Constantinople and Jerusalem. Eventually he became part of a kabbalistic group in Cairo and travelled to Gaza where he encountered Nathan Benjamin Levi who believed Shabbatai was the Messiah. In 1665 his messiahship was proclaimed and Nathan sent letters to Jews in the diaspora asking them to repent and recognize Shabbatai Tzevi as their redeemer. Shabbatai, he announced, would take the Sultan's crown, bring back the lost tribes, and inaugurate the period of messianic redemption. Throughout the entire dispersion, rich and poor made preparations to leave for Palestine.

After a brief sojourn in Jerusalem, Shabbatai went to Smyrna where he encountered strong opposition on the part of some local rabbis. In response he denounced the disbelievers and declared that he was the Anointed of the God of Jacob. This action evoked a hysterical response – a number of Jews fell into trances and had visions of him on a royal throne crowned as King of Israel. In 1666 he journeyed to Constantinople, but on the order of the Grand Vizier he was arrested and put into prison. Within a short time the prison quarters became a messianic court; pilgrims from all over the world made their way to Constantinople to join in messianic rituals and in ascetic activities. Hymns were written in his honour and new festivals were introduced. According to Nathan, who remained in Gaza, the alteration in Shabbatai's moods from illumination to withdrawal symbolized his soul's struggle with demonic powers: at times he was imprisoned by the powers of evil but at other moments he prevailed against them.

The same year Shabbatai spent three days with the Polish kabbalist, Nehemiah ha-Kohen, who later denounced him to the Turkish authorities. Shabbatai was brought to court and given the choice between conversion and death. In the face of this alternative, he converted to Islam and took on the name of Mehemet Effendi. Such an act of apostasy scandalized most of his followers, but he defended himself by asserting that he had become a Muslim in obedience to God's commands. Many of his followers accepted this explanation and refused to give up their belief. Some thought it was not Shabbatai who had become a Muslim, but rather a phantom who had taken on his appearance; the Messiah himself had ascended to Heaven. Others cited biblical and rabbinic sources to justify Shabbatai's action. Nathan explained that the messianic task involved taking on the humiliation of being portrayed as a traitor to his people.

After Shabbatai's act of apostasy, Nathan visited him in the Balkans and then travelled to Rome where he performed secret rites to bring about the end of the papacy. Shabbatai remained in Adrianople and Constantinople, where he lived as both Muslim and Jew. In 1672 he was deported to Albania, where he disclosed his own kabbalistic teaching to his supporters. After he died several years later, Nathan declared that Shabbatai had ascended to the supernal world. Eventually a number of groups continued in their belief that Shabbatai was the Messiah, including a sect, the Dissidents (*Doenmeh*), which professed Islam publicly but nevertheless adhered to their own traditions. Marrying among themselves, they eventually evolved into antinomian sub-groups which violated Jewish sexual laws and asserted the divinity of Shabbatai and their leader, Baruchiah Russo. In Italy several Shabbatean groups also emerged and propagated their views.

In the eighteenth century, the most important Shabbatean sect was led by Jacob Frank, who was influenced by the *Doenmeh* in Turkey. Believing himself to be the incarnation of Shabbatai, Frank announced that he was the second person of the Trinity and gathered together a circle of disciples who indulged in licentious orgies. In the 1750s, disputations took place between traditional Jews and Frankists; subsequently Frank expressed his willingness to become a Christian but he wished to maintain his own group. Although this request was refused by Church leaders, Frank and his disciples were baptized. The clergy, however, became aware that Frank's trinitarian beliefs were not consonant with Christian doctrine, and he was imprisoned for thirteen years. Frank then settled in Germany, where he continued to subscribe to a variant of the Shabbatean kabbalistic tradition.

Spinoza and Anti-Judaism

Amsterdam in the seventeenth century had the largest Marrano community in Europe. In addition to creating a book industry, Marranos there published translations of the Bible for Protestant use as well as a Jewish newspaper, *Gazeta de Amsterdam*. Although their former apostasy was a source of guilt, it was difficult for them to resume a traditional Jewish way of life. As a result, within the Marrano community there was considerable debate about religious practice and belief.

Chief among those who participated in these discussions was Baruch Spinoza. Born in Amsterdam in 1633, his father had been an observant Catholic in Nantes before settling in Holland where he returned to Judaism. A student of the Etz Chaim rabbinical school, Spinoza was influenced by Juan de Prado, who was born in Córdoba, educated in Spanish universities, and later returned to Judaism. In 1656 Spinoza was excommunicated because of his religious views, and several years later he left Amsterdam and went to Leyden. He later settled in Voorburg, near the Hague – he died at the age of forty-four.

During his lifetime Spinoza published the *Tractatus Theologico-Politicus*, and his *Ethics* appeared posthumously. Starting from the heterodox views expressed within the Amsterdam Marrano community, Spinoza in his *Tractatus* developed a critique of Judaism and supernatural religion. Insisting that religious convictions should be judged only on the basis of reason, Spinoza rejected the Mosaic authorship of the Pentateuch and the possibility of prophecy. Supernatural events, he argued, could not occur, and the Bible should be examined solely as a human document. Nature, he believed, is governed by eternal and necessary divine decrees; nothing can occur which is contrary to natural law.

In the *Ethics*, Spinoza presented his philosophy in geometrical form. Beginning with definitions of terms such as "God", "substance", and "attribute" and a series of axioms concerning causality and existence, Spinoza outlined his picture of the world in the form of demonstrations of propositions. God, or nature, he maintained, is the only possible substance, and everything in the world is an aspect of God and can be conceived in terms of one of God's attributes of thought or extension.

Given that God or nature is the only substance, everything else is understood in terms of him and is deducible from his essence. God acts only through law – the world is a logical order and nothing could be different from what it is. God is thus not a being who acts in the world. He lacks nothing and simply is. Due to his being everything occurs of necessity.

In his writings Spinoza made a number of critical observations about the concept of peoplehood. Rejecting the belief that Jews are God's chosen people, he criticized the prerogatives accorded to the Jewish nation:

> He who thinks that his blessedness is increased by the fact that he is better off, or happier and more fortunate, than the rest of mankind, knows nothing of true happiness and blessedness, and the pleasure he derives from such thoughts, unless merely childish, arises only from spite and malice . . . The man who is pleased by such thoughts is pleased by the misfortune of another; he is therefore spiteful and wicked, and knows nothing either of true wisdom or the peace of mind which true living involves.

According to Spinoza, it is not a miracle that the Jewish people have endured through the centuries – rather it was due in large part to their desire to cut themselves off from other people, yet by doing so the Jewish nation evoked hatred from those among whom they lived:

> As for the fact that they have survived their dispersion and the loss of their state for so many years, there is nothing miraculous in that, since they incurred universal hatred by cutting themselves off completely from all other peoples; and not only by practising a form of worship opposed to that of the rest, but also by preserving the mark of

circumcision with such devoutness. Hence the patriotism of the Jews was not only patriotism but piety, and it was so fostered by their daily ritual that it must have become second nature . . . And this must have inspired in the Jews continued and ineradicable hatred, for a hatred which springs from great devotion or piety, and is itself believed to be pious, is undoubtedly greater and more persistent than any other. And the common reason for the continued growth of hatred, i.e., the fact that it is returned, was also present; for the gentiles must have regarded the Jews with the most bitter hatred.

Spinoza's heterodoxy originated in a milieu in which the Marranos' apostasy and return to Judaism led to religious perplexity. Not surprisingly, traditional Jewish dogma came under threat as Marranos struggled to harmonize Jewish teaching with human reason. Unintentionally Spinoza's anti-Jewish polemic provided the basis for anti-Semitism of the modern period: his observations about the Hebrew Scriptures, ceremonial Judaism and Jewish belief were used by Christians to denigrate Judaism and the Jewish people.

CHAPTER NINE

Anti-Semitism in Eastern Europe

In the first millennium, Polish Jewry played an important role in the financial affairs of the country. Unlike their co-religionists in western Europe, Jews in Poland enjoyed considerable tolerance and were granted numerous privileges – they were not confined to ghettos, nor restricted in their occupations. Under such conditions, the Jewish community created an elaborate form of local and national self-government, and rabbinic scholarship reached great heights. Yet despite such general prosperity, the country was subject to Christian anti-Jewish hostility in the late medieval period, and in the seventeenth century Polish Jewry was massacred by Cossacks under Bogdan Chmielnicki. In the wake of this Christian onslaught, the Hasidic movement encouraged religious pietism, but was severely criticized by the traditional rabbinical establishment. As the community was torn by this conflict, attacks were directed against the Jewish population by gentiles. Such hostility in Poland was paralleled in Russia. Initially Jews were prevented from settling in the country, and with the annexation of Polish territories to Russia in the nineteenth century, Jews were regarded by Christians with suspicion and contempt and eventually expelled from the villages where they resided.

Polish Jewry

During the first millennium, the first Jews to penetrate into the area between the Oder and the Dnieper appear to have come from the south-east, the Jewish kingdom of the Khazars, and Byzantium. Given the agrarian economy of the country, they played a major role in activities related to the circulation of merchandise and money. Within this context Jews gained significant influence; indeed, according to legend, a Jew (Saul Wahl) temporarily assumed the throne of Poland.

In 1264, King Boleslav V granted Polish Jewry a charter which paralleled those granted by German princes in previous centuries. Not surprisingly, such positive treatment evoked a hostile response from the clergy. As a result, from the second half of the thirteenth century, Polish ecclesiastical authorities legislated against the Jewish population, and in 1279 an unsuccessful attempt was made to impose the wearing of a Jewish insignia. In the following century there appeared Christian accusations of ritual murder and profanation of the Host. In 1454, Casimir IV abrogated a number of privileges granted to the Jews, and thirty years later the Jews of Warsaw were expelled. This was followed by their expulsion from Cracow and by an attempt to expel them from Lithuania.

Despite the similarities between these events and the treatment of the Jewish community in western Europe in the Middle Ages, Polish Jewry did not endure the same suffering as their co-religionists in England, France, Germany and Spain. Throughout Poland, Jews had succeeded in gaining important economic positions, and thereby were deeply rooted in the social fabric of the country. Jews engaged in a wide variety of trades and created important Jewish communal organizations. Thus the Papal Legate Commendoni observed in 1565:

> In these regions masses of Jews are to be found, who are not subject to the scorn they meet with elsewhere. They do not live in abasement and are not reduced to menial trades thereby. They own land, engage in commerce, study medicine and astronomy. They possess great wealth and are not only counted among respectable people but sometimes even dominate them. They wear no distinctive insignia, and are even permitted to bear arms. In short, they have all the rights of citizens.

Polish Jewry did not live in ghettos, nor were they restricted in their occupations. Instead, they engaged in all aspects of commerce and trade, administration, industrial management and agriculture. A number of Polish Jewish bankers owned considerable lands; others served as stewards, tradesmen, and commercial agents of Polish lords. Some imported wood, wheat, skins and furs. The majority, however, worked as tradesmen, artisans, innkeepers, retail dealers or farmers.

As a consequence of this socio-economic pattern, Polish Jewry was able to establish a form of local and national self-government. The basis of this system was the *kahal* (community) which corresponded to a geographical unit comprising Jews who lived in the city and the surrounding territory. Every year electors (whose names were drawn by lot from the most important members of the community) selected the administrators of each *kahal*. These individuals were responsible for the collection of taxes and customs, the maintenance of public order, the organization of synagogue affairs, and responsibility for the control of the labour market. The *kahal* also appointed the rabbi, who was invested with authority over judicial affairs. In addition, elected commissioners dealt with various charitable activities, including the ransom of prisoners and care of the sick, elderly and needy. Burial societies (*khevkrot kedishah*) were responsible for dealing with the deceased.

Such a coherent and complex communal organization was employed by the Polish authorities for the collection of taxes: it was usual to impose a single annual tax on all Jews, to be allocated among the communities. From the sixteenth century, representatives of each *kahal* gathered in the spring at the Lublin fair, and at the Yaroslav fair in the fall – there they determined their quotas, adjudicated conflicts, and published new laws and decrees. This federal body which met semi-annually was referred to as the "Council of the Four Nations". Through this organizational structure the Polish community enjoyed considerable autonomy and independence from external influence.

Scholarship in Poland

Under such favourable conditions talmudic learning reached great heights in Poland. Beginning in the late fifteenth century, a number of outstanding scholars produced commentaries on talmudic law, and within the *yeshivot* (rabbinical academies) the methods of *pilpul* (dialectical study) and *hilluk* (differentiation and reconciliation of rabbinic opinions) were widely practised. Excerpts from a seventeenth-century chronicle describe the nature of the Ashkenazic educational system which produced such an efflorescence of Jewish learning:

Each community maintained young men and provided for them a weekly allowance of money that they might study with the head of the academy. And for each young man they also maintained two boys to study under his guidance, so that he would orally discuss the *Gemara*, the commentaries of Rashi, and the *Tosafot*, which he had learned, and thus he would gain experience in the subtlety of talmudic argumentation. The boys were provided with food from the community benevolent fund or from the public kitchen. If the community consisted of fifty householders it supported not less than thirty young men and boys. One young man and two boys would be assigned to one householder . . .

There was scarcely a house in all the kingdom of Poland where its members did not occupy themselves with the study of the Torah. Either the head of the family was himself a scholar, or else his son, or his son-in-law studied, or one of the young men eating at his table . . .

The programme of study in the kingdom of Poland was as follows: The term of study consisted of the period which required the young men and the boys to study with the head of the academy in the academy. In the summer it extended from the first day of the month of Iyar till the fifteenth day of the month of Av, and in the winter, from the first day of the Heshvan, till the fifteenth day of the month of Shevat. After the fifteenth of Shevat or the fifteenth of Av, the young men and the boys were free to study wherever they preferred. From the first day of Iyar till the Feast of Weeks and in the winter from the first day of Heshvan till Hanukkah all the students of the academy studied *Gemara* [Talmud], the commentaries of Rashi, and the *Tosafot* with great diligence . . .

In each community great honour was accorded to the head of the academy. His words were heard by rich and poor alike. None questioned his authority. Without him no one raised his hand or foot, and as he commanded so it came to be. In his hand he carried a stick and a lash, to smite and to flog, to punish and chastise transgressors, to institute ordinances, to establish safeguards, and to declare the forbidden. Nevertheless, everyone loved the head of the academy.

During this period, Polish rabbinical authorities were indirectly influenced by Renaissance humanism – textual criticism was used to determine the precise reading of ancient texts and correct errors that had occurred during generations of copying manuscripts. In addition, scholars collected and summarized the legal interpretations of Ashkenazic (eastern European) and Sephardic (western European and oriental) halakhists. Due to the existence of printing presses, rabbinic works were made available to scholars within the *yeshivot*. In the discussions that took place in this milieu the value of Joseph Caro's *Shulhan Arukh* (Code of Jewish Law) became a major issue. A number of authorities were disappointed that this Code was used as the central text for study in the *yeshivot* and as a guide for rabbis. Instead, they argued that the adjudication of cases be based on talmudic sources and the opinions of recent scholars. None the less, the *Shulhan Arukh* was accepted as the basis for rabbinical study since it contained the notes and commentaries of Polish scholars of the sixteenth and seventeenth centuries.

Despite the relative stability of Polish Jewish life and this efflorescence of scholarship, the Jewish community was subject to Christian anti-Jewish outbursts. In 1521 the proconsuls and consuls of Lvov wrote to their fellow consuls in Poznan complaining about Jewish merchants. "The infidel Jews", they charged, "robbed us and our merchant citizens of almost all our sources of livelihood . . . they alone engage in commerce, go out to the small towns and villages, and do not permit anything to reach Christian hands." In 1618 the Jew-hater Sebastian Miczynski, wrote a similar diatribe:

> In Lvov, in Lublin, in Poznan and particularly Cracow, not to mention Vilna, Mohilev, Slutzk, Brest-Litovsk, Lutsk and elsewhere, the Jews have in almost every brick house five, ten, fifteen or sixteen shops. These shops are full of merchandise and all kinds of wares . . . they go to other countries from which they import sundry goods to Poland . . . when goods of any kind reach Poland the Jews quickly purchase everything . . . In addition they export goods . . . to Hungary, to Moravia . . . and to other places. They trade in spices and in all kinds of grain, in honey and sugar, in milk products and other foodstuffs. There is scarcely any kind of goods, from the most expensive to the cheapest, in which the Jews do not trade . . . They do not rest satisfied with sitting in shops and doing business. Some of them actually go round the market, the houses and the courtyards peddling their wares . . . They entice . . . the buyers . . . and attract them to the Jewish shops promising them good bargains.

The Chmielnicki Massacres

In the midst of this general material and spiritual prosperity, the Polish Jewish community was subject in the seventeenth century to a series of massacres carried out by Christian Cossacks of the Ukraine as well as

Crimean Tartars and Ukrainian peasants who rebelled against the Polish nobility. In 1648 Bogdan Chmielnicki was elected hetman of the Cossacks and thereupon instigated an insurrection against the Polish gentry which had previously oppressed the Cossack population. As administrators of noblemen's estates, Jews were slaughtered in these revolts. Estates and manor houses were destroyed and victims were flayed, burned alive and mutilated. Infants were murdered and cast into wells; women were cut open and sewn up again with live cats thrust into their wounds.

According to contemporary Jewish accounts, Jews suffered in the most merciless fashion in this onslaught: "These persons died cruel and bitter deaths. Some were skinned alive and their flesh was thrown to the dogs; some had their hands and limbs chopped off, and their bodies thrown on the highways only to be trampled by wagons and crushed by horses; some had wounds inflicted on them . . . some children were pierced by spears, roasted on the fire, and then brought to their mothers to be eaten." In these massacres thousands of Jews died in towns east of the Dnieper and elsewhere.

As the Cossacks advanced, the Polish king died and was succeeded by John Casimir, who attempted to negotiate with the Cossacks who demanded an independent Ukrainian state. After several more years of battle, Chmielnicki appealed to the Russian allies who invaded north-western Poland, but by the following year a Polish partisan movement drove back these foreign invaders. Finally, in 1667, Russia and Poland signed the Treaty of Andrusovo which distributed the western Ukraine to Poland, and the eastern Ukraine and the Smolensk region to Russia.

During these years of war the Jewish population was decimated by the various opposing forces: the Cossacks and Ukrainian peasants regarded Jews as representatives of the Polish aristocracy; the Russians, who did not allow Jews to settle in their lands, joined the Cossack hordes in this slaughter; and the Polish partisans saw Jews as allied with the Swedes. Approximately a quarter of the entire Jewish community died in this attack, and thousands were ransomed from the Tartars in the slave markets of Constantinople.

In the wake of this catastrophe, the Jewish community went into mourning. In 1650 the Council of the Four Nations proclaimed a national mourning in memory of the victims. For three years Polish Jews were not allowed to wear silk or velvet garments. An annual fast was instituted on the 20th of Sivan as an anniversary of the massacre perpetrated by the Cossacks at Nemirov, where Jews died in masses as martyrs rather than convert to Christianity. New elegies (*selihot* and *kinot*) were written and recited in synagogues following those that traditionally commemorate Jewish suffering during the Crusades. In addition Jews performed acts of penance, seeing in their misery the just retribution for their sins. Thus an appeal from the Council of the Four Nations in 1676 declared: "Gravely have we sinned before our Lord . . . Troubles increase daily, life becomes ever more difficult, our people has no importance among other peoples. It is even surprising that, despite all the disasters, we continue to survive. The only thing left for us to do is to unite in a single alliance and obey the commandments of God and the precepts of our pious teachers and leaders."

As the century progressed, Jewish life in Poland became more insecure due to political instability; nevertheless the Jewish community considerably increased in size during the eighteenth century. Approximately a third of Polish Jewry lived in the countryside in small groups, where they were subject to repeated blood accusations. In the 1730s and 1740s Cossacks known as Haidemaks invaded the Ukraine, robbing and murdering Jewish inhabitants, and finally butchering the Jewish community of Uman in 1768. Throughout this period the Polish *kehillot* (Jewish communities) were heavily taxed, and at times claims were made that the leaders of the Jewish community placed most of the tax burdens on the poor.

In Lithuania, on the other hand, Jewish life flourished, and Vilna became an important centre of rabbinic scholarship. Here Elijah ben Solomon Zalman, referred to as the Vilna Gaon, lectured to disciples on a wide range of subjects and composed commentaries on the Bible, Mishnah, Talmud, midrashim, the *Sepher Yetsirah*, *Zohar*, and the *Shulhan Arukh*. Unlike earlier eastern European sages, he rejected the method of *hilluk* and focused on the simple meaning of the text. In addition his interests extended to secular fields such as algebra, geometry, astronomy and geography. As a symbol of rabbinic learning, he stood out against the excesses of religious piety which began to make an impact on Polish Jewry in the latter half of the eighteenth century.

Hasidism and Later Polish Anti-Judaism

Following the massacres of the seventeenth century, many Polish Jews became disenchanted with rabbinic Judaism and through Hasidism sought individual salvation by means of religious pietism. The founder of this new movement was Israel ben Eleazer, known as the Baal Shem Tov (or Besht). According to tradition, Israel ben Eleazer was born in southern Poland in 1700 and in his twenties he journeyed with his wife to the Carpathian mountains. In the 1730s he travelled to Mezibozh where he performed various miracles and instructed his disciples about kabbalisitic lore. By the 1740s he had attracted a considerable number of disciples who passed on his teaching. After his death in 1760 Dov Baer became the leader of this sect and Hasidism spread to southern Poland, the Ukraine and Lithuania.

The growth of this movement engendered considerable hostility on the part of rabbinic authorities. In particular the rabbinic leadership of Vilna issued an edict of excommunication; the Hasidim were charged with permissiveness in their observance of the commandments, laxity in the study of the Torah, excess in prayer, and preference for the Lurianic (mystical) rather than the Ashkenazic prayerbook. In subsequent years the Hasidim and their opponents (the *mitnagdim*) bitterly denounced one another. Relations deteriorated further when Jacob Joseph of Polonnoye published a book critical of the rabbinate; his work was burned and in 1781 the *mitnagdim* ordered that all relations with the Hasidim cease. By the end of the century the Jewish religious establishment of Vilna denounced the Hasidim to the Russian government, an act which resulted in the imprisonment of several leaders. Despite such condemnation, the Hasidic movement was eventually recognized by the Russian and Austrian governments; in the ensuing years the movement divided into a number of separate groups under different leaders who passed on positions of authority to their descendants.

As the Jewish community was rent asunder by this new movement, anti-Jewish hostility continued to be directed against the Jewish population. In the regions of the Ukraine and White Russia, attacks on Jewry and Judaism continued to take place. Thus Basil Voshtchilo styled himself "Ataman Voshtchilo, grandson of Chmielnicki, grand hetman of the troops, charged with the extermination of Jewry and the defence of Christendom". In a manifesto, he declared:

In their petitions, the Jews claimed that I am fomenting disturbances and that I oppose the government with violence. This is a base lie. I have never had such an intention. I am a Christian. In this region, infidel Jews have not only deprived Christians of their means of existence, but they carry out aggressions, murders, robberies and oppress the holy sacraments. Without their sanction and their written authorization for the priest, no newborn child can be baptized. They bewitch the pans, the lords of the nobility, and thereby gain their acquiescence. They rape Christian women and do many other things that are difficult even to list. Impelled by my fervour for the holy Christian faith, I have decided, in company with other men of honour, to exterminate the cursed Jewish people.

On the eve of the first partition of Poland, massacres became more frequent. Under cover of an imperial decree, insurgents attempted to carry out the extermination of the Jews in the name of the Pravoslavic faith. From the beginning of the eighteenth century, Christian accusations of ritual murder and the profanation of the Host became more frequent. During this period Michael the Neophyte swore on a crucifix that ritual murder was an absolute commandment of Judaism and that he had murdered Christian children – his work, *Revelations of the Jewish Rites before God and the World,* served as the basis for anti-Semitism in following centuries.

Russian Jewry

During the reign of Ivan III in the fifteenth century, the first Jews entered into Muscovy. In about 1470 a Jew, Skharia, arrived in Novgorod, sided with the clergy, and persuaded a number of them of the superiority of Judaism. As a result, Pope Denis, Pope Alexis and several others converted to the Jewish faith. In time a modified form of Judaism was openly practised: although these Judaizers glorified Christ, they denied his divinity as well as the existence of the Trinity, and burned sacred icons. From Novgorod this heresy spread to Moscow and penetrated into the royal court. Ivan III's favourite, Feodor Karitzin, and his daughter-in-law Helena joined the sect. According to a chronicler of the time, "since the time when the Pravoslavic sun first shone in our country, there has never been such a heresy. In the home, in the streets, in the markets, clergy and laymen debated the Faith and no longer trusted the teachings of the Prophets, the Apostles and the Fathers of the Church, but on the arguments of the heretics, renegades of Christianity, sided in friendship with them and accepted instruction in Judaism."

Eventually Ivan III intervened when he recognized the danger of this heresy, and in 1504 the leaders of the sect were burned. Yet their religious views were not uprooted and reappeared in following centuries. In order to protect themselves from future Judaizing influence, the Muscovite authorities quarantined the Jews. Thus in 1526 Demitri Guerassimov proclaimed: "The Jews revolt us most of all, and the very mention of their name horrifies us. We do not permit them to enter our lands, for they are vile and evil-doing men." When Ivan the Terrible (Ivan IV) was urged by the Polish King Sigismund Augustus to allow several Jewish merchants into Moscow, he asserted:

Apropros of what you write to persuade us to allow your Jews to enter our lands, we have already written you several times, telling you of the vile actions of the Jews, who have turned our people away from Christ, introduced poisonous drugs into our state, and caused much harm to our people. You should be ashamed, our brother, to write us about them knowing their misdeeds all the while. In other states, too, they have done much evil, and for this have been expelled or put to death. We cannot permit the Jews to come into our state, for we do not wish to see any evil here. We pray that God may permit the people of our country to live in peace, without any disturbance. And you, our brother, should not write us in the future concerning the Jews.

This policy was maintained by his successors. None the less, in the seventeenth century a number of converted Jews, some of whom still practised Judaism in secret, were allowed to settle in Moscow. Officially, however, Jews were forbidden to enter the city. Thus in 1698 Peter the Great replied to the burgomaster of Amsterdam who requested that he allow certain Jewish merchants to enter Moscow: "You know, my friend, the character and customs of the Jews; you also know the Russians. I, too, know them both, and believe me: the time has not yet come to unite these two peoples. Tell the Jews that I thank them for their offers and I understand the advantages I might have derived from them, but I would have pitied them for having to live among the Russians." This policy was continued by his widow, Empress Catherine I, who two years after his death published an edict which declared: "The Jews of masculine sex and those of feminine sex who are found in the Ukraine and in other Russian cities are to be expelled at once beyond the frontiers of Russia. Henceforth they will not be admitted into Russia upon any pretext, and a very close watch will be kept upon them in all places."

During the following two centuries, Jews entered Russia illegally or with authorization from Poland and Lithuania, occasionally settling in border towns. At this time Russian rulers issued decrees prohibiting the entry of Jewish merchants – treaties between Poland and Russia included these proscriptions. Nevertheless, small Jewish communities existed in the region of Smolensk. In 1742 Tsarina Elizabeth Petrovna expelled the few Jews living in the kingdom. When the Senate attempted to cancel this decree by pointing out the financial loss to the state by this expulsion, she declared: "I do not want any profit from the enemies of Christ."

At the beginning of Catherine II's reign, the question of allowing Jews to enter Russia for trading purposes again became an issue. Although inclined to accede to this request, the Tsarina was compelled to give in to popular opinion. Despite such a setback, some Jews managed to penetrate into Russia, and the authorities did not disturb those living in territories conquered from Turkey in 1768. At the close of the century, however, hundreds of thousands of Jews were placed under the dominion of the Tsarina as a result of the partition of Poland. The Jews who lived in those regions annexed to Russia constituted a distinct social class: many leased villages, flour mills, farms, inns and taverns; others worked as merchants, shopkeepers and tradesmen. The rest were craftsmen working for landowners as well as peasants. The economic position of those Jews living in this region declined in time. After coming under Russian rule, many communities incurred considerable debt, and the burden of taxes drove a considerable number to abandon small towns and settle in villages or on the estates of noblemen.

From the beginning of this annexation of the Polish territories, the Russian government viewed the existence of Jewry in Russia as a serious problem which could only be solved by their assimilation or expulsion. None the less, during the first fifty years of their incorporation, the status of Jews generally remained as it had under Polish dominion. In 1791 a decree was promulgated which contained the right of Jews to reside in the territories annexed from Poland and also permitted their settlement in the uninhabited steppes of the Black Sea shore, as well as in the provinces to the east of the Dnieper. This region, known as the Pale of Settlement, took its final form with the annexation of Bessarabia in 1812. The total area of Jewish settlement extended from the Baltic to the Black Sea, consisting of an area of nearly a million square kilometres, where Jews formed one ninth of the population.

In the regions annexed from Poland, Jews in villages were blamed for the plight of the peasantry, while Jewish autonomy was regarded as undermining the Christian feudal culture of the country. As a result, the first Jewish Statute was promulgated in 1804, which enshrined various economic restrictions. After the promulgation of this Statute, the expulsion of Jewry from the villages began to take place, as did their settlement in southern Russia. In 1822 Jews were systematically expelled from villages, and an unsuccessful attempt was also made to persuade Jews to convert to the Christian faith.

CHAPTER TEN

Western Jewry in the Early Modern Period

During the early modern period the commercial interests of the bourgeoisie, coupled with centuries-old Christian prejudice against Jews and Judaism, evoked considerable hostility toward the Jewish population in western countries. In Germany, merchants protested against the infidels living in their midst. Jewish trade, they believed, would destroy the economic life of the country and pollute the Christian population. Similar attitudes were expressed in France, where the bourgeoisie resisted Jewish settlement despite the fact that the nobility regarded Jews as financially useful. In Great Britain, Jews were also subject to virulent criticism, and attempts to simplify procedures for Jewish naturalization and to authorize Jews to possess land were met with considerable resistance. In the United States, however, Jews gained a broad measure of freedom as the country struggled to achieve its independence from England. None the less, despite many of the advances made in the seventeenth and eighteenth centuries, Jewish life did not alter radically from medieval patterns of existence. Stereotyped as foreign and strange, Jews were subject to discrimination and persecution during the early modern period, and even enlightened Jews such as the philosopher Moses Mendelssohn were unable to escape anti-Jewish sentiment.

German Jewry

At the beginning of the early modern period, Jewish economic progress often conflicted with the interests of the Christian bourgeoisie. As a result, commercial aspirations frequently intermingled with traditional Christian anti-Jewish prejudice. Thus in 1671 Jews were expelled from Vienna by the Emperor of Austria, Leopold I. Initially he adopted a positive attitude to the Jewish population, but in 1669 a series of calamities occurred which altered his attitude: a fire took place in the palace; the heir to the throne died, and the Empress miscarried. According to the Empress's confessor, these events were a divine warning about the Jews, and the Emperor decreed their expulsion on 28 February 1670. When the Prussian Great Elector, Frederick William, heard of this proclamation, he invited thirty rich Jewish families to settle in his state to help develop industry and trade. Jews were granted a special and irrevocable charter which gave them numerous rights and protections. However, such an influx incited the enmity of Christian merchants who complained in 1673: "These infidels run from village to village, from town to town, offer this and take that, whereby they do not only dispose of their discarded and wretched goods and deceive the people with old rags, but they spoil all commerce and particularly the retail trade, especially in silver, brass, tea and copper."

The intermingling of economic interests and Christian religious hostility was further illustrated by an onslaught on the Jewish population which took place in the Prussian town of Halberstadt during the same period. The Jews of the town had built a synagogue without official permission. In response the bourgeoisie of the town devastated the building. In the words of a Jewish petition, these traders, accompanied by armed musketeers, "burst into our synagogue, seized the windows and doors and partially broke them down and razed the whole building to the ground, destroyed and smashed everything, cut it into pieces and caused such violent tumult and confusion, fear and terror that we could not but think that we were to be cut down and chased away to the last man, and then when the mob came running up from every corner we had to have soldiers on guard day and night for our protection."

An investigation of this incident was ordered by the Prussian government. In their defence the Halberstadt bourgeoisie declared that their act was justified, "because it is unfortunately drawn from experience what evil is caused to the Jews and their eternal damnation by the establishment of such seminaries in which superstition and a perverted understanding of all divine prophecy and revelation as well as contempt for Christ and his holy word is inculcated from childhood onwards and thus the way to their conversion is made more difficult and remote; also, this people nowhere grows more numerous than where they are permitted to exercise their damnable religion."

Despite such resentment against the Jewish presence, the princes and nobility regarded Jews as providing substantial economic advantages, even though they were a corrupt influence on the Christian nation. Thus Frederick William advised his son, the future Frederick the Great, how to deal with German Jewry:

> So far as the Jews are concerned there are unfortunately many in our hands who have no letters of protection from me. These you must chase out of the country for the Jews are a locust in a country and ruin the Christians. I ask you, issue no new letters of protection, even if they offer you much money . . . if you need something for your pleasure, then put all the Jews down for 20–30,000 thalers every three or four years, in addition to the protection money they must give you. You must squeeze them for they betrayed Jesus Christ, and must not trust them for the most honest Jew is an arch traitor and rogue.

Throughout the seventeenth and eighteenth centuries, German Jews played an important role in numerous commercial centres. In Leipzig, twenty-five per cent of those participating at fairs in the eighteenth century were Jews; in Hamburg they were actively involved in trade; in Frankfurt, Jewry comprised sixteen per cent of the total population. Confronted by these Jewish tradesmen at the end of the century, Goethe disparagingly described their commercial dealings:

> If you want to buy a suit,
> to the Jew run back.
> Silver dishes, linen, tin –
> anything the households lack,
> you will find the Jew has by him,
> taken as a pledge for loans.
> Stolen goods, abducted items
> with him, make their happy homes.
> Coats and trousers – what you will,
> he will sell it cheap.
> The craftsmen can sell nothing.
> To the Jew all creep.

The traditional Christian identification of Jews as swindlers was reinforced in the literature of this period. Thus Spener, the founder of Lutheran pietism, wrote:

As for the poor amongst them, whose number, as it is amongst the Christians, is always the largest, it is quite impossible for them to live without cunning and ruses for they, having only a few thaler capital, must turn this over through trade so that they can meet the needs of their family as best they may; so the wretched people can day and night think and rack their brains about nothing else than how to spend their miserable lives in cunning, intrigue, deception and theft.

French Antipathy to the Jews

Despite the fact that the old edict (reiterated in 1615 by Louis XIII) banishing Jewry from France had not been repealed, Jews semi-clandestinely settled throughout the kingdom. By the eighteenth century these newcomers were hated by both the bourgeoisie and the general population. Given such anti-Jewish sentiment, whenever the settlement of Jews in a specific town was suggested, the proposal was firmly resisted. Thus in 1708 the minor clergy of Nancy protested to the Duke Leopold of Lorraine:

Are we to lose within minutes what has always so happily distinguished us from the most flourishing kingdoms, and will we, like the nations surrounding us, be forced to mourn the deadly wounds that eternally contagious trade can inflict on a state and a religion? ... How many visions of ruined merchants, devastated fields, oppressed and penniless families rise up before our eyes! Will you grant to the Jews, the most mortal enemies of Jesus Christ, his church and the Christian name, what you have so firmly refused to heretics who have forgotten nothing in order to settle in your states? Will these people, so visibly cursed and damned by God, banished from almost every state, find asylum in yours, Monseigneur?

Although such complaints were made by clergy and tradesmen alike, the royal administration did not stem Jewish settlement and economic activity. Indeed in 1768 a high magistrate defended Jewish trade in Alsace. "Jews can certainly be of some use in Alsace," he stated. "In hard times and when there is war on the frontier, they supply the peasants with the means of supporting their expenses. If they have been pillaged, if they have lost their animals in corvées, the Jews make them advances which put them in a position to buy seeds and animals; these loans are not made cheaply; but in extreme needs, it is better to pass through the usurer's hands than to perish completely." None the less, he did recognize the danger of too large a Jewish population:

> It is therefore no evil for there to be a few Jews in Alsace; but look at the evil too many could entail . . . The Jews do not work at tilling the land, and they occupy a number of houses in the country which could be usefully occupied by agriculturalists. The peasants, finding the Jews have money they can borrow, either to pay their lord's or the King's taxes, become listless and lazy and soon fall into a state of poverty, while their property, ill-cultivated, is sold to pay their creditors.

In the second half of the eighteenth century, the Jewish request for official authorization to engage in commerce in Paris was met with some sympathy. However, the Christian guilds firmly resisted such a proposal, and in 1765 the lawyer Maître Goulleau, representing the merchants and tradesmen, drafted a memorandum outlining the crimes of the Jews throughout history, ranging from ritual murder to the spread of the Black Plague. In another lawsuit of this period, the lawyer Linguet declared: "Habit, religion, policy, reason perhaps, or at least an instinct justified by many reasons, drives us to attach both scorn and aversion to the name of the Jews." Similarly in 1789 the old-clothes men of Montpellier decried the evil of the Jews: "There is no one who does not carry in his heart the conviction of the evil that the Jewish people does throughout the world. The Supreme Being, when he created nature, expressly wished this race to be confined in a specific area, and forbade it to communicate in any way with other nations."

The interests of trade were thus combined with ancient Christian religious antipathy. Both factors produced fear and resentment, as the Minister of State Malesherbes expressed to Louis XVI on the eve of the Revolution: "There still exists in the hearts of most Christians a very strong hatred of the Jewish people, a hatred based on the memory of the crime of their ancestors and corroborated by the custom whereby Jews in every country engage in trade which the Christians regard as their downfall."

Paradoxically, as jealousy and hatred increased among the merchant classes, the nobility surrounded themselves with Jews and protected them from attack. Thus Prince Charles de Ligne wrote a *Mémoire sur les Juifs* in which he stated that Jews are sober, obedient, efficient and loyal. In this work he appealed for their emancipation: "And lastly the Israelites, while awaiting the impenetrable decrees of Providence on their obduracy in the matter of the wrongs of their ancestors, will at least be happy and useful in this world, and will cease to be the meanest people on earth. I well understand the origin of the horror the Jews inspire, but it is time this ended. Eighteen hundred years seems to me long enough for anger to persist!"

Devoid of bourgeois prejudice, aristocratic priests also pleaded the Jewish cause. Thus in 1744 the Abbé de la Varenne de Saint-Saulieu wrote to the Lieutenant of the Paris Police on behalf of a Jewish prisoner:

> I have not forgotten that you told me that I seemed like a rabbi when I spoke to you of this affair; but when you hear that the Jew on whose behalf I am speaking has done at least as much good in the prison where he is as all the charitable offices, when he has been in good health, and that few prisoners have left it without feeling the effects of his liberality, you will probably no longer accuse me of Judaism, and I am even convinced that you will become as much of one (a rabbi) as me, and that your sense of justice will commit you to imitate the Lord who rewards even in this world the good faith of these miserable victims of their blindness.

Such a positive attitude, however, was unrepresentative of the nation as a whole – for the majority of the French Christian populace the Jews constituted a malignant element in the body of the nation.

Jews in Great Britain

In 1656 Cromwell sought to readmit the Jews to the British Isles – yet the proposal was met with fierce opposition. None the less a small group of ex-Marrano merchants settled in London where they subsequently served as financiers and political informers on Spanish affairs. In time, German and Polish immigrant Jews joined their ranks. By 1800 between twenty and twenty-five thousand Jews lived in Great Britain. Unlike their counterparts on the continent, English merchants were not anxious about their presence; only occasionally did British Jewry come under attack.

Despite such an attitude of general tolerance, Jews were subjected to virulent criticism by a number of contemporary authors. Thus in one of his satires Alexander Pope composed a prayer in which he pleaded to be protected from the perfidious Jews: "Keep us we beseech thee, from the hands of such barbarous and cruel Jews, who albeit they abhor the blood of black-puddings, yet thirst they vehemently after the blood of the white ones. And that we may avoid such like calamities, may all good and well-disposed Christians be warned by these unhappy wretches' woeful example, to abominate the heinous sin of avarice." Again, Jonathan Swift emphasized the dangers posed by a Jewish presence: "What if the Jews should multiply and become a formidable party among us? Would the dissenters join in alliance with them likewise, because they agree already in some general principles, and because the Jews are allowed to be a stiffnecked and rebellious people?"

In 1753 the Duke of Newcastle's government (possibly encouraged by rich Sephardim) submitted a Naturalization Bill to simplify procedures for Jewish naturalization and to authorize Jews to acquire land. Although both the House of Lords and the Commons adopted the bill, it was met with fervent agitation from the population as a whole. Petitions were submitted from all sectors of society, defamatory inscriptions appeared in the streets, and pamphlets were issued warning against the settlement of Jews and the ownership of landed property. One of these agitators prophesied that St Paul's Cathedral would be turned into a synagogue, trade would be ruled by obligatory Sabbath observance, pork would be banned, and a Christian naturalization law would be rejected by the Great Sanhedrin. As a result of these charges, the law was repealed after six months. In this rejection of Jewish emancipation, the dark forces of traditional Christian prejudice against the Jews came to the surface: medieval conceptions of the demonic Jew polluting Christian society thwarted all efforts to grant the Jewish people the full rights of man. Such political opposition to Jewish emancipation, however, led to greater solidarity within the Jewish community. From 1760, representatives of the Ashkenazi congregations joined with deputations of the Sephardim to oversee matters of common concern. This development led to the formation of the London Committee of Deputies of British Jews (known as the Board of Deputies) which ultimately comprised representatives of provincial and colonial congregations.

In the next century a number of important families such as the Goldsmids and Rothschilds came to assume an influential role in Jewish affairs. During this period Jewish civil and political disabilities were not overwhelming – Jews enjoyed a considerable measure of social emancipation and were subject to few commercial restrictions. None the less, a number of native-born Jews followed the example of Jewish emancipation in France and sought similar rights for British subjects. In 1829 agitation began for legislation to parallel that which resulted in Catholic emancipation. Such a cause was championed by Robert Grant and Thomas Babington Macaulay in the House of Commons, and the Duke of Sussex in the Lords.

On its second reading in 1833, the Jewish Emancipation Bill was passed by the House of Commons, but rejected by the Lords. Nevertheless minor disabilities were removed by the Religious Opinions Relief Bill of 1846, and in 1858 the House of Commons and the House of Lords were allowed to settle their own form of oath, thereby paving the way for Jews to become members of Parliament.

Jewry in the New World

In 1654, twenty Jews fleeing the Brazilian Inquisition settled in New York; during this time other Jews appeared in Massachusetts, Connecticut, Virginia and Maryland. By the middle of the nineteenth century there were a few thousand Jews, generally of Sephardic origin, who lived in the United States. Occasionally representatives of the colonial power or local assemblies issued complaints about them, but the prevalence of Puritanism tended to curb such attitudes. Such writers as James Adams extolled the Judaism of the Hebrew Scriptures and sought to link Puritan religious values to the Bible. "In spirit," he wrote, "(the Puritans) may be considered as Jews and not Christians. Their God was the God of the Old Testament, their laws were the laws of the Old Testament, their guides to conduct were the characteristics of the Old Testament."

These Puritans, in line with traditional Christian teaching, sought to bring the Jews to the true faith. Hence Cotton Mather celebrated every Jewish conversion and wrote a treatise on the subject. The founder of Methodism, John Wesley, learned Spanish when he resided in America so that he could convert Jews. Again, the Quaker William

Penn asserted that the Jewish nation should be viewed with compassion and converted only with kindness. Other writers, however, were less optimistic about such a possibility. Thus Ezra Stiles noted in his journal: "I remark that providence seems to make everything to work for Mortification to the Jews, and to prevent their incorporating into any nation; that thus they may continue a distinct people ... (It) forbodes that the Jews will never become incorporated with the people of America, any more than in Europe, Asia and Africa."

America was characterized by tolerance for the Jewish people which was reinforced by the communal commitment to clear land and establish settlements in the New World. Religious egalitarianism was a product of common effort and dedication. In such a milieu, Jews were able to obtain civic and electoral rights by the end of the colonial period. Many Jews fought in the War of Independence and became officers; by joining together with gentile countrymen these Jewish patriots won admiration from fellow Americans. In light of such participation, George Washington insisted that all rights be extended to Jews: "May the children of the stock of Abraham who dwell in this land continue to merit and enjoy the good will of the other inhabitants; while every one shall sit in safety under his own vine and fig tree and there shall be none to make him afraid."

Such liberality at the end of the eighteenth century was fuelled by doctrines of liberty and brotherhood proclaimed at the time, yet other factors also served to ameliorate the position of Jewry in the United States. The existence of a sizeable black community provoked the hostility of the white population, thereby deflecting potential animosity away from the Jews. In addition, new waves of immigration brought to the American shores individuals who evoked hostility and xenophobia – all these foreign groups became targets of intolerance and animosity in place of the Jews.

In the post-Revolutionary period many Jews, particularly in South Carolina, were men of education and culture. Yet such distinction was no guarantee against Christian anti-Semitic prejudice, which tended to increase as Jews gained prominence. In Federalist papers those who entered politics and joined the Jeffersonians were vilified as "democrats"; others who sought public office were attacked. Yet despite the prevalence of such attitudes, civil and political emancipation was encouraged in the New Republic. In 1787 the Northwest Ordinance guaranteed Jews the same rights as fellow citizens in all new states, and a year later the Constitution granted equality on the federal level. By 1820 only seven of the original thirteen states granted Jewry full political recognition; ultimately, however, Jews were appointed or elected town councillors, judges of lower courts, and members of state legislatures.

By the first decades of the nineteenth century there were about four thousand Jews in the United States, scattered throughout the country. In the years leading to the Civil War the Jewish population enlarged dramatically. In 1840 the number of Jews was about 15,000; by 1860 it had grown to 150,000. This vast increase was due largely to immigration from German lands. In Bavaria numerous Jewish villages lost their Jewish population to the New World, while in Prussian Poland there was a constant flow of emigrants. German Jews from Bohemia and Hungary also emigrated to the United States. During the 1850s this influx reached a peak when economic recession and the repressive aftermath of the continental revolutions of 1848–49 drove Jews into exile. Over these years, Jewish settlements were established throughout the North American continent. In the New World these immigrants sought the freedoms denied them in their countries of origin. Between 1820 and 1860 American Jews attained considerable social acceptance. In such centres as Charleston, New York City and Philadelphia, a number of individuals entered political life. Overt Judeophobia was uncommon, and conversion to Christianity occurred rarely, despite the missionary activity of US Protestantism.

Life in the Jewish Community

Despite the advances made by a number of Jews in the early modern period, most Jews in western Europe were confined to a ghetto existence not far removed from Jewish life in the Middle Ages. Thus the Prince de Ligne described German Jews as "always sweating from running about selling in public squares and taverns; almost all hunchbacked, such dirty red or black beards, livid complexions, gaps in their teeth, long crooked noses, fearful, uncertain expressions, trembling hands, appalling frizzy hair; knees bare and pocked with red; long, pigeon-toed feet, hollow eyes, pointed chins." In their struggle to earn a living, the Jewish population was subject to innumerable difficulties. In the words of the apologist Zalkind-Hourwitz:

Apart from the expense, the difficulties and the dangers inseparable from a wandering life, they are continually harassed by trade, custom and inspection officials and very often arrested by the mounted constabulary on the slightest suspicion: they are obliged to carry their dishes and meat around with them, those of other nations being forbidden them; this annoys the greedy and intolerant innkeepers who make them pay very dearly for the little they sell them. As oppression makes them suspicious, as people are likewise prejudiced against them, and as moreover they have no fixed domicile, they can barely buy or sell at all except for ready cash.

As in previous centuries, Jews in the early modern period were continually stereotyped – repeatedly the allegation was made that they exuded a particular smell (*foetor judaïcus*) in contrast to the Christian odour of sanctity. This smell was viewed as a sign of their depravity. As reported by the English author and traveller, John Toland: "Yet so strong is the force of prejudice, that I know a person, no fool in other instances, who labor'd to persuade me, contrary to the evidence of his own and my eyes (to mine I am sure) that every Jew in the world had one eye remarkably less than the other, which silly notion he took from the mob. Others will gravely tell you, that they may be distinguish'd by a peculiar sort of smell."

In response to such distortion and antipathy, based on ancient Christian stereotypes, the Jewish community turned inward, despising those who denigrated them. As Zalkind-Hourwitz explained, Jewry viewed Christians and Christianity with equal contempt:

What must the Jews think of the people who oppress them solely because of their religion, and treat as friends all who abjure it, that is to say cease to be Jews, without worrying if they become Christians, or if they are decent people; what, I say, must the Jews think of this behaviour? Behaviour which, in this enlightened century, they can no longer attribute either to fanaticism or bad policy. Are they not right in concluding from it that Christianity ordains it, or that Christians, even the most honest and enlightened, are less zealous about moral principles and their own religion, than hostile to Judaism, and consequently to God its author?

In the intimacy of the Jewish community, Jews mistrusted the Christian world, rejected its values, and were indifferent to its views.

Believing in their own moral superiority, they held firmly to the conviction that God had chosen them as his special people. Devoted to the Covenant, they adhered to ancient laws and customs of the Jewish tradition. In response, Christians reviled these foreigners living in their midst. Even such enlightened individuals as Moses Mendelssohn were subject to discrimination. Remarking that he preferred to stay at home rather than venture out into the streets, Mendelssohn stated:

> Everywhere in this so-called tolerant country I live so constricted, hemmed in on all sides by true intolerance that for the sake of my children I must shut myself up the whole day in a silk factory. At times of an evening, I talk of it with my wife and children. "Father," an innocent child asks, "what does that fellow have against us? Why do people throw stones after us? What have we done to them?" "Yes, father dear," another says, "they chase after us in the streets and abuse us: Jews! Jews! Is it then such a reproach in people's eyes, to be a Jew? And how does that hamper other people?" Oh I close my eyes and sigh to myself: Men! Men! How have you come to this?

During this period the very word "Jew" was invested with emotive intensity – it evoked hatred and disgust. Thus although an increasingly large number of gentile defenders of Jewish rights appeared in these centuries, popular Christian anti-Semitism remained a powerful force in society. The Christian age-old conception of the Jew as a demonic and evil force animated Christian consciousness and evoked considerable resistance to proposals for the acceptance of Jewry as equal citizens in the modern world.

CHAPTER ELEVEN

The Enlightenment in England, France and Germany

Under the banner of the Enlightenment, English free-thinkers sought to ameliorate the condition of the Jews. Such attempts, however, were countered by other writers who attacked Jewry on grounds consonant with the spirit of a rationalist and scientific age. In France, Protestants influenced by the Enlightenment attempted to refute charges against the Jewish population. Yet despite such progressive attitudes, they were unable to free themselves from traditional Christian assumptions about Jewish guilt and divine retribution. In addition, many of the major thinkers of the age encouraged Judeophobia. In Germany an attempt was made to present Jews in a more positive light, but here as well the rise of national self-confidence provoked antipathy toward the Jewish population. Such philosophers as Kant, Fichte and Hegel wrote disparagingly of both Jews and Judaism. In order to escape such hostility, a number of enlightened Jews – primarily in Berlin –dissociated themselves from the Jewish way of life, and others sought to gain acceptance by becoming a new Jewish–Christian Protestant sect.

English Free Thinkers

The English Civil War and the rise of the commercial middle class resulted in economic and cultural expansion. Most English thinkers of the eighteenth century supported traditional Christian doctrine, yet some writers sought to reconcile the Christian faith with the new scientific spirit. Religion, they argued, must be rational and natural. John Toland, for example, issued a formal indictment of the Fathers of the Church whom he accused of corrupting true Christianity. The original form of the faith, he insisted, was that which was practised by the Ebionites (whom he referred to as the Nazarenes or simply as Jews):

The true Christianity of the Jews was over-borne and destroyed by the more numerous Gentiles who, not enduring the reasonableness and simplicity of the same, brought into it by degrees the peculiar expressions and mysteries of Heathenism, the abstruse doctrines and distinctions of their Philosophers, an insupportable pontifical Hierarchy, and even the altars, offerings, the sacred rites and ceremonies of their Priests, tho they would not so much as tolerate those of the Jews.

Such philo-Semitic attitudes led Toland to advocate Jewish immigration to the British Isles. In 1714 he published *Reasons for Naturalizing the Jews in Great Britain and Ireland* in which he criticized the xenophobia of those who resisted their entry. "The vulgar, I confess," he wrote, "are seldom pleased in any country with the coming in of foreigners among 'em: which proceeds, first, from their ignorance, that at the beginning they were such themselves; secondly, from their grudging at more persons sharing the same trades and business with them, which they call taking the bread out of their mouths; and thirdly, from their being deluded to this aversion by the artifice of those who design any change in the government."

Toland's liberalism, however, was unrepresentative of Christian free-thinkers of the period. Rather, those who were critical of traditional Christian teaching blamed the Jews for the errors of the Church. The mathematician William Whiston, for example, attempted to integrate biblical chronology and astronomic time. Unable to achieve this result, he ascribed mathematical inconsistencies in his researches to the malevolent intentions of Jewish scribes. In a work entitled *Essay Towards Restoring the True Text of the Old Testament* published in 1722, he charged that "The Jews, about the Beginning of the Second Century of the Gospel greatly alter'd and corrupted their Hebrew and Greek copies of the Old Testament; and that, in many places, on purpose; out of Opposition to Christianity." Again, in *Christianity as Old as Creation: or the Gospel, a Republication of the Religion of Nature*, Matthew Tindal argued that Christianity is the natural religion which Moses had perverted.

Another writer of the period, Thomas Morgan, defended Gnosticism as consistent with the teaching of Christ and ridiculed the idea that the Jews are God's chosen people:

To imagine that a Company of poor, contemptible egyptianiz'd Slaves, who having been delivered from one Yoke of Priesthood, were now to be put under another; a People scarce known to the rest of Mankind, and were never to mix or converse with them, but to be mew'd up in a little bye Corner of the Earth; that such a People, under such Circumstances, were intended in the divine Counsel and Wisdom, as a Light to the Gentiles, and the Means of preserving and keeping up the true Knowledge and Worship of God in the World, and of the true Religion or Way to Salvation; this, surely, is supposing what we speak with Scorn, that God was as much disappointed of his End, and took as wrong Measures to obtain it, as Moses himself.

Another figure who attacked the Jewish people was the pastor Woolston, who maintained that the world was full of stinking Jews. Drawing on medieval tradition, he wrote:

. . . and the World, according to the Proverb, and common belief of Mankind, may be said to stink with them. Hence Ammianus Marcellinus very appositely to the purpose before us, speaking of the Jews, calls them Tumulating and stinking Jews. How this mark of Infamy was first fixt upon the Jews, whether from any ill smell that proceeds from them, according to the common Opinion, or otherwise; It is all one to the Prophesie and Type of them; and if their Bodies neither do, or even did stink living; Yet their blasphemies against Christ, their Maledictions of his Church, and false Glosses on Scripture, are enough to make their very Name odious and abominable."

Such attacks were grounded in the traditional conception of the Jew as a demonic, dark, polluting force. Though critical of traditional Christianity, these English polemicists targeted Jews as corrupters of the pure faith: enriched by the language of conventional anti-Jewish sentiment, they kept alive the Christian anti-Semitic attitudes which they infused with contemporary notions consonant with the scientific age.

The French Protestant Reaction

In eighteenth-century France, the general opinion concerning the Jews was reflected in sentiments expressed by Mme de Sévigné who declared: "This hatred felt for them (the Jews) is extraordinary. But from where does this stench which confounds all perfumes come from? It is probably that unbelief and ingratitude smells bad as virtue smells good . . . I feel pity and horror for them, and I pray God with the Church that he remove from their eyes the veil which prevents them from seeing that Jesus Christ has come." None the less, despite such prevailing views, an increasing number of individuals sought to ameliorate the position of the Jewish population under the influence of the Enlightenment.

Among French Protestants in particular such aspirations were pronounced, since they themselves had suffered indignities as a minority living in Catholic society. The Calvinist Jaques Basnage, for example, intended to write a history of the Jewish people beginning with the destruction of the second Temple – his aim was to provide a factual historical narrative. "We are reporting accurately and faithfully everything we have been able to unearth which refers to the Jews", he wrote. "The Christian ought not to find it strange that we very often exonerate the Jews from various crimes they are not guilty of, since Justice demands it; and to accuse of injustice and violence those who have pursued Justice is only to show bias."

Basnage's aim was to refute numerous false charges that had been levelled against Jews and Judaism, despite the fact that he believed that God had rejected them because they had crucified Christ. Even though they merited God's anger, to his mind the punishment they had endured through the centuries was excessive:

> If the punishment had fastened on the heads of the guilty, it would not be surprising; but it has passed from generation to generation, from century to century. Seventeen hundred years of wretchedness and captivity have already flowed by, with no prospect of relief . . . this unfortunate nation can find almost nowhere on the whole earth where it can lay its head or set its feet. It passes through torrents of blood which it has shed, and does not perish.

This positive evaluation of Jewry was found among other Protestant writers of the time. In their theological reflections they rejected the previous denigration of Jews and Judaism. The Marquis Jean-Baptiste d'Argens, for example, was of Catholic origin, but under the influence of two Protestant publicist pastors he attacked the established

Churches and praised the Jewish faith for approximating to the true natural religion. In one of his *Lettres juives* he wrote:

> Everyone who is called a free-thinker here (in Paris), fashionable people, society ladies, only practise the religion of Nazareth externally; very few of them are really convinced at the bottom of their hearts. They are satisfied to believe in God; several think that the soul is immortal; many others, like the Sadducees, claim that it is subject to death. I regard these latter as people labouring under a misapprehension; as for the former category, I do not know if we can deny them the title of Jews. They believe in God who created the Universe, who rewards the good, and punishes the bad. What more do we believe? Is not this the whole of our religion except for a few ceremonies which our scholars and priests have prescribed for us?

Yet despite this conception, d'Argens endorsed the traditional Christian idea that God had punished the Jews for their crimes. In another of his *Lettres*, he portrays an ex-rabbi who admits the ritual crimes of the Jews and endorses other allegations made against them. Discoursing on their guilt, this ex-rabbi states:

> When I think of the ills our father suffered, I am tempted to believe that they were guilty of some great crimes, knowledge of which has not come down to us; and I must confess to you that, if I was not as confident as I am of the truth of my religion, when I examine the ills which have overwhelmed us since the birth of Nazareanism, I would find it easy to believe that the prophecies had been fulfilled and that the God of Israel had abandoned his people, and chosen another. Is it possible . . . that the Divinity should expose a people to such great ills if they did not deserve them because of crimes which required such severe punishment?

Thus although such enlightened Protestant writers as d'Argens and Basnages attempted to defend Judaism from traditional Christian vilification, they were unable to free themselves from Christian prejudice: their portrayal of Jews and Judaism was tinged by implicit assumptions about Jewish guilt and divine retribution.

The Jews and the French Enlightenment

During this period a number of French thinkers influenced by the Enlightenment championed tolerance and understanding and advocated a more benevolent attitude toward the Jewish people. Thus in *L'Esprit des lois*, Montesquieu viewed Christian intolerance as the source of Jewish ills and the cause of their peculiar practices. According to Montesquieu, Jews should be treated as Christians want others to treat them, as a Jew declares in Montesquieu's "A Most Humble Remonstrance to the Inquisitors of Spain and Portugal": "We conjure you, not by the mighty God whom both you and we serve, but by that Christ who, you tell us, took upon him a human form, to propose himself for an example for you to follow; we conjure you to behave to us, as he himself would behave was he upon earth." Such a view of Jewry is a reflection of the new spirit that had flourished in France since the death of Louis XIV.

Other writers of the Enlightenment, however, encouraged Jewish hatred, and their works mirror ancient and medieval Christian vilifications of Jews and Judaism. In his *Profession de Foi*, Voltaire, for example, contrasted his conception of God with the Jewish view found in the Hebrew Scriptures and denigrated the Jewish people:

> The morals of theists are of necessity pure; since they always have the God of justice and purity before them, the God who does not descend upon the earth to order people to rob the Egyptians, to command Hosea to take a concubine in exchange for money and to live with an adulterous woman. Also one does not see us selling our wives like Abraham. We do not get drunk like Noah, and our sons do not insult the respectable member which gave them birth.

Again, in his *Dictionnaire Philosophique*, Voltaire included thirty articles which attacked Jews who are described as "our masters and our enemies . . . whom we detest", and "the most abominable people in the world". The Jews are, he wrote, "an ignorant and barbarous people, who for a long time have combined the most sordid greed with the most detestable superstition and the most invincible hatred for all the peoples who tolerate them and enrich them." Although Christians are culpable of crimes against the Jewish people, the Jews themselves are guilty as well: "The only difference is that our priests have had you burned by laymen, and that your priests have always sacrificed human victims with their sacred hands."

Similar attitudes are reflected in the writings of Jean-Jacques Rousseau. In his works, he pleaded for tolerance for the beleaguered

Jewish nation and expressed admiration for Moses. Yet, like Voltaire, he was horrified by the biblical conception of the deity:

"If then it (the Divinity) teaches us what is absurd and unreasonable, if it inspires us with feelings of aversion for our fellows and terror for ourselves, if it paints us a God, angry, jealous, vengeful, partial, hating men, a God of war and battles, ever ready to strike and to destroy, ever speaking of punishment and torment, boasting even of the punishment of the innocent, my heart would not be drawn towards this terrible God.

At times he also speaks of the Jew in conventional Christian anti-Semitic terms: "the vilest of peoples"; "the baseness of (this people), incapable of any virtue".

Those who contributed to Diderot's *Encyclopédie* were also frequently contemptuous of Judaism. The article on "Hebraic (language)" for example, implicitly denigrates the Jews for their blindness: "It is not for us, blind mortals, to question Providence; also let us not ask it why it pleased it only to speak to the Jews in parables: why it has given them eyes so that they do not see, and ears so that they do not hear, and why of all the nations of antiquity it chose particularly the one whose head was hardest and coarsest." In an article dealing with medicine, Chevalier de Jaucourt raged against the Jews in the name of science: "The ancient Hebrews, stupid, superstitious, separated from other peoples, unversed in the study of physics, incapable of resorting to natural causes, attributed all their diseases to evil spirits . . . in a word, their ignorance of medicine caused them to turn to soothsayers, magicians, enchanters or finally to prophets." Another criticism of Jewish superstition was made by Nicholas Boulanger:

The monarch, with the obdurate Jews and with all the other nations, was regarded less as a father and a God of peace than as an exterminating angel. The motive behind theocracy would therefore have been fear: this was also true of despotism . . . The true God of the Hebrews was also obliged, because of their character, perpetually to threaten them . . . The Judaic superstition which fancied that it could not pronounce the terrible name of Jehovah, which was also the great name of its monarch, in this was transmitted to us one of the conventions of this primitive theocracy.

Pastor Polier de Bottens, a disciple of Voltaire, added to this contempt. In an article on the Messiah, he castigated the Jews for blaspheming against the Christ: "If the Jews disputed Jesus Christ's role of Messiah and divinity, they have also neglected nothing to make him appear contemptible, to cast on his birth, his life and his death, all the ridicule and all the opprobium that their cruel relentlessness against this divine Saviour and his heavenly doctrine could imagine."

Other writers in the eighteenth century published anti-clerical polemics which echoed such Judeophobic sentiments. *La Moïsade* by Nicholas Fréret, for example concludes with a curse on Moses and the Jewish nation: "Die, Moses, die, destructive tyrant", he proclaimed. "Let the Heavens crush you with thunderbolts of vengeance! Let the earth, as angry as the Heavens with your treachery and cruelty, open beneath your guilty feet and swallow you, abominable monster . . . and you, raging, senseless people, vile, coarse men, worthy slaves of the yoke you bear, go back to your books; and keep away from me!" A contemporary of Freret, Jean-Baptiste de Mirabaud, argued that the disrepute into which the Jewish nation had fallen preceded the curse of Christ:

> You will therefore see from this that, a long time before they had brought down upon themselves this curse, which is now regarded as the cause of their wretchedness, they were generally hated and generally despised in every country which knew them: after which you will agree that there is no mention of them in the old books except in connection with this concept, and in relation to the general aversion felt for them.

Thus, although France in the Enlightenment championed liberty and tolerance, many of the illustrious figures of this period were unable to free themselves from Judeophobia. Their advocacy of reason and anti-clericalism was accompanied by a parallel denigration of the Jewish faith and the Jews.

Stirrings in Germany

In Germany the new spirit of the age took firm root. German Protestant pastors in particular propagated ideas of science and progress and revised their theology in the light of biblical criticism. Among advocates of the Enlightenment a special case was made for tolerance of the Jews. Such attitudes were promoted by descendants of court Jews such as Aaron Salomon Gumpertz, a member of the Berlin Gumpertz dynasty, who asked the writer Gottsched for permission "to come and graze under your wings, to suck the sweet milk of the sciences . . . it is you whom we Germans have to thank for so varied intellectual writings."

Prominent among those writers who sought to assimilate Jews into German society was the playwright Lessing, whose *Die Juden* depicts the noble character of a Jewish traveller who saves a baron and his daughter (the Fraulein) from bandits. In gratitude the baron offers him his daughter's hand. Unable to accept, the traveller declares:

Traveller:	I am a Jew
Baron:	A Jew! What cruel mischance . . .
Lisette:	A Jew!
Fraulein:	What difference does that make?
Lisette:	Shush, Fraulein, I'll tell you the difference afterwards.
Baron:	So there are cases when Heaven itself prevents us from being grateful!
Traveller:	It would be superfluous because you wish to be.
Baron:	But I wish to do at least as much as fate allows me. Take all my fortune. I would rather be poor and grateful than rich and ungrateful.
Traveller:	This offer is in vain for the God of my fathers has given me more than I need. As sole reward all I ask is that in future you judge my people more kindly and do not generalize. I did not conceal myself from you because I am ashamed of my religion. No! But I saw that you looked favourably on me but unfavourably on my people. And a man's friendship, be he what he will, has always been inestimable to me.

During this period other dramatists also presented Jews in a positive light, and the Jews became a symbol of the struggle against prejudice. In reaction, some writers disputed these claims. Jews, they believed, were incapable of attaining noble qualities. Thus the theologian Johann David Michaelis argued that no Jew like Lessing's Traveller could exist. Lessing replied that in fact there were such individuals, and he published a letter from the philosopher Moses Mendelssohn to demonstrate his point:

Is the cruel judgement of Michaelis justified? How shameful for the human race! And how shameful too for the author. It is not enough for us that we must suffer the attacks of the cruel hatred that the Christians have for us; and must this injustice be justified by a slander? Let them continue to oppress us, let them allow us to live in subjection amidst free and happy citizens, let us be exposed to the scorn and contempt of the whole world; but do not let them try to challenge our virtue, the sole solace for unhappy souls, the sole comfort of the abandoned ... In general, certain human virtues are met with more frequently amongst Jews than Christians. Think of the unutterable horror that they have of murder. You cannot quote a single example of a Jew (except for professional bandits) having killed a man. How easily many a worthy Christian will kill a man for a simple insult. They say this is because of cowardice amongst the Jews. So be it! If cowardice spares human blood, then cowardice is a virtue!

In the course of this discussion the Swiss Pastor Lavater called on Mendelssohn to refute Christian doctrine or, if unable to do so, to convert to Christianity. Although he did not issue a public reply, Mendelssohn communicated his views privately to the Duke of Brunswick. His reason, he explained, prevented him for accepting the mysteries of Christianity. Lavater's challenge was met by the publication of Mendelssohn's *Jerusalem*, in which he argued for a secular state in which the political and juridical rights of the Churches would be abolished (as well as the judicial autonomy of Jewish communities). In this work his principal aim was the granting of civil rights to all Jews.

With the death of Moses Mendelssohn, the era of tolerance for the Jewish population ended. The revival of national self-confidence aroused considerable Christian anti-Semitism, and a number of German philosophers of the period wrote disparagingly of the Jewish people. Following the lead of such rationalist theologians as Michaelis, Immanuel Kant declared that Judaism is not a religion. Instead, he asserted, it is "merely a union of a number of people who, since they belonged to a particular stock, formed themselves into a commonwealth under purely political laws and not into a church." Describing the Jews as "Palestinians", he inveighed against their dishonesty:

> The Palestinians living amongst us are, since their exile, because of their usurious spirit not unjustifiably renowed for their deceitfulness, so far as

the great majority is concerned. It does indeed seem disconcerting to conceive of a nation of usurers; but it is just as disconcerting to conceive of a nation of pure mercantilism, by far the largest part of which is bound together by a superstition recognized by the state in which they live and do not seek any civic honour. But they try to compensate for this lack by the advantages of outwitting the people amongst whom they find shelter and even by deceiving each other.

Kant's disciple Fichte advocated the expulsion of the Jews as the only means of protecting the German nation. "To protect ourselves against them", he wrote, "I see no other way than to conquer for them their promised land and see them all there . . . But to give them civic rights – I see no means to do that except, one night, to cut off all their heads and give them new ones in which there would not be one Jewish idea." Echoing such antipathy, Hegel added his invective against the Jewish nation who "saw in Jesus only the man, the Nazarene, the carpenter's son whose brothers and kinsfolk lived among them; so much he was, and more he could not be, for he was only one like themselves, and they felt themselves to be nothing. The Jewish multitude was bound to wreck his attempt to give them consciousness of something divine, for faith in something divine, something great, cannot make its home in a dunghill." Not surprisingly, such views laid the foundations for the reign of terror which was to come two centuries later.

The Berlin Haskalah

Berlin at the end of the eighteenth century contained a number of rich Jews who built large homes in which they entertained Prussian society. These individuals, who had assimilated into Western culture, were highly critical of Orthodoxy. Adopting the principles of the Enlightenment, they sought to reform the mass of Jewry. A number of Jews who moved in these circles wrote disparagingly of the stultifying atmosphere of traditional Jewish life. The philosopher Solomon Maimon, for example, decried the oppressive atmosphere of Polish Jewish life which he had endured as a youth. In his *Autobiography* he wrote:

My life in Poland from my marriage to my emigration, which embraced the springtime of my existence, was a series of miseries with a lack of all facilities for the promotion of culture, and consequently an aimless application of my powers . . . The general constitution of Poland at the time; the condition of our people in it, who, like the poor ass with the double burden, are oppressed by their own ignorance and religious prejudices, as well as by the ignorance and prejudices of the ruling classes; the misfortunes of my own family – all these combined to hinder the course of my development and to check my natural disposition.

To remedy this situation, reformers advocated a revision of educational training in accordance with the principles of reason. Only in this way, they believed, would Jewry be able to recognize the absurdity of Jewish beliefs and practices. To this end such modernists as the Kantian Bendavid ran a school for Jews in which worship was conducted in German. Other figures of this period celebrated the Jewish contribution to the Enlightenment. Thus Moses Herschel declared:

Thanks to our philosophical century, the age of barbarism has passed away, when one must expect a contemptuous grimace at the mention of the word Jew . . . The man who is capable and worthy, whatever his faith and religious opinions, can henceforth lay claim to the affection and respect of those who think differently . . . The Christian and the Jew can love each other with a brotherly love, esteem each other, and honour each other.

Although most of these de-Judaized Jews retained some vestige of their ancestral faith, others converted to Christianity. Among Moses Mendelssohn's descendants, his youngest son converted to Protestantism, and Abraham, the father of the composer Felix Mendelssohn, had his children converted. His brother-in-law, Bartholdy, was convinced that this was the right course of action.

Do you think you have done something wrong in giving your children that religion which you think the better for them? It is a real tribute which you and we all are paying to your father's efforts for true enlightenment in general, and he would have acted like you have done for your children, perhaps as I have done, for my part. One can remain faithful to an oppressed, persecuted religion; one can force it on one's children in expectation of a life-long martyrdom – so long as one believes it to be the only religion that can save you. But if one no longer believes this; then it is barbarous.

As for Mendelssohn's daughters, Recha remained Jewish while the youngest, Henriette, opened a boarding school for Parisian society girls. Her elder sister Dorothea married a banker, Simon Veit, but became attached to the writer Friedrich Schlegel and in 1804 converted to Protestantism. This couple met at the Berlin Jewish salon held by Henriette Herz, the wife of Dr Herz who was a friend and disciple of Kant. Famous for her beauty, she attracted a circle of admirers. In her old age, she described the impact of these Jewish salons. "There," she wrote, "there was no mediation of a tradition, of a culture transmitting itself from generation to generation, keeping pace with the spirit and knowledge of the time; and also none of the prejudice formed by such a train of culture. The lavishness, the arrogance, the transcendence of accepted forms in expression is to be attributed to a similar nature of this spirit and the awareness of this in those women who embodied it. But it was undeniably very original, very powerful, very piquant, very exciting and frequently, with its astounding mobility, of great profundity."

Another salon of the time which attracted young romantics, royalty and diplomats was held by Rahel Levin, whose central aim in life was to escape from her Jewishness. Such an obsession was a major theme of her correspondence. In a letter to a childhood friend, David Veit, she declared: "I have a strange fancy: it is as if some supramundane being, just as I was thrust into this world, plunged these words with a dagger into my heart: 'Yes, have sensibility, see the world as few see it, be great and noble, nor can I take from you the faculty of eternal thinking. But I add one thing more: be a Jewess!' And now my life is a slow bleeding death." Again, in a letter to her brother, she stated: "I do not forget this same for a single second. I drink it in water, I drink it in wine, I drink it with the air; in every breath, that is . . . The Jew must be extirpated from us, that is the sacred truth, and it must be done even if life were uprooted in the process." In 1814 this magnetic figure converted and married the Prussian diplomat and writer, August Varnhagen von Ense.

During this period a number of Jews sought to transcend their Jewishness through collective conversion, yet unlike other Christian converts they wished to form a new Judeo-Christian sect. In 1799, under the leadership of David Friedlander (a follower of Mendelssohn), a group of the heads of enlightened Jewish families declared their willingness to submit to baptism as long as they were not obligated to accept traditional Christian dogma. "If the religion of the Protestants prescribes certain ceremonies," they stated, "then we can well submit ourselves to these as pure forms which are demanded for entry into a society; it being well understood that these ceremonies are only demanded as actions, as customs, to demonstrate that the member admitted has accepted the eternal truths and, as man and citizen, subordinated himself to the duties flowing from them, but not as a sign that the person who performs these actions admits that he accepts in faith the dogmas of the church of this society."

This request was addressed to Pastor Wilhelm Teller of the Lutheran Consistory in Berlin, who responded that he would grant baptism, but only if certain conditions were fulfilled: "To be Christian you must at least accept the sacraments of baptism and communion and acknowledge the historical truth that Christ is the founder of the most sublime moral religion. It is possible to grant you freedom of religious opinions, which moreover differ with the Church itself, but not as far as the dogmas are concerned." Once this Jewish appeal was made public, numerous Christian objections were raised. The theologian Friedrich Schleiermacher, for example, charged the Jewish petitioners with hypocrisy, contending that these individuals were motivated solely by material concerns. Thus, though the ideals of the Enlightenment animated many Christians to see the improvement of German Jews, undercurrents of Christian anti-Semitism flowed just beneath the surface of public life.

CHAPTER TWELVE

The Emancipation of the Jews

At the end of the eighteenth century the spirit of the Enlightenment stimulated Christian Europe to seek the amelioration of Jewish life. With the establishment of the Napoleonic era, Jewish existence was revolutionized. The summoning of a Great Sanhedrin in France paved the way for Jewish emancipation, and the position of Jewry improved throughout the continent. In the midst of such social upheaval, German Jewish reformers such as Israel Jacobson attempted to adapt Jewish worship to modern conditions. To the consternation of the Orthodox, Reform temples appeared throughout Germany. Yet ironically, many enlightened Jews influenced by the Romantic movement were uninterested in what Reform Judaism had to offer. Instead of providing a basis for the resurgence of Judaism, the movement undermined confidence in traditional belief and practice and intensified Christian antipathy to the Jewish way of life. In Russia, the aim of emancipation was to bring about the assimilation of the Jewish population – the programme of the Tsars was driven by centuries-old Christian hostility to the Jews. From the Jewish side, responses to these moves throughout Europe to improve the plight of Jewry were mixed: traditionalists tended to fear that such steps would undermine Torah Judaism, whereas progressives enthusiastically welcomed new freedoms and opportunities. The gentile reaction was equally ambivalent. Although liberals ardently campaigned for equal rights, many Christians feared the consequences of such agitation, and at the end of the second decade of the nineteenth century outbursts against the Jewish population spread from country to country.

The French Experience

In the wake of the Enlightenment, the emancipation of the Jews began to take place at the end of the eighteenth century. From western

Europe to the Russian Empire humanist ideals began to stir the consciousness of the Christian population. In France, the last remnants of Jewish legislation were abolished in 1782. Yet throughout the country complaint books were composed, listing a wide variety of grievances against the Jewish community. The book of the clergy of Colmar, for example, portrayed Jews in demonic terms and advised that only eldest Jewish sons be allowed to marry. In Alsace the rural proletariat attacked the Jewish populace, driving thousands of Jews to seek refuge in Switzerland.

When, in 1789, the French Constituent Assembly enfranchised Protestants, Jews were refused such rights, and even advocates of emancipation agreed that the Jews constituted a fallen nation. None the less, some reformers sought to regenerate French Jewry. As Robespierre declared: "The Jews' vices are born of the degradation you have plunged them into; they will be good when they can find some advantage in so being!" Others, however, viewed Jews as incorrigible and argued against ameliorating their condition.

Despite the opposition against granting the Jewish community civil rights, on 27 September 1791 the Constitutional Assembly provided for the total emancipation of French Jewry. In general the Jewish community did not express enthusiasm for the Revolution, but with the establishment of the Napoleonic era their lives were revolutionized, as were those of Jews elsewhere in Europe. At the beginning of the nineteenth century, France had assumed the role of protector and emancipator of European Jewry. According to Napoleon, the Jews were "an objectionable people, chicken-hearted and cruel". Their evil, he believed, "primarily comes from that indigestible compilation called the Talmud, while their true biblical traditions are found side by side with the most corrupt morality as soon as their relations with Christians are involved."

The remedy for this condition was to dissolve the Jewish race into the population as a whole. In 1806, Napoleon summoned Jewish representatives to a General Assembly in Paris, to whom he addressed a series of questions about the Jewish attitude toward France and the French people, the authority of autonomous institutions, and the problems of usury and of Jewish occupations. To conciliate the authorities the Assembly appointed a committee to formulate their replies. In 1807 the Great Sanhedrin was convened, consisting of rabbis and leading Jewish figures, to give religious sanction to the

Assembly's replies. In March 1808 two edicts were issued to regularize the position of Jews in the country. According to the first, a hierarchical organization of communities was to be introduced into France – all individual and communal Jewish affairs were to be concentrated in a central consistory in Paris. A second edict (the Infamous Decree) imposed control over Jewish loans, introduced permits to engage in trade, forbade Jews to settle in other areas in north-east France, and prohibited the provision of replacements for military service.

Although these edicts paved the way for Jewish emancipation, they did impose serious restrictions on the Jews and ensured that the state enjoyed preference over religion. The organizational code of the consistories engaged the rabbis to make certain that Jews "should regard military service as a sacred task, and they should inform them that during the period in which they dedicate themselves to service the Torah exempted them from observing religious injunctions which cannot be reconciled with it." Jewish assimilation was the goal of such legislation, as the final paragraph of the Infamous Decree makes clear:

> The instructions in this order will be implemented over a period of ten years in the hope that at the end of this period, under the influence of the various measures undertaken with regard to the Jews, there will no longer be any difference between them and other citizens of our Empire. But if, despite all this, our hope should be frustrated, implementation will be extended for whatever length of time seems appropriate.

After Napoleon's defeat, there was a strong European reaction against the legislation enacted during this period. In several of the Italian states Jews were deprived of their rights and returned to ghettos. German Jewry was similarly treated – in Frankfurt, Jews were forced to live in the ghetto, and in Lübeck a total expulsion occurred. The Germanic Federation, however, discussed the Jewish question at the Congress of Vienna in 1815 and agreed not to return to the conditions before Napoleon's conquest. Instead, it decided to discuss the means of achieving civil amelioration. During the debate which took place, a number of states proposed granting to the Jews those rights accorded to them by the French under Napoleon; most, however, were unwilling to maintain laws that had been forced upon them. Thus the French experiment in civil liberty, which had spread beyond its borders under Napoleon, eventually culminated in a regression to previous Christian hostile attitudes to Jews and Judaism.

German Emancipation

During the time of Napoleon's conquests, the position of Jewry in German lands significantly improved. In some areas, Jewish emancipation was dictated by French occupational authorities; in other places it was due to the French example or to the influence of prominent Jewish figures. The financier and communal leader Israel Jacobson, for example, initiated a programme of religious reform. He founded a boarding school for boys in Seesen, Westphalia, in 1801, and subsequently established other schools throughout the kingdom. In these new foundations general subjects were taught by Christian teachers while a Jewish instructor gave lessons about Judaism. The consistory of which Jacobson was president also introduced external reforms to the Jewish worship service, including choral singing, hymns and addresses, and prayers in German.

In 1810 Jacobson built the first Reform temple next to the school, which was dedicated in the presence of Christian clergy and dignitaries. In his address at the dedication ceremony, he proclaimed: "Our ritual is still weighed down with religious customs which must be rightly offensive to reason as well as to our Christian friends. It desecrates the holiness of our religion and dishonours the reasonable man to place too great a value upon such customs; on the other hand he is greatly honoured if he can encourage himself and his friends to realize their dispensability." After Napoleon's defeat, Jacobson moved to Berlin where he attempted to put these principles into practice by founding the Berlin Temple.

In Hamburg in 1817, a Reform temple was opened in which a number of innovations were made to the liturgy, including prayers and sermons in German as well as choral singing and organ music. To defend these alterations, Hamburg reformers cited the Talmud in support of their actions. In 1819 the community issued its own prayerbook, which omitted repetitions of prayers as well as medieval poems and changed some of the traditional prayers related to Jewish nationalism and messianic redemption. Israel Jacobson, to whom this prayerbook was dedicated, was instrumental in obtaining a number of rabbinic opinions in support of this temple. The Hungarian rabbi Aaron Chorin declared that it was not only permissible but obligatory to free the liturgy from its adhesions, to hold the service in a language understandable to the worshipper, and to accompany it with organ and song.

Not surprisingly, such innovations provoked the Orthodox establishment to issue a proclamation condemning the Hamburg reformers. Eleazer Fleckeles, of the Beth Din of Prague, stated: "These people (of the Hamburg Temple) really have no religion at all. It is their entire desire to parade before the Christians as being more learned than their brothers. Basically, they are neither Christians nor Jews." In a personal attack on Aaron Chorin, Rabbi Eliezer of Triesch in Moravia declared: "We know this rabbi Aaron Chorin. He is a man of mediocre knowledge in Talmud and commentaries, and far be it from us to lean on his pronouncements."

The central aim of these early reformers was to adapt Jewish worship to contemporary aesthetic standards. For these innovators, the informality of the traditional service seemed foreign and undignified, and they therefore insisted on greater decorum, more unison in prayer, a choir, hymns and musical responses, as well as alterations in prayers and the length of the service. Yet from the perspective of Jewish and Christian avant-garde writers and thinkers in the first two decades of the nineteenth century, the rationalism of the Enlightenment was out of date. The Enlightenment was viewed as shallow, unhistorical and anaemic in comparison with the values of the Romantic movement. In a period of reaction against the French Revolution and French cultural models, the advocates of German Romanticism and nationalism regarded such rationalistic reforms as irrelevant. No mere external reform of Judaism could win respect for the Jewish faith as a vibrant religious tradition.

For those inspired by the ideals of the Romantic Movement, subjective religious experience was of central importance. Such aspirations were absent from a Jewish religion of reason. Thus the reformers, in their quest to provide a modernized form of Judaism for an enlightened age, failed to satisfy the spiritual longings of German-assimilated Jewry. Instead, those who sought to reform the Jewish faith inadvertently provided the basis for a critique of traditional Judaism which was seized upon by anti-Semites. The destructive impact of their criticism of talmudic Judaism and the traditional Jewish way of life intensified antipathy for what Christians regarded as an outdated religious tradition.

Jews and the Russian Empire

With the partition of Poland at the end of the eighteenth century, vast numbers of Jews became Russian subjects and were confined to the Pale of Settlement. Anxious not to offend the gentile population, Catherine the Great kept previous Jewish restrictions in force. None the less, mistrust of these foreigners provoked further anti-Jewish measures. In 1799, White Russia was devastated by a famine, and an inquiry was charged with discovering its causes. The investigator Gabriel Derzhavin's report provided an unflattering picture of the Jewish population. "The Yids", he wrote, "are clever, perceptive, quick-witted, alert, polite, obliging, sober, modest, simple, not lascivious, etc., but on the other hand they are unpleasant, stinking, lazy, idle, cunning, covetous, pushful, sly, malicious, etc. . . . And besides, so many of them look the same, have the same name . . . and they all wear a uniform black dress; the memory is befuddled and the understanding confused when it is a question of counting them or distinguishing them, especially when claims or inquiries are concerned. It is difficult to detect the guilty; all present themselves and no one is the right man. This must also be an example of their cunning."

The conclusion of his report was reminiscent of Christian medieval accusations against the Jews:

> In accordance with these earlier and more recent views on the Yids and varied opinions concerning them, I find: their schools are nothing more than a nest of superstition and hatred for Christians; the communities are a dangerous state within the State, which a well-organized political body is not obliged to tolerate; their excommunications are an impenetrable sacrilegous cover for the most terrible abuses committed to the detriment of the community.

According to Derzhavin, reform was imperative, and he drew up a plan which advocated civic status for the Jews, the abandonment of traditional clothing, encouragement of craft and agriculture, and the transfer of a number of Jews to the steppes of New Russia. In addition, he emphasized the importance of Western education. Citing the example of Moses Mendelssohn in Germany, he stated:

> In order to expose the superstition of misguided zealots of his faith, that is to say the deceived deceivers, he (Mendelssohn) has taught some of his brethren the pure Jewish language and, by translating the Scriptures into everyday German, he has made ordinary people read them. They have been understood, the veil has fallen and the reign of the Talmuds has ended. Since then, the numbers of erudite Jews, second to none amongst the most learned men in Europe, have multiplied on German soil.

To remedy the situation in Russia, Derzhavin proposed the establishment of an educational programme in which only children up to the age of twelve be allowed to study in *heders* (Jewish primary schools); older children would be required to attend schools in which secular knowledge would be transmitted by Jewish teachers trained in Germany. After Tsar Paul I's assassination in 1801, his successor, Alexander I, created a Committee for the Reorganization of Jewish Life along the lines suggested by Derzhavin. In 1804 a law was promulgated which restricted the autonomy of Jewish communities, permitted Jews to attend schools and universities, made the study of European languages compulsory in Jewish schools, and specified territory in western Russia where the Jews would be allowed to reside (the Pale of Settlement). After several attempts to expel Jews from the countryside the Tsar, in 1817, initiated a new policy of integrating the Jewish community into the population by founding a society of Israelite Christians which extended legal and financial concessions to baptized Jews.

In 1824 the deportation of Jews from villages began. In the same year Alexander I died and was succeeded by Nicholas I, who adopted a severe attitude to the Jewish community. In 1827 he initiated a policy of inducting Jewish boys into the Russian army for a twenty-five year period in order to increase the number of converts to Christianity. Nicholas I also deported Jews from villages in certain areas; in 1827 they were expelled from Kiev and three years later from the surrounding province. In 1835 the Russian government propagated a revised code of laws to regulate Jewish settlement in the western border. In order to reduce Jewish isolation, the government set out to reform education in 1841; a young Jewish educator, Max Lilienthal, was asked to establish a number of reformed Jewish schools in the Pale of Settlement, which incorporated western educational methods and a secular curriculum. Initially, Lilienthal attempted to persuade Jewish leaders that by supporting this project the Jewish community could improve their lot, but when he discovered that the intention of the Tsars was to undermine the Talmud he left the country. These new schools were established in 1844, but they attracted a small enrolment, and the Russian government eventually abandoned its plans to eliminate traditional Jewish education.

In the same year, Nicholas I abolished the *kehillot* and put Jewry under the authority of the police as well as municipal government. Despite this policy it was impossible for the Russian administration to carry out the functions of the *kehillot*, and it was recognized that a Jewish body was needed to recruit students for state military schools and to collect taxes. Between 1850 and 1851 the government attempted to forbid Jewish dress, men's sidecurls, and the ritual shaving of women's hair. These various steps toward emancipating the Jewish people were thus part of a general policy to undermine the traditional Jewish way of life. Rather than attempting to liberate Jewry from oppression and discrimination, the programme of the Tsars was driven by centuries-old Christian hostility toward Judaism and the Jewish people.

The Jewish Reaction

Although many European Jews welcomed emancipation, others were more cautious. In Comtat-Venaissin (the district of Avignon), for example, some Jews did not wish to give up wearing the yellow hat which singled them out as belonging to the Jewish community. In France there were similar signs of reluctance. As Laumond, the Prefect of the Bas-Rhine, commented concerning Alsatian Jewry: "As for the Hebraic mob, it continues to wallow in the same ignorance and the same lowliness as before. Its religious principles, which in some way separate it from the rest of the nations, and which nothing up till now has been able to eradicate, are an almost insuperable obstacle to the rapprochement that the public good would require." These Jews, he concluded, "cannot lose the idea that they are foreigners every-where, and this old prejudice will prevent them from thinking of settling permanently for a long time to come."

Despite the Jewish voices raised against emancipation, the assimila-tion of the Jewish population proceeded with rapidity. Throughout Europe communal autonomy was abolished and education radically transformed. Jewish children were required to attend school and subsequently conscripted into the army. As adults they were no longer subject to rabbinical authority; freed of former disabilities, they were able to take advantage of widening opportunities. Within only one or two generations, the ideals of the emancipation had penetrated into all levels of Jewish life, and Jews came to regard themselves as citizens like everyone else.

Throughout Europe, changes in status were noted by Jews and non-Jews alike. In France, for example, the Prefect of the Seine depicted the progress of Jewish emancipation. "It is common know-ledge in all Paris," he wrote, "that the Jews of the capital, freed from the fetters which have for so long hampered them in the exercise of their industry, with the hope held out of being raised to the rank of other citizens, only took advantage of their first moments of enfranchisement to prove that they were worthy of it . . . For example, they are to be seen lining up under the colours, cultivating science and the arts, embracing professions, establishing useful institutions, and indulging in specula-tions distinguished by honour and probity."

In other lands, emancipation was less advanced. As a consequence, alternative routes were followed to assimilation and opportunity. In Germany a considerable number of Jews adopted the Christian faith in order to secure social and professional advancement. Eduard Gans (a friend of Hegel), for example, embraced the Church so that he could be appointed to a chair of philosophy at the University of Berlin. Although the writer Heinrich Heine criticized Gans' decision, Heine himself later converted in order to register at the Hamburg bar. Such a step, he declared, was an "admission ticket to European culture". A contemporary of Heine, Ludwig Borne, similarly converted so he could run a newspaper. "The three drops of water that were administered to me were not even worth the small amount of money they cost me," he remarked. According to Rahel Varnhagen-Levin, who herself became a convert, half the members of the Berlin Jewish community had already converted by 1823.

Like the Marranos of previous centuries, these Jewish apostates remained Jews socially in the eyes of the Christian community. As the practising Jew Gabriel Riesser remarked: "Believe me, hate like the angel of death can find its man, it can recognize him by whatever name he calls himself." In addition, these neo-Marranos, although abandoning their ancestral faith, could not avoid feelings of guilt and admiration for traditional Jewish ways. Thus Heine, who described Judaism as "that misfortune, that family illness of German Jews", declared: "The Greeks were only beautiful adolescents, the Jews on the other hand were always . . . strong and unyielding, not only in the past, but until today, despite eighteen centuries of persecution and hardship . . . martyrs, who have given the world a God and a code of morality, and who have fought and suffered on all the battlefields of thought." In the same vein the Alsatian, Alexandre Weill, who expressed hatred of the Talmud and the rabbis, none the less declared that "more ingenuity, more spirit was expended in one day in the Jews' street in Frankfurt than in all the rest of Germany in a year . . . for centuries, this street represented a civilized life, amidst barbarism, where in an oppressed society, faith, charity, and justice reigned."

This internal conflict between contempt and affection was symptomatic of the period. Prior to the Enlightenment, Jews lacked full citizenship rights. Nevertheless, they were able to regulate their own affairs through an organized structure of self-government. Within such a context Jewish law served as the basis of communal existence, and rabbis were able to exert power and authority in the community. But as a result of social and political emancipation, Jews entered the mainstream of modern life, taking on all the responsibilities of citizenship: the rabbinical establishment thereby lost its status and control and the Jewish legal system became voluntary. Further to gaining access to secular institutions, the influence of the surrounding culture pervaded all aspects of Jewish life. Emancipation was thus both a blessing and a curse. Although it resulted in the amelioration of the condition of European Jewry, it led to widespread disillusionment with traditional ways as well as considerable confusion about Jewish identity.

The Gentile Response

Within the non-Jewish world the Age of Enlightenment led to considerable religious upheaval: some of those who engaged in theological speculation envisaged the Jewish nation in terms reminiscent of an earlier Christian age. The Swedish prophetic figure Emmanuel Swedenborg, for example, maintained that the Jews were an idolatrous people. "The character of this nation," he declared, "is such that, more than the other nations, they worship externals as well as idols, and that they want to know absolutely nothing about internals; in fact, of all the nations, they are the most miserly, and greed like theirs, which consists of loving gold and silver as gold and silver and not for some purpose is the most worldly affection."

Like Luther, Swedenborg believed that it would be easier to convert stones than Jews to the true faith. Because of their hard-heartedness the Jewish nation would be denied everlasting reward; instead Hell would be set aside for this despicable people. Depicting Hell as a town, he proclaimed it would be a place where they would "flock, crowing up together; but this town is foul and covered with filth, consequently it is called the defiled Jerusalem. There, they run about in the mud and in filth above their heads, moaning and lamenting." In this realm they would eat "cadaverous matter, putrid, excremental, and stercoral, foul and urinous". Other writers such as the occultist Claude de Saint-Martin, issued similar invectives against the Jewish people. "If the Jews were brought back as a national body in this world," he warned, "no one could hope for eternal salvation, because the divine circle of the supreme operations would thereby be fulfilled and closed in time."

Such Christian anti-Jewish sentiment – which was evoked in response to steps toward Jewish emancipation – intensified with the onset of revolution. When Napoleon convened the Great Sanhedrin, it was feared that the Emperor had concluded a pact with the forces of evil. Thus in 1807 the Holy Synod decreed that a proclamation was to be read in all Russian Churches accusing Napoleon of seeking to destroy the Christian faith.

In order to complete the degradation of the Church, he has convened the Jewish synagogues in France, restored the rabbis to their dignity, and laid the foundations of a new Hebrew Sanhedrin, the same infamous tribunal which once dared to condemn Our Lord and Saviour Jesus Christ to the cross. And now he is daring to bring together all the Jews whom the anger of God had dispersed over the face of the earth, and launch all of them into the destruction of the

Church of Christ, in order, Oh unspeakable presumption, greater than any heinous crime, that they should proclaim the Messiah in the person of Napoleon.

According to a number of German theosophists, Napoleon's efforts to enfranchise Jewry was a final struggle between Good and Evil. In Great Britain, millenarian French émigrés depicted Napoleon as the Anti-Christ. In their principal organ, *L'Ambigu*, they asked: "Is he (Napoleon) claiming to pass himself off and be acknowledged by them (the Jews) as the Messiah they have waited for, for so long? This, time will tell. Nothing remains for us but to see this Anti-Christ struggle against the eternal decrees of the Divinity: this must be the last act of his diabolical existence." In France, the appearance of the Great Sanhedrin was viewed by many Christians as a conspiracy against the Church.

With the defeat of Napoleon, such propaganda ceased. Yet the fear that Jews were seeking world dominion through their emancipation continued to inspire fear and contempt. As a result of such sentiment, outbreaks against Jews began in August 1819 in Würzburg and spread throughout German towns and the countryside. Similar excesses took place in Bohemia, Alsace, the Netherlands and Denmark. The populace was aroused by travelling rioters whose cry was, "Hep! Hep!" In response the Christian mob armed with axes and iron bars proceeded to the Jewish quarter and demolished the synagogue. In Berlin a contemporary account related:

The excesses which have been committed against the Jews in several towns in Germany have given rise to fear amongst the Israelites in this capital; there have even been some small scenes here already. A few of the Jews' enemies paid a fair number of ne'er-do-wells to cry Hep! Hep! under the windows of the country house of a banker of that nation. An old Israelite pedlar of ribbons and pencils was chased by delinquents in the street which echoed with the ominous cry; he made the best of it like a man with a sense of humour and continued on his way laughing and even shouting Hep! Hep! incessantly himself, but having taken it into his head to peer into a shop and shout inside, a woman who happened to be on the threshold dealt him a violent box on the ears, to which he immediately replied with another. A police employee, who was within call, took him under his protection and, to get him out of reach of the ill-treatment to which he was still exposed, conducted him to the police station . . . The famous Hep! Hep! has already caused some tumultuous scenes in several public places.

As a result of these incidents, Jews sought refuge in other countries. Thus, although the spirit of emancipation had freed Jews from the fetters of the past, Christian Europe continued to inflict suffering on the Jewish nation.

CHAPTER THIRTEEN

Judeophobia in
the Early Nineteenth Century

In the enlightened environment of the nineteenth century, Jewish apologists sought to ameliorate the condition of the Jewish population. In England Benjamin Disraeli, the Tory Prime Minister, formulated a theory of the Jewish race which served as the basis for his quest to grant civil rights to British Jewry. His advocacy of Jewish emancipation, however, provoked a hostile response from such critics as Robert Knox, who denigrated Jewry in terms reminiscent of previous centuries. Such disparagement was similarly a central feature of French life, as evidenced by the Damascus Affair in which the President of the French Council sided with the French consuls in Damascus who accused Jews there with ritual murder. Despite the peaceful conclusion of this matter, this medieval Christian charge gave rise to widespread anti-Jewish sentiment in France. In addition, the Christian myth of the Wandering Jew who was driven from his homeland for having rejected Christ became a predominant image in French literature of the period and stimulated French Judeophobia, as did the anti-Jewish allegations of French socialists. In Germany the advocates of German racism as well as metaphysical writers critical of Jews and Judaism generated considerable ill-will. Such hostility reached its climax in the diatribes of the composer Richard Wagner, whose critique of Judaism paved the way for the Nazi onslaught in the following century.

The English View

Since the eighteenth century, English Jews had had a similar status to Catholics and Nonconformists – their only disability consisted in exclusion from political and honorary offices. In 1829, Catholics were granted full civil rights, but such privileges were denied to the Jewish population. Thus, despite the generally tolerant environment in the country, the presence of Jews continued to arouse public antipathy: the image of Shakespeare's Shylock in his *Merchant of Venice* and Fagin in Dickens' *Oliver Twist* reinforced Christian stereotypes of Jewish behaviour and generated prejudice against the Jews.

During this period Benjamin Disraeli, the Tory Prime Minister of Jewish origin, formulated a theory of race which became the cornerstone of his political views. In his novel *Coningsby*, a philo-Judaic doctrine of Semitic superiority, based on purity of race, is formulated by Sidonia who acts as mentor to Coningsby. To Lord Coningsby Sidonia declares:

> The fact is, you cannot destroy a pure race of the Caucasian organization. It is a physiological fact . . . And at this moment, in spite of centuries, of tens of centuries, of degradation, the Jewish mind exercises a vast influence on the affairs of Europe. I speak not of their laws, which you still obey; of their literature, with which your minds are saturated; but of the living Hebrew intellect. You never observe a great intellectual movement in Europe in which the Jews do not greatly participate.

In view of such attitudes, Disraeli pressed for the admission of Jews to the House of Commons. In a speech of 1847 he declared:

> On every sacred day you read to the people the exploits of Jewish heroes, the proofs of Jewish devotion, the brilliant annals of past Jewish magnificence. The Christian Church has covered every kingdom with sacred buildings, and over every altar . . . we find the tables of the Jewish law. Every Sunday – every Lord's day – if you wish to express feelings of praise and thanksgiving to the Most High, or if you wish to find expression of solace in grief, you find both in the words of the Jewish poets . . . All the early Christians were Jews. The Christian religion was first preached by men who had been Jews until they were converted; every man in the early ages of the Church by whose power, or zeal, or genius, the Christian faith was propagated, was a Jew.

In defence of Jewish interests Disraeli continued:

> In exact proportion to your faith ought to be your wish to do this great act of national justice. If you had not forgotten what you owe to this people,

if you were grateful for that literature which for thousands of years has brought so much instruction and so much consolation to the sons of men, you as Christians would be only too ready to seize the first opportunity of meeting the claims of those who profess this religion. But you are influenced by the darkest superstitions of the darkest ages that ever existed in this country. It is this feeling that has been kept out of this debate: indeed, that has been kept secret in yourselves – enlightened as you are – and that is unknowingly influencing you as it is influencing others abroad.

Such remarks provoked a hostile reaction from a number of writers. In his *The Races of Man*, for example, Robert Knox criticized Disraeli's analysis. "A respect for scientific truth", he wrote, "forbids me refuting the romances of Disraeli; it is sufficient merely to observe here that, in the long list of names of distinguished persons who Mr Disraeli has described of Jewish descent, I have not met with a single Jewish trait in their countenance, in so far as I can discover; and therefore they are not Jews, nor of Jewish origin." In addition, Knox queried Disraeli's contentions about the Jewish people. "Where are the Jewish farmers, Jewish mechanics, labourers?", he asked. "Can he not till the earth, or settle anywhere? Why does he dislike handicraft labour? . . . The real Jew has no ear for music as a race, nor love of science or literature; he invents nothing, pursues no inquiry; the theory of *Coningsby* is not merely a fable as applied to the real and undoubted Jew, but is absolutely refuted by all history." Despite such disagreement about the nature of the Jewish nation, Disraeli and his critics accepted the presupposition that race is a fundamental feature of social and cultural life – the point at issue was whether the Jewish race enriched civilization or polluted it.

French Hatred

As in England, French Jewry came to enjoy full civil rights and a number of prominent Jewish figures attempted to crush the last vestiges of Judeophobia. The Jewish statesman Adolphe Crémieux, for example, praised the advances that the Jewish population had made. "Cast your eyes over this France, the homeland of all liberal feelings," he declared. "See the Israelites launching into all the honourable careers and distinguishing themselves by all the virtues which make good citizens ... Let men cease therefore to make the name of the Jewish nation echo within their boundaries, if indeed the Jews can be regarded as a nation at all since they have the good fortune to be blended into the great family of the French people."

Jews who prospered in this enlightened environment were those who had managed to gain great wealth. In the nineteenth century money became the dominant factor in determining social acceptance and esteem – thus the richest Jew, the Austrian consul James de Rothschild, took on the role of leadership of French Jewry. Many of those opposed to this new order criticized his influence. Ludwig Börne, for example, sarcastically remarked:

> Rothschild has kissed the Pope's hand ... Order has at last been restored such as God intended when he created the world. A poor Christian kissed the Pope's feet and a rich Jew kissed his hand. If Rothschild had received his Roman loan at 60 per cent instead of 65 per cent and so been able to send the Cardinal-Chamberlain ten thousand ducats more, then he would have been allowed to embrace the Holy Father. Would it not be the greatest boon for the world if all kings were chased off their thrones and the Rothschild family installed in their place?

The disparagement of Jewry also occurred when Jews were embroiled in public scandal. In 1832, when the Duchesse de Berry was betrayed to Louis Philippe's government by the convert Simon Deutz and arrested, the writer Chateaubriand denounced Deutz as a traitor in the Christian image of Judas Iscariot: "Let the descendant of the Great Traitor, let Iscariot into whom Satan had entered, *intravit Satanas in Judam*, say how many pieces of silver he received for the deal." In the same vein Victor Hugo employed the Christian concept of the Wandering Jew to describe Deutz, the apostate: "He is not even a Jew! He is a filthy pagan, a renegade, the disgrace and outcast of the world, a foul apostate, a crooked foreigner ... Move on, wandering Jew."

Another event of this period had far reaching consequences for French Jewry as well as Jews in other lands. In 1840 a Capuchin monk, Father Thomas, disappeared mysteriously in Damascus. Two French consuls (Ratti-Menton and Cochelet) maintained that this disappearance was due to the Jewish community and charged its leaders with the

Christian medieval accusation of ritual murder. After a period of torture, false confessions were obtained. However, some of the accused were Austrian subjects, and the Austrian consuls came to their aid. This affair aroused intense feelings throughout Europe, and in Syria representatives of England, Prussia and Russia assisted their Austrian colleagues.

In France a number of prominent Jews (including Adolphe Crémieux and James de Rothschild) were vitally concerned with the plight of their Syrian co-religionists. The President of the Council of Ministers, however, made common cause with the French consuls and the governmental newspaper *Le Messager* was instructed to claim that the superstitions of oriental Jews advocated ritual murder, and to encourage French Jewry to remain silent about the incident. Remarking on the ignorance of the French President of the Council of Ministers, Heinrich Heine wrote:

> The most distressing thing that the bloody Damascus question has brought to light is the ignorance of eastern affairs which we observe in the present President of the Council of Ministers . . . a glaring ignorance which might one day make him commit the most serious mistakes, when it will no longer be this small bloody question of Syria, but really the major bloody world question, the fatal and inevitable question that we call the Eastern question which will have to be solved.

In defence of his actions, the President made his view clear to the Chamber of Peers. "Should I not believe M. Cochelet's words," he declared, "rather than that of a sect which I respect for its energetic efforts to vindicate itself, but which after all is itself a party to the suit?" Endorsed by the President of the Council, the story of the Damascus Affair was publicized in the press. In Paris only two papers defended the Jews, but in other western countries, particularly Great Britain, public opinion generally supported the Jewish cause. Organizing themselves internationally, Jewish leaders met in London to formulate a common policy. Protesting against his own countrymen, Crémieux (the delegate for France) proclaimed: "France is against us!" In defence of the Jewish faith, one of the Jewish dignitaries, Bernard van Oven, recommended that European rabbis swear publicly that the Jewish religion does not prescribe human sacrifice. Eventually it was agreed that a mission composed of Crémieux, Moses Montefiore, and the orientalist Solomon Munk, be sent to the Sultan and the Viceroy of Egypt, Mehemet Ali, to plead the Jewish cause. Fortunately for world Jewry, this crisis was peaceably settled. None the less, this event – recalling the Christian medieval charge against the Jewish population – served as a reminder that anti-Jewish hatred was still present in the modern age.

The Wandering Jew and French Socialism

Despite the improvement in Jewish life in the nineteenth century, French Jewry was well aware of the undercurrents of anti-Semitism: the wretched Christian stereotype of the Jew continued to haunt Europe. According to the *Archives israélites*, the leading writers continued to perpetrate the myth of the demonic Jew:

> Everyone of them at least once in his lifetime is determined to cut himself a doublet in Middle Ages style and, when their imagination runs dry, they knock up a history of the Jews. There is not a novelist, a would be short story writer, not the most wretched manufacturer of *feuilletons* who has not got a fantastic picture of the Jews of yore in his bag . . . At the theatre, from Shakespeare to Scribe; in novels, from Ivanhoe to Paul de Kock; in the newspapers ever since there have been writers to perpetrate *feuilletons* and a public which is willing to swallow a lengthy daily rigmarole, everywhere in fact, in this world of printed paper . . . crack, a Jew is knocked up for you as an egg would be fried.

Such protests were in vain – the disfigurement of the Jew remained an important literary theme. In particular the Christian legend of the Wandering Jew – which had spread in Europe in the sixteenth century – gained universal popularity. According to this Christian myth the Jewish people were driven from their homeland for having rejected Christ. Like Cain, the Jew is a fugitive, destined to wander throughout the world. In his own eyes, he is blameless, yet his crime was to view Christ as a criminal and refuse to help him on his way to Calvary. In a ballad from 1800 the Wandering Jew explained:

> Churlishly, rebelliously,
> I said to him irrationally,

> "Get you gone, criminal
> From outside my house,
> Move on, get going
> For you shame me."

The fault of the Jew was his unbelief, a fault which he regretted, even desiring to become a Christian:

> It was a cruel presumption
> Which caused my misfortune;
> If my crime is expiated,
> I would be too fortunate:
> I have treated my Saviour
> Too harshly.

In 1833, Edgar Quinet in *Ahasvérus* made the Wandering Jew a symbol of human suffering; this work was the inspiration for a publication, *Le Juif Errant, Journal* which decreed in its first issue: "The wandering Jew! at this name, the whole world stops and bows down in terror before the majesty of God: children, peasants, noblewomen . . . The wandering Jew, according to the orthodox priest, is the Jewish race, eternally dispersed amongst the nations, without merging with them, without becoming a sister to them, alone amongst the peoples of the earth, thus fulfilling the prophecies of the divine curse."

This legend captured the imagination of numerous authors of the period, causing them to caricature Jewry. Thus in *Rabbi Manassé ben Israël*, Victor Hugo remarked that Jews thirsted for Christian blood: "Of the two rival parties, what does it matter which succumbs? Christian blood will flow in waves. I hope so anyway." In *Jocelyn*, Lamartine portrayed the fate of a poor despised Jewish pedlar:

> The poor pedlar died last night.
> No one wanted to give the planks for his coffin;
> The blacksmith himself refused a nail.
> "It's a Jew," he said, "come from I don't know where,
> An enemy of God whom our land worships
> And who if He returned, would outrage him again."

Chateaubriand rejoiced in the perils of the torturers of Christ: "Happy Jews," he declared, "crucifix dealers, who rule Christianity today . . .

Ah! if you wanted to change skins with me, if I could at least slide into your strongboxes, rob you of what you have stolen from gilded youth, I would be the happiest of men."

While such literary figures were caricaturing the Jewish people, anti-Semitism, based on previous Christian stereotypes, was also being promoted by French socialists. Hostile to the industrialization of the modern world, these propagandists castigated the pernicious influence of Jewry. In his *Fable of the Jew Iscariot and the Six Christians*, for example, Charles Fourier attacked Jewish commercialism:

> The Jew Iscariot arrives in France with a hundred thousand pounds in capital which he gained from his first bankruptcy: he sets up as a merchant in a town where there are six accredited and respected rival firms. To take away custom from them, Iscariot begins by selling all his goods at cut prices; this is a sure means of attracting the mob; Iscariot's rivals soon start shouting: Iscariot smiles at their complaints and cuts prices even further. Then the people exclaim in admiration: long live competition; long live the Jews, philosophy and fraternity; the price of all goods has fallen since Iscariot arrived; and the public says to the rival firm: "It is you, gentlemen, who are the real Jews, and who want to make too much money. Iscariot is an honest man, he is content with a modest profit, because his household is not as splendid as ours." In vain do the old traders point out that Iscariot is a rascal in disguise.

After Fourier's death, his followers continued the diatribe against the Jewish population. Thus in his *Juifs, rois de l'époque*, his disciple Toussenel wrote: "I call by this despised name of Jew every trader in cash, every unproductive parasite, living off the substance and work of others." For these socialist thinkers the Jew personified evil. In the words of Pierre Proudhon,

> The Jew is by temperament unproductive, neither agriculturalist nor industrialist, not even a genuine trader. He is an intermediary, always fraudulent and parasitical, who operates in business as in philosophy, by forging, counterfeiting, sharp practices. He only knows the rise and fall of markets, transport risks, uncertainties of returns, hazards of supply and demand. His economic policy is always negative; he is the evil element, Satan, Ahriman, incarnated in the race of Shem.

Echoing Christian sentiments of previous centuries, Proudhon recommended a course of action similar to what was carried out by the Nazis a century later:

Jews. Make a provision against that race, which poisons everything, by butting in everywhere, without ever merging with any people. – Demand its expulsion from France . . . Abolish the synagogues, allow them to enter no employment, finally proceed with the abolition of this religion. Not for nothing have the Christians called them deicides. The Jew is the enemy of mankind. That race must be sent back to Asia or exterminated.

German Racism and Metaphysical Thought

In Germany, obsession with purity of the blood resulted in intense Judeophobia. Thus the writings of the two major proponents of Germano-Christian racism, Ernst Moritz Arndt and Friedrich Ludwig Jahn, perpetrated the myth of the supremacy of the German people. According to Arndt, it is the Germans who possess the divine spark. "I do not think", he wrote, "I am mistaken in stating that the powerful and ardent wild stock called German was the good species into which the divine seed could be implanted to produce the most noble fruits. The Germans, and the Latins impregnated and fertilized by them, are the only ones to have made the divine germ flower, thanks to philosophy and theology, and as rulers to animate and guide . . . the surrounding peoples, belonging to foreign species."

Such Germanness must be protected from contamination, and it was Arndt's desire that the Jews disappear as a separate people; this, he believed, could occur through their conversion to Christianity. "Experience shows," he stated, "that as soon as they abandon their disconcerting laws and become Christian, the peculiarities of the Jewish character and type rapidly grow indistinct and by the second generation, it is difficult to recognize the seed of Abraham." Similarly, for Jahn the struggle against foreign blood is a battle of life and death for German society and culture: "Hybrid animals have no real capacity for reproduction; similarly, mongrel peoples have no national survival of their own . . . he who strives to bring all the noble peoples of the world into one herd runs the risk of ruling over the most despicable outcast of the human race."

In the midst of such racial and patriotic sentiment, the Wartburg festival was held in 1817 to commemorate the tricentenary of the Reformation and the tenth anniversary of the Battle of Leipzig. Delegates from fourteen primarily Protestant universities gathered together at Jena to found the *Allgemeine deutsche Burschenschaft*. A solemn procession took place, followed by a divine service and an *auto-da-fé* of books and other objects regarded as anti-German. A letter from a Heidelberg student, Richard Rothe (who later became a theologian), described the event:

> The people in Jena want a Christian–German *Burschenschaft* but we had always wanted till then a general one in the strictest sense of the word and we therefore decided to give entry to Jews and foreigners as to anyone else if they had acquired academic rights through matriculation. Thereupon the Germans – there were about twenty of them – flew into a terrible rage. Since then they form a sect in the *Burschenschaft* and at general meetings are mainly distinguished by forming a perpetual opposition . . . They keep strictly together and have a way of their own . . . They are not too keen on their studies and act as if they have found the philosopher's stone, and meditate on how they will one day become Germany's saviours and redeemers.

Alongside such patriotic attitudes which fostered the disparagement of Jewry, German metaphysicians castigated Judaism and the Jewish action in terms reminiscent of previous Christian centuries. The theologian Friedrich Wilhelm Ghillany attempted to expose what he believed to be Jewish cannibalism. According to Ghillany such cannibalism was evidenced by the ritual murder of Jesus as well as subsequent ritual murders in Jewish history. In the light of such barbarism, he believed that it would be misguided to grant the Jewish people civil rights: "How can political rights be granted to such men, who adhere so rigidly to old inhuman prejudices, who regard us as impure, like serfs and dogs, just as their ancestors did, even if they do not flaunt it to our face? It is men such as these who claim full civil rights, the right to exercise functions of government, to become the superiors of Christians, judicial and administrative officers!" The philosopher Ludwig Feuerbach also attacked the Jewish people:

> The Israelites only opened their gastric senses to nature. They only enjoyed nature through their palate. They only became aware of God through the enjoyment of manna . . . Eating is the most solemn act or even initiation into the Jewish religion. In the act of eating the Israelite celebrates and renews the act of creation. In eating, man declares nature to be a nullity in itself. When the seventy elders climbed the mountain

with Moses, then "they saw the God of Israel . . . they stayed there before God; they ate and they drank" (Exodus 24:10–11). The sight of the highest being therefore only amused their appetite.

With similar contempt the Hegelian Arnold Ruge emphasized the pernicious influence of Jewry on German society. They are "maggots in the cheese of Christianity who are so unutterably comfortable in their reflective and stock-jobbing skin that they believe in nothing and precisely for this reason remain Jews." Another Hegelian, Bruno Bauer, polemicized against Jewish emancipation. In his *Die Judenfrage*, he criticized the Jewish people "for having made their nest in the pores and interstices of bourgeois society". The Jews' crime resided in "not recognizing the purely human development of history, the development of human conscience".

Finally, Karl Marx in his writings attacked the Jewish influence on bourgeois society. Material concerns, he argued, form the basis of Jewish life. "The bill of exchange is the real God of the Jew," he declared. "His God is only an illusory bill of exchange. That which is contained in an abstract in the Jewish religion – contempt for theory, for art, for history, and for man as an end in himself – is the real, conscious standpoint and the virtue of the man of money . . . The chimerical nationality of the Jew is the nationality of the trader, and above all the financier." According to Marx, what is required in modern society is not the emancipation of the Jew, but the emancipation of the world from Jewry: "As soon as society succeeds in abolishing the empirical essence of Judaism – huckstering and its conditions – the Jew becomes impossible . . . The social emancipation of the Jew is the emancipation of society from Judaism."

Richard Wagner

German hostility toward the Jewish people in the nineteenth century reached its culmination in the writings of the composer Richard Wagner. In exile in Switzerland from 1849 to 1851 he studied Germanic myths. In his first book he presented an Aryan theory of the origin of humanity based upon these studies: "Upon this island, i.e. these mountains, we have to seek the cradle of the present Asiatic peoples, as also of those who wandered forth to Europe. Here is the ancestral seat of all religions, of every tongue, of all these nations' Kinghood." Focusing on the legend of the Niebelungen he wrote, "Research has shown the basis of this saga, too, to be of religio-mythic nature: its deepest meaning was the un-conscience of the Frankish stem, the soul of its royal race ... compelling respect."

Later, Wagner identified the God Wotan with the Christian conception of the Son of God: "The abstract Highest God of the Germans, Wotan, did not really need to yield place to the God of the Christians; rather could he be completely identified with him ... for in him was found the striking likeness to Christ himself, the Son of God, that he too died, was mourned and avenged."

Such convictions served as the general background of his *Das Judentun in der Musik*. In this work Wagner stated that the quest to emancipate the Jews was based on idealistic notions rather than on a personal familiarity with the Jewish population:

> Even when we strove for emancipation of the Jews, however, we were more the champions of an abstract principle than of a concrete case: just as all our liberalism was not very lucid mental sport – since we went for freedom of the Folk without knowledge of that Folk itself, nay, with a dislike of any genuine contact with it – so our eagerness to level up the rights of Jews was far rather stimulated by a general idea, than by any real sympathy.

For Wagner, the Jew was a degenerate element in society; even those who had been emancipated were incapable of making a positive contribution. With his patron the Jewish musician Meyerbeer in mind, Wagner declared:

> Whoever has observed the shameful indifference and absent-minded-ness of a Jewish congregation, throughout the musical performance of Divine Service in the Synagogue, may understand why a Jewish opera-composer feels not at all offended by encountering the same thing in a theatre audience, and how he can cheerfully go on labouring for it; for this behaviour, there, must really seem to him less unbecom-ing than in the House of God ... In general, the uninspiring, the truly laughable, is the characteristic mark whereby this famed composer shows his Jewhood in his music.

With the publication of *Oper und Drama*, Wagner continued his diatribe against Meyerbeer. "As a Jew, he owned no mother tongue, no speech inextricably entwined among the sinews of his innermost being: he spoke with precisely the same interest in any modern tongue you chose, and set it to music with no more concern for its idiosyncrasies than the mere question of how far it was ready to be a pliant servitor to Absolute Music."

For Wagner, hatred of the Jews became a driving obsession. In 1853, Liszt described to Princess Wittgenstein Wagner's passionate contempt: "He flung his arms round my neck, then he rolled on the ground, caressing his dog Pepi, and talking nonsense to it, in between spitting on the Jews, who are a generic term with him, in a very broad sense." Twenty years later the Gobinist Ludwig Schemann presented a more detailed picture of Wagner's hostility:

> His laments at the unutterable misery wrought by the Jews against our people culminated in the description of the fate of the German peasant who would soon no longer own a square inch of his own soil . . . I have never seen him exhibit such a flare-up of holy wrath; after his last words, quite beside himself, he flung himself out into the winter night, and only returned after an interval, when the paroxysm had died down.

Throughout Wagner's life virulent anti-Semitism was a constant theme; thus in 1881 he warned the King of Bavaria about the threat of a Jewish nation. "I regard the Jewish race as the born enemy of pure humanity and everything that is noble in it; it is certain that we Germans will go under before them, and perhaps I am the last German who knows how to stand up as an art-loving man against the Judaism that is already getting control of everything." Such ardent Judeophobia was a modern manifestation of ancient Christian attitudes to the Jews. Conceived in racist terms, it eventually fuelled the passion of Nazism which sought to solve the Jewish problem by means of the gas chambers.

CHAPTER FOURTEEN

Modern Images of the Jew in Germany, France and Russia

During the latter half of the nineteenth century, the Jewish community suffered further outbreaks of Christian anti-Semitism. In Germany, numerous racist publications denigrated the Jewish people, leading to the creation of political parties which propagated anti-Jewish attitudes. At the same time the researches of Christian biblical scholars tended to undermine the traditional Jewish belief in the authority of Scripture. Similar anti-Jewish attitudes were expressed in France: such writers as Chevalier Gougenot des Mousseaux, Edouard Drumont, and Jules Soury denounced both Judaism and the Jewish nation. Such hostility provided the background to the Dreyfus Affair which erupted at the end of the century. Falsely accused of treason, Alfred Dreyfus was sentenced to life imprisonment, but subsequently exonerated. The hatred engendered by his trial led a number of Jews to question whether Jewry could ever be secure without its own land. Inspired by the vision of a Jewish homeland, Theodor Herzl embarked on a vigorous campaign to convince world leaders of the necessity of a Jewish state. Only in this way, he believed, could the problem of anti-Semitism be solved. During this period Russian Jewry also experienced widespread persecution, culminating in the pogroms of 1881. Profoundly affected by such massacres, many Jews emigrated to distant lands; others sought to ameliorate their condition through revolutionary struggle. Aware of such agitation, the Russian authorities became increasingly alarmed. Such concern was intensified by the publication of *The Secret of Judaism* and the fraudulent *Protocols of the Elders of Zion*, which alleged that the Jewish people conspire against society to achieve world domination. The revival of the ritual murder charge at the beginning of the next century further inflamed Russian antipathy toward the Jews.

German Anti-Semitic Campaigns

The second half of the nineteenth century witnessed the manifestation of Christian anti-Semitic agitation throughout Germany and Austria. In 1871 *The Jew of the Talmud* was published by Canon August Rohling, a Professor at the Imperial University of Prague. This work, based on *Judaism Unmasked* by Johann Andreas Eisenmenger, revived the Christian myth of ritual murder. The twelve ritual murder trials of Jews in German regions held between 1867 and 1914 were largely due to Rohling's influence.

Another major figure of this period was Wilhelm Marr, who is credited with coining the term "anti-Semitism". In his *The Victory of Judaism over Germanism* Marr argued that Judaism had been victorious in the modern world. "They (Jews) do not deserve any reproach," he wrote. "They have struggled for 1800 years against the western world. They have beaten it and subjugated it. We are the losers and it is natural that the winners should shout *Vae victis*. We are so Judaized that we are beyond salvation and a brutal anti-Semitic explosion can only postpone the collapse of our Judaized society, but not prevent it." On the basis of such views, Marr founded an Anti-Semitic League in 1871. Similar attitudes were expressed in a series of articles by the journalist Otto Glagau in the magazine *Die Gartenlaube*: "The Jewish tribe does not work," he stated. "It exploits the manual or intellectual production of others. This foreign tribe has enslaved the German people. The social question is basically the Jewish question. All the rest is fraud."

In 1878 the minister Adolf Stoecker, chaplain of the Imperial Court, founded the Christian Socialist Workers' Party which promulgated anti-Semitism as a central policy. In consequence violence erupted in Berlin in 1880–81. Mobs assaulted Jews in the streets, drove them from cafés, and smashed their store windows; in the provinces synagogues were burned. At the same time, Bernhard Förster, Nietzsche's brother-in-law, who had visited Wagner's Bayreuth, organized a petition which called for a census of the Jews in Germany and their exclusion from the teaching profession. Over 200,000 signatures were obtained.

Through the influence of the historian Heinrich Treitschke, anti-Semitism gained considerable respectability, and anti-Semitic movements and parties became increasingly common. International conferences were held, and various fraternities refused to admit Jewish students. In addition, the German custom of the student duel was denied to Jews. Numerous anti-Semitic treatises also began to circulate at the end of the century, such as *Die Judenfrage als Rassen-Sitten- und Kulturfrage* and *Der Ersatz der Religion durch Volkommeneres und die Ausscheidung des Judentums durch den modernen Völkergeist* by Karl Eugen Dühring. All these works were eventually overshadowed by *The Foundations of the Nineteenth Century* by the Anglo-German writer, Houston Stewart Chamberlain. In his study Chamberlain maintained that the antiquity and mobility of the Jewish nation illustrates the confrontation between superior Aryans and parasitic Semites. On the political front Karl Lueger, the leader of the Austrian Christian party, publicly espoused anti-Semitic policies in 1887 with the encouragement of Pope Leo XIII and Cardinal Rampolla. Eventually he was elected mayor of Vienna. In Germany the *Antisemitsche Volkspartei* won four seats in 1890: three years later its number in the Reichstag increased to sixteen.

Such political activities were accompanied by the researches of Christian biblical theologians which undermined the central tenets of traditional Judaism. According to rabbinic tradition, the Five Books of Moses were dictated by God to Moses on Mount Sinai. This doctrine implies that the entire text – including precepts, theology and history – is of divine origin: all of its contents are inerrant. Such a belief guarantees the validity of the legal system, the Jewish view of God, and the concept of Israel's pre-eminence among the nations. It was precisely these views which the discoveries of Christian theologians called into question. In the middle of the nineteenth century, sustained investigation by two German scholars, Karl Heinrich Graf and Julius Wellhausen, concluded that the Five Books of Moses are composed of four main documents which once existed separately but were later combined by a series of editors or redactors. By utilizing this framework, Graf and Wellhausen maintained that it is possible to account for the manifold problems and discrepancies in the biblical text. Subsequently the Graf-Wellhausen hypothesis was modified by other German scholars, yet despite the varying interpretations of textual origins there was a general recognition that the Five Books of Moses was not written by Moses – rather the Pentateuch was seen as a collection of traditions originating at different times in ancient Israel. Orthodox Jewish scholars protested against the findings of these Christian higher critics, referring to their views as "Higher

Anti-Semitism". Thus on the threshold of the twentieth century, Jews and Judaism were beseiged on all sides as they had been through centuries of Christian discrimination and persecution.

Before Dreyfus

After the Revolution of 1789, French Jewry was accused of conspiring against Western society – to defend their co-religionists the *Alliance Israélite Universelle* was established in 1860, with headquarters in Paris. Yet despite such allegations, from 1846 to 1878, under the pontificate of Pius IX, French Catholics and others adopted a relatively moderate policy toward the Jewish population. None the less, during this period Christian anti-Semitism continued to fester, as evidenced by the publication of *Le Juif, le judaïsme et la judaïsation des peuples chrétiens* by Chevalier Gougenot des Mousseaux. This tract (which received the blessing of Pius IX) collected anti-Jewish charges concerning the Talmud and kabbalistic sources, the activities of the *Alliance Israélite Universelle*, and a plot allegedly conceived in Italy by the Jewish Mason Piccolo Tigre.

According to Gougenot, Jews continually conspire against Christians and encourage revolution in consonance with Talmudic prescriptions: "This savage code (the Talmud), which combines the precepts of hatred and plunder with the doctrine of cabbalistic magic, which professes high idolatry . . . That is why the Jews will remain unsociable beings until the Talmud is destroyed." In the light of such a conception, Gougenot argued that "the Middle Ages had the good sense to isolate in restricted quarters and to compel (Jews) to wear a special attire that allowed everyone to avoid them. When one was forced to deal with this scum it was hidden like a disgrace for which one sought all possible purification. Shame, and the danger of contact, had been the Christian antidote to their pestilence since God wanted to perpetuate this vermin."

From 1880 to 1881 this theme of a Jewish conspiracy was promulgated by the Catholic review, *Le Contemporain*, which published the work of Calixte de Wolski. According to this author, the Jews themselves were responsible for the Russian pogroms of this period since "they have been pursuing from time immemorial, and by every means, the idea of ruling the earth". This contention was based on the writings of the Russian convert, Jacob Brafman, and the forgery, *The Rabbi's Speech* taken from a novel by Hermann Goedsche. In 1882 *La revue des questions historiques* stated that: "Judaism rules the world, and we must therefore conclude either that the Masons have become Jewish or that the Jews have become Masons." Such an allegation was based on the bi-monthly magazine *Civilità cattolica*, which began a virulent anti-Semitic campaign in 1880. During this period such hostility was intensified by the Catholic Eugène Bontoux, founder of the bank Union Générale, who blamed the bankruptcy of the bank on the intrigues of the Rothschilds. This charge was widely believed and became the subject of numerous literary works. The 1880s also witnessed the proliferation of a wide range of anti-Semitic publications such as the periodicals *L'antijuif* in Paris, in 1881, and *L'antisémitique* in Montdidier in 1883.

In 1886, Edouard Drumont's *La France juive* denounced the Rothschilds as well as other prominent Jewish figures, and thereby fostered further manifestations of Christian anti-Semitism. In the first page of this work he linked the Revolution with the Jews: "The only one who benefited from the Revolution", he wrote, "was the Jew. Everything came from the Jew. Everything returns to the Jew." Attributing what he saw as the Judaization of France to Jewish emancipation, he contrasted the scheming character of the Semite with the chivalrous nature of the Aryan: "Semite, mercantile, greedy, scheming, devious and the Aryan, enthusiastic, heroic, chivalrous, disinterested, frank, trusting to the point of naïveness. The Semite is earthbound ... the Aryan is a son of heaven ... The Semite sells glasses or grinds lenses like Spinoza, but he does not discover stars in the immensity of heaven."

As a consequence of such racist propaganda, a number of official Catholic publications became openly anti-Semitic, and the Jewish problem became a major theme for novelists and journalists. In 1890 *La Croix* declared that it was "the most anti-Semitic newspaper in France". Philosophical works as well denounced Jewry as an inferior race. According to the materialist philosopher Jules Soury:

The product fertilized in the egg of an Aryan or a Semite will reproduce the biological characteristics of the race or the species, body and spirit, as surely as the embryo, the foetus, the young, or the adult of any other mammal. Raise a Jew in an Aryan family from birth, and neither the nationality nor the language will modify one atom of the genes of the Jew, and consequently, of the hereditary structure and texture of his tissues and organs.

Such attitudes permeated French society and fuelled the passions inflamed by the Dreyfus Affair which attracted world-wide attention at the end of the century.

The Dreyfus Affair and Zionism

In the last decades of the nineteenth century a relatively large number of French Jewish men had embarked on a military career: more than three hundred Jews out of 40,000 were members of the officer corps. Such an influx led to suspicion and mistrust – this situation served as the background to the Dreyfus Affair which erupted in the 1890s. In 1892 Alfred Dreyfus became a captain on the General Staff. Two years later a secret memo sent by a French officer to Colonel von Schwartzkoppen (the military attaché of the German embassy in Paris) came to the attention of the French Intelligence Service. On the basis of an examination of the handwriting, the heads of the Intelligence Service, including Major H. J. Henry, accused Dreyfus of treason. Tried before a court-martial, Dreyfus was found guilty and sentenced to life imprisonment. On 5 January 1895 he was demoted in a public ceremony during which he proclaimed his innocence. Incited by the anti-Semitic press, the onlookers fulminated against Dreyfus and the Jewish community. Subsequently Dreyfus was exiled to Devil's Island in French Guinea, off the coast of South America.

In desperation Dreyfus' brother enlisted the writer Bernard Lazare, who sought to overturn the verdict. In November 1886 Lazare published a pamphlet, *The Truth about the Dreyfus Affair*, and sent copies to prominent politicians and public figures. The same year the Intelligence Service seized a letter which Schwartzkoppen had written to a French major, Ferdinand Walsin Esterhazy. On the basis of the evidence the new head of the French Intelligence Service, Lieutenant-colonel Georges Picquart, concluded that the original letter incriminating Dreyfus had in fact been written by Esterhazy. Major Henry forged further documents to demonstrate that Dreyfus' court-martial had been correct in its judgement, and Picquart was dismissed and dispatched to Africa.

However before departing, Picquart communicated the facts of the case to friends who passed on the information to Auguste Scheurer-Kestner, who declared in the Senate that Dreyfus was innocent and accused Esterhazy instead. Although Prime Minister F. J. Méline refused to accept this testimony, the case became a *cause célèbre*. Subsequently Esterhazy was tried and acquitted, and Picquart was punished with sixty days' imprisonment. None the less, on 13 January 1898, the newspaper *L'Aurore* published an open letter by Emile Zola to the President of the Republic entitled: *J'accuse!* In this declaration those who had denounced Dreyfus were charged with libel. Zola was, however, eventually found guilty of defamation, and officers of the General Staff threatened to resign if Dreyfus were acquitted.

Throughout the country, anti-Semitic outbreaks took place, and the Dreyfus Affair became a public issue. In the summer of 1898 a new war minister, Cavaignac, decided to reopen the case. Henry's forgeries were discovered, and he was arrested. Later he committed suicide. The government decided to request an annulment of the verdict and a retrial. During a second trial the army officers repeated their original testimony, and on 9 December 1899 the court-martial decided that Dreyfus had committed treason, sentencing him only to five further years of imprisonment because of extenuating circumstances. Although Dreyfus was eventually granted a pardon by the President of the Republic, he demanded a fresh investigation in 1904. After re-examining the case, the court of appeal decreed that the evidence against him was unsubstantiated and that it was thus unnecessary to order a further trial.

The Dreyfus Affair had a profound effect on Jewry world-wide, and in particular on the thought of Theodor Herzl, the Paris correspondent of the Vienna *Neue Freie Presse*. On 5 January 1895, Herzl witnessed the outcry of the mob when Dreyfus was stripped of his military rank. Hearing the rabble shout "Death to the Jews", he became convinced that there was no way anti-Semitism could be eliminated: the only solution for the Jewish people was to resettle in a territory of their own. In the same year, he completed the first draft of his *Der Judenstaat*. This work was initially addressed to the Rothschilds – Herzl was convinced that their capital could only be safeguarded by the establishment of a Jewish state. "There exists only one solution," he wrote. "We are talking about a simple old matter – the exodus from Egypt."

Subsequently Herzl revised the work for the general public; his central thesis was that the Jewish problem cannot be solved by assimilation because of the persistence of anti-Semitism. Jews are inevitably marginalized in the lands where they reside: "In vain are we loyal patriots, our loyalty in some places running to extremes; in vain do we make the same sacrifices of life and property as our fellow citizens; in vain do we strive to increase the fame of our native land in science and art, or her wealth by trade and commerce; in countries where we have lived for centuries we are still cried down as strangers." Only the creation of a Jewish state could relieve Jewry of such an insecure existence.

In 1887 the first Zionist congress took place in Basle, which called for a national home for Jews based on international law. At this congress Herzl stated that the emancipation of the Jews had been an illusion: Jews were everywhere objects of contempt and hatred. The only remedy to the Jewish problem, he argued, was the re-establishment of a homeland in Palestine. In the same year the Zionist Organization was created, with branches in Europe and America. After establishing these basic institutions of the Zionist movement, Herzl embarked on diplomatic negotiations. In 1898 he met with Kaiser Wilhelm II, who promised he would take up the matter with the Sultan. When nothing came of this, Herzl attempted to arrange an interview, and a meeting with the Sultan took place in 1901. This was followed by meetings with Joseph Chamberlain, the British Secretary of State for Colonial Affairs.

After a trip to the Pale of Settlement in 1903, where he encountered poverty and deprivation, Herzl reluctantly agreed to Chamberlain's proposal for a Jewish state in Uganda as a place of temporary asylum. At the next Zionist conference in Basle this plan was presented for ratification. When the resolution was passed by a small margin, the delegates from eastern Europe walked out of the auditorium. During the next few days the Zionist movement was threatened by schism; at the end of the proceedings the Russian Jews set off for Kharkov where they convened their own conference committing themselves to the idea of Palestine. In England, public opinion was opposed to the transference of Uganda to the Jews, and the offer was eventually withdrawn. In the following year Herzl died, and the Zionist movement was led by a new President (David Wolffsohn) who attemped to heal the rifts between competing factions. At the 1907 congress a resolution was passed which pledged the movement to the quest for a charter, the physical settlement of Palestine, and the revival of the Hebrew language. Thus the Dreyfus Affair and its aftermath highlighted the precarious position of modern Jewry. After 1800 years of persecution in Christian lands, many Jews came to see their salvation in terms of social and political isolation.

Russian Protests

After the annexation of the major part of Poland at the end of the eighteenth century, Russian authorities turned their attention to the charge of ritual murder. Although Derzhavin's investigation had revealed that Jewish law does not prescribe such a practice, the Damascus Affair of 1840 had revived Christian fears. Thus the Tsar assigned officials to conduct a new investigation. In a lengthy report published in 1844, the folklorist Vladimir Dhal concluded that although ritual murder was not practised by the vast majority of Jews, it did take place among the Hasidim. Subsequently trials for ritual murder occasionally occurred, as for example in Kutays in 1879. At the same time the former Polish priest Hippolytus Lutostanski published a work on this subject which he sent to the future Tsar Alexander III, and the Russian daily *Novoye Vremya* printed a study of ritual murder in the Ukraine by Nikolai Kostomarov.

The latter half of the nineteenth century also witnessed counter-emancipatory tendencies among Russian writers. In the 1860s the Slavonic theoretician Ivan Aksakov protested against Jewish emancipation. "The real question", he stated, "is not the emancipation of the Jews, but the liberation of the Russians of the south west from the Jewish yoke." Later the convert Jacob Brafman, professor of Hebrew at the Orthodox Seminary of Minsk, published a series of articles on Jewish life which were collected in two volumes. In the *Book of the Kahal*, Brafman sought to illustrate the procedures by which Jews excluded other religious groups from trade and industry:

We learn that each Christian landowner is sold by the *kahal* (Jewish community) to a Jew. Yes, sold like an investment, both in his person and in his property. It is not just a way of speaking, but a legal term because the transaction is sealed by a special sales contract. Similarly villages, whole sections with their inhabitants, are bought and sold. Under the cover of our civil laws there exists a radically different legal code, secret and negative, that rules over and subjects to the jurisdiction of the Jews not only the Jews but also the Russians, without their knowledge.

In *Local and Universal Jewish Brotherhoods*, Brafman further explained the nature of Jewish communal organization: "The brotherhoods are the major arteries of Jewish society . . . They link all the Jews scattered over the globe into one powerful and invincible body."

For many Russian Jews, including the intelligentsia, the Jewish presence became increasingly problematic. Thus in the summer of 1879 the writer Fëdor Dostoevski, who was undergoing his yearly cure for emphysema in Bad Ems, complained in a letter to Pobyedonostzev, the procurator of the Holy Synod, about the number of Jews he encountered. "Everything is completely foreign," he declared. "It's unbearable. It is supposed to last five weeks. And note this. Literally half are Yids. On my way through Berlin I also noticed that Germany, or at least Berlin, has become Judaized." In response Pobyedonostzev asserted that the Jews had become a threatening force in Russia as well. "What you write about the Yids is perfectly correct. They have invaded everything . . . They are at the root of the Social Democratic movement and tsaricide. They control the press and the stock market. They reduce the masses to financial slavery. They formulate the principles of contemporary science, which tends to dissociate itself from Christianity . . . And nobody dares say that here the Jews control everything." In the same year *Novoye Vremya* published extracts from Wilhelm Marr's *The Victory of Semitism over Germanism*; this was followed in 1880 by the publication of *The Yid is on the March*.

Given such a climate of Judeophobia it is not surprising that when Alexander II was assassinated, Jews were suspected of plotting his death. As a consequence a pogrom took place during the Holy Week of 1881 in Elisavetgrad, followed by others in Kiev, Odessa and elsewhere. These events were described by Anatole Leroy-Beaulieu, a French expert on Russian affairs:

> Anti-Jewish riots took place on a set day, almost everywhere in accordance with the same procedure, not to say the same programme.

They began with the arrival by train of a gang of troublemakers. Often, on the previous evening posters had been hung accusing the Jews of nihilism and the murder of Emperor Alexander II. To arouse the masses, the agitators read in the streets or cabarets articles from anti-Semitic newspapers . . . the rumour spread that the Tsar had granted three days to pillage Jewish property. In many localities the negligence of the police and the indifference of the officials . . . helped to confirm this legend.

In May 1881 the Tsar assured the Jewish community that he would protect them from further violence, yet he regarded Jewish exploitation of the masses as the cause of these disturbances. In the following year the Tsar issued a series of decrees to protect Christians from such abuse: the Pale of Settlement was decreased in size and Jews were forbidden to settle in the countryside as well as in certain cities. In 1884 General Drenteln (Governor-General of the south-western region) closed the vocational school in Zhitomir, giving as his reason the privileged position of the Jewish populace: "In view of the fact that in the cities and localities of the south-west the Jews constitute the greatest group of artisans and, consequently, prevent the development of crafts among the native populations exploited by them, a vocational school for which there is no Christian equivalent becomes in Jewish hands an additional weapon for the exploitation of the native population." Outside the Pale where a number of Jews had managed to settle during the reign of Alexander II, police raids were aimed to reduce their numbers. In defence of this policy Alexander III stated to a high official: "We must never forget that the Jews crucified Christ and shed his precious blood."

Revolution and Ritual Murder

The pogroms which took place at the end of the nineteenth century produced a profound change in Jewish consciousness. Beginning in 1881, Jews petitioned the government to legalize emigration, and articles and letters were published in Jewish periodicals protesting against this new wave of anti-Semitism. A typical example stated: "When I think how we were treated, how we were taught to love Russia and Russian letters, how we were manoeuvred into introducing the

Russian language into our homes, so that now our children know no other, and how nowadays we are hunted and persecuted, my heart is filled with the most corrosive despair."

At this time a number of young Jews formed a Zionist organization, Lovers of Zion (*Hoveve Tzion*), and some of its members settled in Palestine. Other Jews sought refuge elsewhere, primarily in the United States. Alarmed by such mass immigration, the US government commissioned an official report on the plight of Russian Jewry. In the conclusion of this document, the authors recommended that a formal protest be made about Jewish persecution:

> Considering the fact that restrictive measures against the Jews in Russia affect from five to seven million individuals, who are therefore forced to emigrate, and who, for various reasons (mostly individual and religious freedom) choose our country, we have devoted more time to the study of Jewish emigration than any other ... Russian emigration is a consequence of official policies. It can be slowed down by an imperial decree or an official order to stop the persecutions.

Yet despite such disapproval of Russian policies, the plight of Jewry grew worse.

Although for many Russian Jews emigration served as the solution to their problems, many young Jews became partisans in the revolutionary struggle. In his *Der Antisemitismus in Russland*, Ivan Tolstoy described these young revolutionaries:

> Jewish young people who, after graduating from high school, have acquired the legal right to a university education but are barred from it through administrative prohibitions, enter practical life deeply frustrated, full of resentment and hatred against authorities who deprive them of their rights. It is these embittered groups who organize and swell the ranks of the revolutionary parties, and the universities barricaded against their influx, are helpless against their propaganda.

As a result of such agitation, Nicholas II came to identify Jews with revolutionary ferment.

During this period Russian hostility toward the Jews was intensified by the tracts which propagated the myth of a Jewish world conspiracy. After the coronation of Nicholas II in 1895, *The Secret of Judaism* appeared in the files of the police, alleging that in ancient times the doctrine of monotheism was known by a small number of Egyptians who refused to enlighten the masses. Yet Moses transgressed this ban and passed on such teaching to the Hebrews in order to give them an exalted position among the nations. Later, when Christ sought to impart divine knowledge to humanity, the Jews crucified him and were thereby punished. This was the origin of the Jewish plot against humanity:

> The only method within human limitations that seemed capable of changing the tragic fate of the Jews, punished by God, was to hasten as much as possible the spiritual evolution of the rest of mankind. This premise implies two types of activities:
>
> (a) Creative: to contribute to the rapid spread of Christianity throughout the world.
> (b) Destructive: to undermine at all cost the ethical foundation of Christianity among the believers.
>
> This is the programme that became the cornerstone of the whole subsequent history of the Jewish people ... How can we help admiring a people that was able to subordinate all its thoughts, passions, enthusiasms, and even every routine detail of its life to a master plan?

Ten years later, when the situation appeared to justify the dire prediction contained in this anti-Semitic tract, the *Protocols of the Elders of Zion* made its appearance. This forgery was written at the end of the nineteenth century by an unknown author working for the Russian secret police. Adapted from an old French political pamphlet by Maurice Joly (which ascribed ambitions of world domination to Napoleon III), it alleged that the leaders of world Jewry controlled the policies of various European states. The aim of this Jewish body was to achieve world power by reducing the gentiles to slavery. The purpose of both these works was to enlighten Russian society to the evil influence of Jewry and their leading role in the Revolutionary movement.

The ancient Christian accusation of ritual murder accompanied such charges. On 20 March 1911 the body of a thirteen-year-old boy, André Lushchinsky, was discovered in the suburbs of Kiev. After the anti-Semitic press accused the Jews of this murder, an inquest was initiated. Eventually Mendel Beilis, a foreman in a brickyard near where the body was found, was accused of the crime. However the editor of the newspaper *Kievskaya Mysl* embarked on his own investigation and tracked down the true culprits – a gang of thieves who killed the child because they feared he would act as a witness against them. In September a trial took place. During the proceedings Father Pranaytis, a Catholic priest who had published a pamphlet on ritual murder, reiterated the medieval legend of the punishment of the Jewish people and its remedy:

> The Jewish people was cursed by Moses, who said: "God will strike you with all the plagues of Egypt." It is clear that this curse was accomplished since all European Jews have eczema on their posteriors, all Asiatic Jews scabies on their heads, all African Jews boils on their legs, and American Jews a disease of the eyes that drives them insane. The perverse rabbis have found a cure for these diseases. They rub the affected parts with Christian blood. When Jews kill Christians, they respond to a triple motive. First, they satisfy the hatred they bear Christians, and they believe that this crime is a sacrifice pleasing to God. Second, it allows them to perform magical acts. Third, since the rabbis are not sure that the Son of Mary is not the Messiah, they believe that by sprinkling themselves with Christian blood they may find salvation.

Although Beilis was later acquitted of this crime, the trial appeared to substantiate the charge of ritual murder. Thus the Tsar proclaimed: "Undoubtedly, there has been a ritual murder, but I am happy that Beilis was acquitted, since he is innocent."

CHAPTER FIFTEEN

Prelude to the Holocaust

In the years leading up to World War I, Jews became scapegoats for the problems afflicting German society. Objections were raised against the assimilation of German Jewry, and numerous Christian writers protested against the pernicious influence of Jewish attitudes. Although Germany prospered after the war, over six million were unemployed between 1930 and 1933 – such a situation led to the rise of Nazism with its policies of rabid anti-Semitism. In Russia during the war years Christian anti-Semites accused Jews of espionage and collaboration with the enemy. With the onslaught of the Revolution, Russian authorities condemned what they believed to be an international Jewish conspiracy, and pogroms occurred throughout the country. In the years following the war a series of forgeries were produced to implicate Jews with the Revolutionary movement and illustrate the existence of a world-wide Jewish conspiracy. During this period British writers also vilified Jewry for their dishonesty as well as participation in the Revolutionary struggle. After the war, the publication of *The Protocols of the Elders of Zion* reinforced the Christian myth of international Jewish intrigue. In the United States, Jews were also subject to discrimination, and a number of Christian writers blamed the Russian revolution on the involvement of Jewish activists. In response, the American Jewish Committee and the Anti-Defamation League were established to protect Jewish interests. French Judeophobia was similarly animated by the perception of the Jewish influence on world affairs: once the Bolsheviks were successful, the French press blamed the Jews. Such images of a universal Jewish conspiracy paved the way for the growth of Nazism and the horrors that were to follow in the years of Nazi rule.

The German Reaction

On the evening of 4 August 1914 when the British government abandoned its neutrality, the German Jewish poet Ernst Lissauer wrote "The Hymn of Hate Against England":

> And some day we will sign a peace treaty.
> But you, we will hate you with an enduring hatred.
> Never is our hatred going to abate.
> Hatred on the sea, hatred on land,
> Hatred of the head, hatred of the hand,
> Hatred of the blacksmith, hatred of the prince,
> Ferocious hatred of seventy million.
> United in love, united in hate,
> They have only one enemy,
> England.

Although Willhelm II decorated the author, a number of anti-Semites attacked Lissauer because of his racial origins. Thus Houston Stewart Chamberlain criticized Lissauer for belonging to a people who have always cultivated hatred. Such antipathy was symbolic of the age: once the realities of World War I had become evident, Jews became the scapegoats for all the ills afflicting German society. In this environment of Judeophobia the philosopher Max Hildebert Boehm drafted a bill of indictment in the *Jahrbücher* protesting against Jewish assimilation. In a subsequent article, "Emancipation as Will to Power in Modern Jewry", he declared: "Nowadays, they, the cosmopolitan Jews, hold the universe in the palm of their hands, and they have no intention of letting go." Dostoevski's visionary eye had already seen that their power would grow during a great European catastrophe: "Like a vast, tightening net, the power of assimilated Jewry stretches over the whole world, and no matter where we set foot, we are caught in it... We must struggle to our last drop of blood against the insidious Judaization of Europe, and especially of Germanism."

Other writers echoed similar fears. In *The Decline of the West*, Oswald Spengler contrasted "Faustian nations" (pre-eminently Germany) and "Magian nations" which included the Jews. According to Spengler, there can be little comprehension between these two peoples:

Even when the Jews consider themselves members of the host country and share in its destiny, as was the case in most countries in 1914, in reality they do not live this event as their own destiny, but they side with it, judge it as interested bystanders, and the ultimate meaning of the struggle must for this very reason remain incomprehensible to them . . . The belief in the inevitability of this mutual misunderstanding leads finally to a frightening hatred, deeply concentrated in the blood, attaching itself to symbolic signs such as race, lifestyle, profession, language, which leads both sides to bloody explosions.

During the last days of World War I, the assembly at Weimar drafted a new constitution which transformed Germany into a federal republic. Immediately this new regime faced opposition from the extreme right and left. During 1922–23 there was massive inflation, but for the next five years there was greater stability as well as important intellectual and cultural developments. This period of prosperity was followed by the Great Depression – over six million were unemployed between 1930 and 1933. As a consequence the communists and the Nazis gained considerable support. To cope with this crisis, the government began to rule by presidential decree. After several ineffective conservative coalitions, Field-Marshall Paul von Hindenburg appointed Adolf Hitler as Chancellor of Germany on 30 January 1933.

According to Hitler, the Jews are parasites and degenerates. Germany, he believed, had lost the war because of treachery by Jewish socialists, liberals and pacifists. Further, he argued that the Bolshevik revolution was part of a world-wide Jewish plot. Such a fusion of anti-Jewish sentiment and anti-communism provided a justification for the belief that the Germans were entitled to greater living space in eastern Europe: the Jews had taken control over the Slavs and therefore the struggle against communism (defined as Jewish Bolshevism) was synonymous with the attack on Jewry itself. Hitler saw himself as the leader of an heroic battle against a malignant part of Europe – an Aryan victory would provide Germany with control of an empire which it rightly deserved. During the 1920s Hitler's party was a minor force in Germany. In November 1923 the Nazis attempted a coup in Munich, which failed. But the Depression gained Hitler the support of several sectors of society: German industrialists who feared communism; those who were insecure about their social positions; and boisterous youth. In 1928 the Nazis achieved 810,000 votes; in 1930 they had 6,380,000; and 14,000,000 in 1932. On 5 March 1933 the Nazis won

44 per cent of the vote. These events were the prelude to catastrophe for European Jewry.

Russian Hostility

At the beginning of World War I, many Russian Jews proclaimed their allegiance to the Fatherland. Hence in 1914 the Jewish deputy Friedmann declared to the Duma: "In spite of the discriminatory legislation that governs us, we have always felt like citizens of Russia, and we are faithful sons of the fatherland. No force on earth can separate the Jews from the fatherland, from this land to which they are bound by ancient links. The Jews are going to defend it, not only out of a sense of duty, but also because of deep affection."

Despite such protestations of loyalty, Christian anti-Semites accused Jews of espionage and collaboration with the enemy. Frequently traditional Jewish customs were misinterpreted to support allegations of treason. As one report of the period stated:

> It is an old Jewish practice to keep in the synagogue of small communities a piece of wire or a rope long enough to surround the whole village on Saturday. When an area is thus roped off, everyone is allowed to carry his usual possessions on Saturday, that is to say, the day of rest. According to a convention of Jewish law, a city surrounded by a rope is considered a courtyard. The soldiers, not understanding the function of that rope, believe that its function was to telephone the enemy.

In this atmosphere of suspicion it was not uncommon for Russian officers to foster hatred of Jews. Such attitudes are reflected in the instructions given in July 1915 by Lieutenant-General Zhdanovitch, commander of the First Infantry Brigade. "During the present patriotic war," he wrote, "all the numerous nationalities that settled in Russia, with the exception of the Yids, have united so thoroughly that national differences have been completely forgotten. The Yids could have taken advantage of this exceptional, historical moment to restore the reputation of their people, to give proof of their human dignity, and to obtain equal rights, since they claim to be the object of unfair treatment." Yet such aspirations were not Jewish aims. Instead, he asserted, "Russian Yids exhausted every trick to keep from participating in the defence of the homeland. Anger and hatred will then find an outlet infinitely more dangerous for them than the risks that they run by fulfilling their military obligation, and popular resentment will turn not only against those who through their criminal behaviour helped the enemy but also against their relatives and innocent children."

In their antipathy to the Jewish people, the Russian authorities invoked the spectre of an international Jewish conspiracy. With the onslaught of the Revolution of 1917, pogroms broke out in provincial cities and excesses took place elsewhere. In Ekaterinodar a "Slavic Group" was formed to carry out an anti-Semitic campaign in the countryside, and the Ukraine witnessed widespread anti-Jewish activity. So extensive were these hostilities that in June the regional prosecutor of Petrograd emphasized the need for an anti-pogrom law. "According to my information," he wrote, "there is a growing incitement to riots in the markets and other gathering places of the public. It is in Vitebsk and Petrograd that the calls for pogroms are the loudest. The pogromists insist that the Jews control the militia, the Soviets, and the District Dumas, and threaten to assassinate certain political figures." The Soviets themselves accused the counter-revolutionaries of blind prejudice: "This anti-Jewish militancy, often marked by radical rallying cries, constitutes an enormous danger, not only for the Jewish people, but also for the whole revolutionary movement, for it threatens to drown in blood the whole cause of the liberation of the people, and cover the revolutionary movement with an indelible shame."

For many Russians the Jews were viewed as responsible for the revolutionary struggle. Added to this charge was the allegation that influential Jewish capitalists played a central role in these events. In a series of forgeries sold in Petrograd by the journalist Eugen Semyonov to the American diplomat Edgar Sisson, it was claimed that the Bolsheviks were controlled by a "Rhenish-Westphalian syndicate" through the agency of the Jewish banker Max Warburg and the Bolshevik Jew Fürstenberg. Convinced of their authenticity, the American Government published these documents under the title *The German-Bolshevik Conspiracy* in 1918. It was also asserted that the Tsar and his family had been murdered on the order of the Jew Jacob Sverdlov and under the direction of the Jews Yurovsk and

Goloshtshekin. According to the British military attaché, General Alfred Knox: "There were two camps in the local soviet. One wanted to save the royal family. The other was directed by five Jews, two of whom were adamantly in favour of the murder." In response to such claims, an anti-Jewish crusade was initiated by the White armies. The total number of Jews killed in the Ukraine from 1918 to 1920 numbered more than sixty thousand.

In the years following World War I, various forgeries were produced to implicate the Jews with the Revolutionary movement and demonstrate the existence of a world-wide Jewish conspiracy. Thus in an alleged secret report of the French government (which was in fact fabricated in New York by a Russian emigré) a list of Communist leaders (all of whom except Lenin were Jews) described their plans for universal Zionist domination: "The Jews have already secured the formal recognition of a Jewish state in Palestine. They have also succeeded in organizing a Jewish republic in Germany and in Austro-Hungary. These are the first steps toward the future domination of the world by the Jews, but it is not their last attempt." Another forgery, *The Report of Comrade Rappoport* published in May 1920, focused on the Zionist manipulation of the Russian masses:

> After the fiasco of national co-operation, Ukrainian nationalism lost its economic base. The discount banks runs by our comrades Nazert, Gloss, Fischer, Krauss, and Spindler play the major role in this case. The Russian landowning class, frivolous and stupid, will follow us like sheep going to the slaughter. As representative of the Poale Zion, I must acknowledge to my great satisfaction that our party and the Bund have become centres of activity manipulating the immense flock of Russian sheep.

The most important forgery of this period was *The Protocols of the Elders of Zion*: this text was circulated by propagandists who sought to incite the general population against the "Jewish Revolution". After the defeat of the White armies, Russian emigrés publicized this document in the West. Thus within and without Russia, Jewry was viewed as a demonic force, fermenting revolution and chaos.

British Anti-Semitism

At the time of the Dreyfus Affair, the British public was outraged by French Judeophobia. Yet with the coronation of Edward VII in 1901, the climate of opinion in the country began to change. Although the king's banker was a German Jew, Ernest Cassel, British officials attempted to undermine Cassel's projects, particularly when he went to Constantinople to reorganize the finances of the Ottoman Empire. Eventually a journalistic campaign took place in 1911–12 which alleged that the Turkish Revolution was due to a Zionist conspiracy. Additional unrest was caused by a financial scandal (the Marconi Affair) concerning two leading Jewish politicians: Rufus Issacs who was appointed Attorney General in 1909 and Herbert Samuels, the first non-Christian member of a British Cabinet. In 1912 Lloyd George and other liberals were accused of mishandling funds, as the magazine *Eyewitness* reported: "Issac's brother is the president of the Marconi Company. Issacs and Samuels have privately arranged to have the British people pay the Marconi Company a considerable sum of money through the intermediary of Samuels, and for Issacs' benefit."

Although the Jews involved were cleared by a parliamentary commission of inquiry, the scandal had a profound impact on British thought. In the wake of these events the writer Rudyard Kipling dedicated a hymn of hate ("Gehazi") to the affair. Based on the biblical story about Naaman's servant Gehazi, who is portrayed in 2 Kings 5 as a greedy and crafty character who was punished with leprosy for his deceit, the poem was intended to illustrate the cunningness of these Jewish politicians:

> Whence comes thou, Gehazi,
> So reverend to behold,
> In scarlet and in ermines
> And chain of England's gold?
> From following after Naaman
> To tell him all is well,
> Whereby my zeal hath made me
> A Judge in Israel . . .
> Thou mirror of uprightness
> What ails thee at thy vows?
> What means the risen whiteness
> Of the skin between thy brows?

The boils that shine and burrow,
The sores that slough and bleed
The leprosy of Naaman
On thee and all thy seed?
Stand up, stand up, Gehazi,
Draw close thy robe and go,
Gehazi, Judge in Israel,
A leper white as snow!

Such hostility was aggravated by an influx of Jews from eastern Europe into London. In 1902 the Bishop of Stepney compared this mass of Jewry to a conquering army that "eat the Christians out of house and home". With the coming War, suspicions were raised about these immigrant foreigners. In 1915 the sinking of the *Lusitania* led to further anti-Jewish hostility. The *Times* attributed this war crime to the Jew Albert Ballin, Wilhelm II's courtier, and a campaign was launched to strip Sir Ernest Cassel of both his citizenship and his titles. In response the London Jewish newspapers protested against describing all Jews as Germans. Despite such Jewish outrage, the dailies and the weeklies sought to incite racial hatred. In the *New Witness* for example, C. G. Chesterton invoked the ancient Christian image of ritual murder. Mr Thompson in *The Clarion* claimed that "the Prussians like the Jews, came from a tiny, rocky and arid land, and they, too, conquered the place in the sun through robbery. The Prussians, like the Jews, have a tribal God, whose principles are based on the fear he inspires." Again, in the *National Review*, Leo Maxse argued that the international Jew, having learned of the departure of Lord Kitchener for Russia, informed the German High Command. This Jew, he stated, was a "miserable, calculating creature, without king or homeland."

Similar antipathy was echoed by leading figures of the day. Despite his support for a Jewish homeland, Lord Balfour complained to his mistress, Lady Elcho:

In Brighton, at the Sassoons, I met Rosebery, Devonshire, and H. Farquhar. We found out, to our profound indignation, that we had been invited under false pretences. The Prince of Wales had dedicated a hospital in the morning, and he stayed at Reuben Sassoon's until Monday. The two evenings, we were forced to attend a long, hot and pompous dinner, crowded with innumerable Sassoon young ladies.

Although I have no prejudices against the race (far from it) I began to understand the point of view of those who are opposed to foreign immigration!

Lord Robert Cecil remarked that the enthusiasm of Chaim Weizmann "overshadowed his rather repulsive, even sordid, physique". Joseph Chamberlain commented to the Italian minister of foreign affairs, Sonnino, that he despised the Jews. "They are all physical cowards," he declared. Reporting on the events taking place in Russia, the British press accused the Jews of playing a major role in the Revolution. Thus the *Times* of 11 September 1917 reported that the Soviet leadership was composed of Jewish partisans: "The Petrograd soviet is an organism accredited only by itself, composed of idealists, theoreticians, and anarchists . . . most of the time typical international Jews, and including no soldiers or workers. A few of them are known to be in the pay of the Germans." The *Morning Post* similarly interpreted these events:

From the very beginning, German influence in the soviet was barely disguised. Some time ago, we published a list of the members of this remarkable council who thought it useful to change names, and the number was considerable. These conspirators were obviously Russian Jews of German extraction, and we fear that it will be said that Russian Jews betrayed Russia. It used to be said that the Spanish Jews had been expelled from Spain because they opened the gates to the Moors. Indeed, it would be unfortunate for the Jews of the entire world if it could be said that Russian Jews have opened the gates of Russia to the Germans.

Such allegations led to widespread animosity, and in 1918 the *Herald* recorded various outbreaks of anti-Semitism:

Our attention has been called to the terrorism practised against the Jews and foreigners in some parts of East London. We are informed that all kinds of mean persecutions prevail, that men with long beards are insulted in the streets by having their beards pulled, that shopkeepers are obliged to submit to what is nothing more nor less than organized blackmail . . . This kind of thing is directly traceable to the free distribution of incitements, which the police allow to be circulated, and to the venomous attacks on foreigners appearing in the yellow press.

After the war the publication of *The Protocols of the Elders of Zion* provoked a storm of controversy. On 8 May 1920 the *Times* questioned its authenticity, but in terms that suggested that a secret international organization might exist: "What is this *Protocols*?" it asked. "Is it authentic? Did a gang of criminals really prepare such a project and gloat over their exposition? Is it a forgery? If so, whence comes the uncanny note of prophecy, prophecy in part fulfilled, in part far gone in the way of fulfilment? Have we been struggling these tragic years to blow up and exterminate the secret German organization of world domination only to find beneath it another more dangerous because more secret? Have we, by straining every fibre of our national body escaped a *Pax Germanica* to fall into a *Pax Judaica*?" The *Morning Post* subsequently printed a series of articles which explored the thesis of a Judeo-Germano-Bolshevik conspiracy. In defence of Jewry the *Jewish Chronicle* attempted to refute such allegations, yet the myth of a world Jewish conspiracy continued to haunt British life.

Anti-Semitism in the United States

Despite the general acceptance of the Jewish community in the United States, the European stereotype of the Jews was not unknown in the New World. As waves of immigrants penetrated into North America, discrimination against Jewry became increasingly widespread. Thus in 1876 a New Jersey hotel announced in New York newspapers that it would not admit Jews. In the following year the hotelier John Hilton refused to allow the millionaire Joseph Seligman to stay in his Saratoga resort. At the end of the century such discrimination spread to country clubs, Masonic lodges and colleges. In response, prominent Jews publicly protested against acts of intolerance. When, for example, the librarian Melvil Dewey founded a club in New York which excluded Jews, a number of Jewish notables addressed a letter of complaint to the State:

> More than 750,000 Jews reside in this state. The majority are taxpayers who fulfil their obligations for the maintenance of state institutions and the payment of salaries of state employees, including Mr Melvil Dewey as head librarian. They are proud of this state and its administration. They strive to raise its cultural level, to facilitate education, and to

promote the arts, science, and literature. They have worked for the cause of education as much as any other group of citizens in this community. They, therefore, feel they have the right to demand that a man, as a public official representing the whole population of the state, be prohibited as a state employee from showing the vile prejudice to which a man can stoop.

The Jewish community also established organizations to protect their interests, such as the American Jewish Committee and the Anti-Defamation League.

In their efforts to defend the rights of American Jews, the American Jewish Committee fought successfully against attempts to limit Jewish immigration, and on the international scene pressurized the Russian government to issue entry visas to Americans of Jewish origin. In addition, the American Jewish Committee sought to ensure that Jews were fully accepted as Americans. Such an undertaking was needed to counter the views of writers such as Madison Grant who argued in *The Passing of the Great Race* that the Jews posed a serious threat to the American populace:

> The old-time American is being replaced in many rural regions by foreigners, just as he is being literally chased from the streets of New York by swarms of Polish Jews. These immigrants borrow the language of the original Americans, adopt their dress, steal their names, and begin to take their women . . . New York is in the process of becoming a *cloaca gentium*, which will produce numerous and strange hybrids and ethnic horrors that future anthropologists will not be able to sort out.

With the American entry into World War I, Jews were viewed as participants in international conspiracy. In a report, *Bolshevism and Judaism*, which appeared in November 1918, it was alleged that the decision to overthrow the Tsar was made on 14 February 1916 in the Jewish section of New York by a revolutionary group headed by Jacob Schiff. Quoting a section of *The Protocols of the Elders of Zion*, the report stated that the Elders were convinced that they could stop any rebellion of the "*goyim*". Finally the report listed thirty-one leaders – all of whom were Jews except for Lenin – who ruled Russia. The fears evoked by these revelations were compounded by a succession of strikes in the United States in 1919, including that of the garment workers, most of whom were Jewish. In response, Citizens' Committees and Patriotic Organizations flourished.

Although the Russian revolution was heralded by a number of Americans, many others abhorred the new system in Russia. In their condemnation, they spoke bitterly of the Jewish influence on the course of events. Some witnesses even maintained that the ringleaders of the revolution were Jews from New York. Thus in a conversation with American senators, the Rev. George A. Simons of the English Methodist Church in Russia gave evidence that the Bolshevik movement was aided by American Jews:

Mr Simons:	We were told that hundreds of agitators who had followed Trotsky-Bronstein came from the East Side of New York. I was surprised to find a great number of these men going up and down the Nevski. Some of them, when they learned that I was the American minister in Petrograd, stopped me and seemed happy to find someone who spoke English. But their bad English showed that they were not real Americans. Some came to visit me. We were struck by the predominance, from the beginning, of the Yiddish element in this affair, and it soon became evident that half the agitators were Yiddish.
Senator Nelson:	Hebrews?
Mr Simons:	Hebrews. Jewish apostates. I don't want to speak of Jews as such. I am not in sympathy with anti-Semitism. I never was and never will be. I hate pogroms of any type. But I am firmly convinced that this business is Jewish.
Senator Overman:	Wouldn't it be remarkable if it turned out that the Bolshevik movement was born in our country, financed by Germans?
Mr Simons:	I don't think that the Bolshevik movement would have been successful in Russia without the help of certain New York elements, what is known as the East Side.

Such charges encouraged American patriots to defend their country from the pernicious influence of Jewry. In 1922, after a trip to the United States, Hilaire Belloc reported on these activities:

Even in New York, defence organizations are just beginning. (In Great Britain) a certain proportion of Jews has become generally necessary to the ruling circles . . . Nothing of the sort in the United States. The Jews are barely admitted in major country clubs, and most of the time they are barred. Their talents are rarely used on the General Staff of the army. They have no real civic standing. They are excluded from I don't know how many hotels. As I have just stated, the major country clubs refuse to admit them. The universities, particularly Harvard, have openly organized their defences against the invasion of new Jewish students.

In literary circles writers commented on the evils of Jewish influence. Thus in F. Scott Fitzgerald's *The Beautiful and the Damned*, the character Anthony Patch described the Jewish impact on life in New York:

Down in a tall, busy street he read a dozen Jewish names on a line of stores. In the door of each stood a dark, little man watching the passers by with intent eyes, eyes gleaming with suspicion, with pride, with clarity, with cupidity, with comprehension. New York – he could not dissociate it now from the slow upward creep of this people. The little stores, growing, expanding, consolidating, moving, watched over with hawks' eyes and a bee's attention to detail. They slathered out on all sides.

The most vociferous critic of Jews during this period was the industrialist Henry Ford. In an interview Ford explained the origins of his views:

On the ship there were two very prominent Jews. We hadn't travelled two hundred miles (when) these Jews started telling me about the power of the Jewish race and the way they manipulated the world through their control of the gold supply. The Jews, and only the Jews, could stop the war. I refused to believe this, and I told them so. They went into details to describe how the Jews controlled, and how they owned the money.

Having uncovered this Jewish plot, he felt compelled to share such revelations with others. On 22 May 1920 the *Dearborn Independent*, which Ford had purchased two years earlier, denounced the economic power of the Jewish community. Subsequently, Ford's newspaper began to quote passages of *The Protocols of the Elders of Zion*, and an American version of the text was published in 1921. In the same year a protest against such slurs about the Jewish population was issued by leading American figures including Presidents Taft, Wilson, and Harding. Yet despite such objections, anti-Jewish sentiment, drawing on previous Christian stereotypes, continued to fester beneath the surface of everyday life, poisoning the body politic of the American people.

French Judeophobia

Despite the patriotism of French Jewry during World War I, anti-Semitism persisted during the war years; as in other countries, the Russian revolution was viewed as inspired by Jewish activists. Thus in July 1917, when the Bolsheviks attempted to gain power, the Jews were accused by *La Libre Parole* for their role in these tumultous events: "It is impossible to understand anything about the great tremors that are tearing society apart if we neglect the Jewish factor . . . Austro-Boche or Franco-German Jews will raise the flag of Israel over the ruins of the vanquished." A month before the revolution became successful, *L'Heure* (basing its information on the *Morning Post*) incriminated the Jews in the plot against the Tsar:

> Even those who are not anti-Semitic cannot help making a small observation on the composition of the Petrograd soviet and the background of its members. The real name of Chernov, the former minister of agriculture, who is now Kerensky's bitterest opponent, is Feldman. The real name of Steklov, the well-known author of Order Number One to the Russian army, the one that abolished discipline, is Nahinkes, German Jew . . . As for Lenin, everybody knows that his name is Zederblum.

Once the Bolsheviks were successful, the French press blamed the Jews. As Maurice Barrès noted: "Russia is disappearing because it is infested with Jews." Added to such allegations were the claims of the politician Georges Clemenceau who attacked the Jewish population for their involvement:

> Without patriotism, how can there be a homeland? What is a people that no longer has a homeland? Alas, we can see it in this mob of German Jews who, unable to keep the land of their ancestors, appeared at the

instigation of their brothers in Germany to derussify Russia, whose first reaction was savage pogroms, the supreme aggravation of all barbarisms. One must not kill, for killing is not an answer. Among others, before and after him, the Nazarene proved it. It is sufficient not to be led, that is, misled, by the suggestions of a people that once was great, but now shows itself incapable of creating this homeland that its atavistic concepts considered secondary, the way the fox of the fable convinced others to disdain an appendage of which it had been deprived.

In December 1918, the vilification of the Jews intensified: Jewish Bolshevism was perceived as a major threat to national stability. In addition, Zionism was seen as posing a serious danger to the Christian world. Thus in March 1919 *La Documentation catholique* stated that the Jewish "claim to universal domination does not prevent the Jews from pursuing the reconstruction of their own special kingdom." Several months later this publication listed a series of remedies for the Jewish peril:

> We must create a public opinion in Christian countries . . . We must echo the moving complaint of the Holy Father: we must speak to these Christian nations of the Christian ideal, of the disgrace of allowing the cradle of their religion to fall under the domination of the Jews, whether disguised or not. A second remedy . . . persuade the peasants not to sell their land to the Jews by pointing out that this land will increase in value. A bank that would give mortgages . . . would be extremely helpful. Finally (I ought to say, above all), union between Christians and Muslims is required as an essential for salvation.

In May 1920 *Le Petit Parisien* reported on events taking place in Russia: "It would be easy to see the organization of the great Asiatic crusade against the British. The Jew Braunstein (sic), known as Trotsky, surrounded by his Semitic or Oriental cabal, dreams of becoming the Napoleon of the East. He is the undisputed head of the immense international secret society that aspires to overthrow European civilization and expel the British from their possessions in Asia." Again, the reporter Albert Londres commented in *L'Excelsior*:

> The proletarians are led by the nose. Who rules, then? The activities of socialist conventions, the grimy exiles, the moles of the world's libraries,

wasting their youth on books dealing with pauperism to find ways to cope with their material needs, the Siberians, the Mongolians, the Armenians, the Asiatics, and in the labyrinths of hallways, in the police stations, under the wastepaper baskets, the king: the Jew. Ah! the charming little massacre that is brewing on the horizon.

The campaign against the Jews continued in the years that followed. Thus in 1921 Roger Lambelin proclaimed in *Le règne d'Israël chez les Anglo-Saxons* that Jewry was determined to prevail over those among whom they lived. "The documents I have consulted," he wrote, "the examination of English, American and Jewish newspapers and periodicals, testimonies gathered in Egypt and Palestine, and data furnished by reliably informed correspondents on certain Jewish manoeuvres have put me in a position to follow rather closely the steps toward the creation of Jewish rule over the Anglo-Saxons." Some observers concluded that the Judeo-German conspiracy had increased its grip on power. According to André Chéradame:

> The people of the Entente are caught in the formidable pincers held by pro-German leaders. The first branch of this pincer is represented by the international financial activities of the Judeo-German syndicate operating on the upper strata of the countries of the Entente to recruit accomplices through corruption. The second branch is represented by the activities of the Bolsheviks or Socialists of Bolshevik leanings acting on the labouring classes of the Allied countries.

Such attitudes paved the way for the horrors that were to follow in the years of Nazi rule.

CHAPTER SIXTEEN

The Death Camps

Christian anti-Semitic attitudes of the war years crystallized in Adolf
Hitler's conception of the Jewish people as an evil race seeking world
domination. Once the Nazis gained power, they instituted a series of
anti-Jewish policies culminating in *Kristallnacht* (the Night of Broken
Glass) during which Jewish property and buildings were destroyed.
This event was followed by the invasion of Poland in September 1939,
where Jews were massacred. The next stage of Hitler's plan of
extermination took place with the invasion of Russia in 1941. Initially,
mobile killing battalions began the devastation of Russian Jewry; this
method of killing was supplemented by the death camps where Jews
were gassed. The first gassing took place in Auschwitz Block II, then at
Birkenau, followed by Chelmno, Belzec, Sobibor, Majdanek, and
Treblinka. As the destruction of European Jewry progressed, resistance spread. In the Warsaw ghetto the Jewish Fighting Organization
engaged in acts of sabotage; however in May 1942 this uprising was
suppressed. The final stage of Nazi terror proceeded without pause:
Jews continued to be transported to their deaths as World War II drew
to a close. During these years of horror many Church members, within
and without Germany, refused to help the Jews, including those in
positions of ecclesiastical influence. Once the war ended, the Vatican
and others close to it helped a number of war criminals to escape from
the Allies.

Hitler and the Jews

At the beginning of his activity in Munich in 1918, Hitler was allied
with the anti-Semitic publicist Dietrich Eckart. After his death an
incomplete book was produced under Eckart's name which contained
Hitler's views on the Jewish problem. These ideas were developed in

Hitler's *Mein Kampf* as well as in numerous speeches. The various elements of his myth of the Jew were previously used by German and Austrian Christian anti-Semites at the end of the nineteenth century and are also contained in *The Protocols of the Elders of Zion*.

According to Hitler, the Jews were a malevolent race whose aim was to gain world domination and destroy the Aryan race. To achieve this end Jews were intent on gaining political power and thereby exerting their economic influence. They also promoted wars and instigated revolutionary struggles. With contempt and disgust he described the nature of the Jewish people:

> With satanic joy in his face, the black-haired Jewish youth lurks in wait for the unsuspecting girl whom he defiles with his blood, thus stealing her from her people. With every means he tries to destroy the racial foundations of the people he has set out to subjugate. Just as he systematically ruins women and girls, he does not shrink back from pulling down the blood barriers of others, even on a large scale. It was and it is Jews who bring the Negroes into the Rhineland, always with the same secret and clear aim of ruining the hated white race by the necessarily resulting bastardization, throwing it down from its cultural and political height, and himself rising to be its master . . . In Russia he killed or starved about thirty million people with positively fanatical savagery, in part amid inhuman tortures, in order to give a gang of Jewish journalists and stock exchange bandits domination over a great people.

According to Hitler the Jews had subjugated Germany to achieve their own ends: "The leadership of our destinies has, since the end of the War, been quite openly furnished by Jews . . . Conscious purpose is destroying our nation. And once we examine the apparent madness of our nation's leadership in the field of foreign affairs from this standpoint, it is revealed as the subtlest, ice-cold logic, in the service of the Jewish idea and struggle for world conquest." During the 1920s the Nazi party was a minor force in Germany. However the Depression of the 1930s enabled Hitler to gain the support of various sectors of society. Eventually on 5 March 1933 the Nazis won 44 per cent of the vote. When the Nazis gained power, they dissolved a number of social institutions and absorbed others. In the spring and summer of 1933 all political parties were eliminated, strikes were outlawed, and trade unions were replaced by a government- and employer-controlled labour front. In May 1933 book burnings took place and scientists, scholars and artists were arrested. In June 1934 a purge of the SA eliminated the party's social radicals and made way for the expansion of the SS. Under Heinrich Himmler, the SS troops took over many of the functions of the police including the Gestapo as well as the running of the concentration camps.

After Hindenburg's death in August 1934, Hitler became the party chief and head of state. In September 1935 all sexual liaisons between Jews and non-Jews were described as crimes against the state. In 1938 Jewish communal bodies were put under the control of the Gestapo, and Jews were forced to register their property. Later in the year the Nazi party organized an onslaught against the Jewish population. This event, known as *Kristallnacht*, was a prelude to the terrors of the death camps. Jews throughout Germany were victims of this massacre. In Hoengen, a small village near Aachen, the synagogue was destroyed. According to a witness who observed these events:

> The stormtrooops were joined by people who were not in uniform; and suddenly with one loud cry of, "Down with the Jews", the gathering outside produced axes and heavy sledgehammers ... the little synagogue was but a heap of stone, broken glass and smashed up woodwork ... Where the two well-cared-for flowerbeds had flanked both sides of the gravel path leading to the door of the synagogue, the children had lit a bonfire, and the parchment of the Scrolls gave enough food for the flames to eat up the smashed-up benches and doors, and the wood, which only the day before had been the Holy Ark for the Scrolls of the Law of Moses.

The Destruction of Polish and Russian Jewry

The first stage of the Nazis' plan for European Jewry began with the invasion of Poland in September 1939. In every conquered town and village the Germans forced Jews to hand over jewellery, to clear rubble, carry heavy loads and scrub floors and lavatories with their prayer shawls. In addition the Germans cut off religious Jews' beards and sidelocks with scissors, or tore them from their faces. When the Jewish population was forced into what Hitler referred to as a huge Polish labour camp, a massive work programme was initiated. The nightmare of these camps was described by numerous eye-witnesses, such as this record of a mass slaughter of Jews at a camp in the village of Stutthof during the Passover of 1940:

> All the Jews were assembled in the courtyard; they were ordered to run, to drop down and to stand up again. Anybody who was slow in obeying the order was beaten to death by the overseer with the butt of his rifle. Afterwards Jews were ordered to jump right into the cesspit of the latrines, which were being built; this was full of urine. The taller Jews got out again since the level reached their chin, but the shorter ones went down. The young ones tried to help the old folk, and as a punishment the overseers ordered the latter to beat the young. When they refused to obey, they were cruelly beaten themselves.

The surviving Jews from this camp were subsequently sent to another smaller camp at Gransdorf; only one survivor, a sculptor, was left behind. In the words of a witness to these events:

> The SS men took all his works, put him to a carriage loaded with sand, and forced him to run while flogging him with a lash. When he fell down they turned the carriage over on him; and when he nevertheless succeeded in creeping out of the sand they poured water on him and hung him; but the rope was too thin and gave way. They then brought a young Jewess, the only one in the camp, and with scornful laughter they hanged both on the rope.

The next stage in the plan of extermination began with the invasion of Russia in 1941. This was designed to destroy what was described by the Nazis as the "Jewish-Bolshevik conspiracy". At first mobile killing battalions of 500 to 900 men (the *Einsatzgruppen*), under the supervision of Reinhard Heydrich, began the slaughter of Russian Jewry. Of the 4,500,000 Jews who resided in Soviet territory, more than half fled before the German invasion; those who remained were concentrated in large cities, making it easier for Heydrich's troops to carry out their task. Throughout the country the *Einsatzgruppen* moved into Russian towns, sought out the rabbi or Jewish council and obtained a list of all Jewish inhabitants. The Jews were then rounded up in market places, crowded into trains, buses and trucks and taken to woods where mass graves had been dug. They were then machine-gunned to death. A typical example of such killings was depicted by a civilian works engineer in the 1945 Nuremberg trials:

> People were closely wedged together, lying on top of each other so that only their heads were visible. Nearly all had blood running over their shoulders from their heads. Some of the people shot were still moving. Some lifted their arms and turned their heads to show that they were still alive. The pit was already two-thirds full. I estimated that it held a thousand people.

In this slaughter the Jews attempted to escape the onslaught by hiding under floorboards and cellars, but they were buried alive or blasted out with grenades. A few girls offered themselves to stay alive; they were used during the night but killed the next morning. In the initial sweep between October and December 1941, these troops killed over 300,000 Jews; in a second stage that lasted throughout 1942, over 900,000 were murdered.

The Death Camps

Other methods were also employed by the Nazis. Mobile gas vans were sent to each battalion of the *Einsatzgruppen*. Meanwhile the mobile killing operations were being supplemented by the use of fixed centres, the death camps. Six of these were at Chelmno and Auschwitz in the Polish territories, and at Treblinka, Sobibor, Majdanek and Belzec in the Polish "General Government". Construction of this mass murder industry began in 1941. Two civilians from Hamburg went to Auschwitz to teach the staff how to use Zyklon-B gas. In September 1941 the first gassing took place in Auschwitz Block II; then work began at Birkenau, the central killing centre in Auschwitz. The first death camp to be completed was Chelmno near Lodz, which started functioning in December 1941. Subsequently Belzec became operational and the building of Sobibor began in March 1942. At the same time Majdanek and Treblinka were transformed into death centres.

The horrors of the rounding up of Jews and the journey and arrival at the camps have been depicted in numerous accounts. According to a Polish pharmacist who witnessed the Jews of Cracow being gathered together in the Cracow ghetto:

Old people, women and children pass by the pharmacy window like ghosts. I see an old woman of around seventy years, her hair loose, walking alone, a few steps away from a larger group of deportees. Her eyes have a glazed look; immobile, wide-open, filled with horror, they stare straight ahead. She walks slowly, quietly, only in her dress and slippers, without even a bundle, or handbag. She holds in her hands something black, which she caresses fondly and keeps close to her old breast. It is a small puppy – her most precious possession, all that she saved and would not leave behind. Laughing, inarticulately gesturing with her hands, walks a young deranged girl of about fourteen, so familiar to all inhabitants of the ghetto. She walks barefoot, in a crumpled nightgown. One shuddered watching the girl laughing, having a good time. Old and young pass by, some dressed, some only in their underwear, hauled out of their beds and driven out.

Crowded together, Jews travelled to their deaths as the pace of murder accelerated. As a local Pole later recalled, the trains carrying these victims were horrifying:

The small windows were covered with planks or lots of barbed wire, and in some places planks were missing from the walls, which was proof of desperate struggles taking place inside. Through the cracks in the planks and through the wired-up windows peered scared human faces. Sometimes we could tell that a train was approaching, although it was still far off, because of the shooting by the guards; they were standing on the buffers of the wagons and shooting those who tried to escape. When such a train stopped at Zwierzyniec station in order to allow another train to pass through, screams, laments and cries could be heard from all the wagons, "Water, water!" The Jews were holding out bottles and money fastened to sticks or broken parts of planks – but no one was allowed to approach the wagons. The Germans were shooting without warning all those who begged for water, as well as those who tried to give it to them. Soldiers were marching along the train breaking the bottles with sticks and pocketing the money. Women were throwing rings, earrings and jewellery through the windows and cracks, begging for a glass of water for their children who were dying of thirst.

One of the survivors of a convoy of Jews who travelled from Paris to Auschwitz later recounted the terrors of this journey:

Piled up in freight cars, unable to bend or to budge, sticking one to another, breathless, crushed by one's neighbour's every move, this was already hell. During the day, a torrid heat, with a pestilential smell. After several days and several nights, the doors were opened. We arrived worn out, dehydrated, with many ills. A newborn baby, snatched from its mother's arms, was thrown against a column. The mother, crazed from pain, began to scream. The SS man struck her violently with the butt end of his weapon over the head. Her eyes haggard, with fearful screams, her beautiful hair became tinted with her own blood. She was struck down by a bullet in her head.

On arrival at the camps, Jews were ordered out of the train and separated into groups. According to a survivor of Treblinka, women and children were sent to the left, men to the right:

The women all went into the barracks on the left, and as we later learned, they were told at once to strip naked and were driven out of the barracks through another door. From there, they entered a narrow path lined on either side by barbed wire. This path led through a small grove to the building that housed the gas-chamber. Only a few minutes later we could hear their terrible screams, but we could not see anything, because the trees of the grove blocked our view.

At Treblinka the women on arrival were shaved to the skin; their hair was later packed up for despatch to Germany. At the Nuremberg Tribunal one of those who survived gave an account of this procedure:

Because little children at their mothers' breasts were a great nuisance during the shaving procedure, later the system was modified and babies were taken from their mothers as soon as they got off the train. The children were taken to an enormous ditch; when a large number of them were gathered together they were killed by firearms and thrown into the fire.

Here, too, no one bothered to see whether all the children were really dead. Sometimes one could hear infants wailing in the fire. When mothers succeeded in keeping their babies with them and this interfered with the shaving, a German guard took the baby by its legs and smashed it against the wall of the barracks until only a bloody mass remained in his hands. The unfortunate mother had to take this mass with her to the "bath".

The most horrible of all horrors were the gas chambers. An eyewitness to the killings at Belzec later recounted a typical occurrence:

A little before seven, there was an announcement: "The first train will arrive in ten minutes!" A few minutes later a train arrived from Lemberg: forty-five carriages with more than six thousand people; two hundred Ukrainians assigned to this work flung open the doors and drove the Jews out of the cars with leather whips. A loudspeaker gave instructions: "Strip, even artificial limbs and glasses. Hand all money and valuables in at the 'valuables' window. Women and girls are to have their hair cut in the 'barber's' hut." Then the march began. Barbed wire on both sides, in the rear two dozen Ukrainians with rifles.

Stark naked men, women, children and cripples passed by . . . SS men pushed the men into the chambers . . . Seven to eight hundred people in ninety-three square metres. The doors closed . . . Twenty-five minutes passed. You could see through the window that many were already dead, for an electric light illuminated the interior of the room.

All were dead after thirty-two minutes . . . Jewish workers on the other side opened the wooden doors. They had been promised their lives in return for doing this horrible work, plus a small percentage of the money and valuables collected.

The people were still standing like columns of stone, with no room to fall or lean. Even in death you could tell the families, all holding hands. It was difficult to separate them while emptying the room for the next batch. The bodies were tossed out, blue, wet with sweat and urine, the legs smeared with excrement and menstrual blood. Two dozen workers were busy checking mouths they opened with iron hooks . . . Dentists knocked out gold teeth, bridges and crowns with hammers.

Jewish Resistance

By September 1942 German troops had conquered most of Europe. Yet as the murder of Jews continued, resistance spread. On 24 September the Jews of the White Russian town of Korzec set the ghetto on fire and a number of Jews established a partisan band. On 25 September, in Kaluszyn near Warsaw, the chairman of the Jewish Council in Lukow near Lublin collected money from Jews assembled in the main square in the expectation that he could use the funds to ransom the Jewish community. When he discovered the deportation would take place, he shouted: "Here is your payment for our trip, you bloody tyrant." Tearing the money into shreds, he slapped the German supervisor in the face and was shot on the spot by the Ukrainian guards. In the same month a former Jewish soldier in the Polish army, who was being held with several hundred other prisoners in a prison camp in Lublin, escaped with seventeen Jews, forming a small partisan group.

In the Warsaw ghetto, the Jewish Fighting Organization prepared itself for action. On 29 October a member of the Organization killed the commander of the Jewish police in the ghetto. In the Bialystok ghetto resistance was also taking place with the assistance of German soldiers from whom they obtained weapons. Near Cracow six members of the Jewish Fighting Organization set off for the forests armed with pistols and a knife, but were betrayed by local peasants. The next month the Jewish Fighting Organization in Cracow sabotaged railway lines, raided a German clothing store, and killed several Germans. In Marcinkance the chairman of the Jewish Council called out to the Jews who had been brought to the railway station. "Fellow Jews, everybody run for his life. Everything is lost!" As the Jews ran towards the ghetto fence, attacking the guards with their fists, over a hundred were shot. Yet despite the insurmountable odds, some Jews in other situations did manage to escape from the Nazis. As one survivor recounted:

The moans of the elderly, the screams of the children . . . were being drowned by the clatter of the death train as it moved through the French countryside of contrasting bucolic beauty and serenity . . . We chose the moment of escape very carefully. It had to come at a time when the train would slow down for a curve. It also had to avoid the floodlights which the guards were aiming over the entire length of the concave curvature of the train during the period of reduced speed . . . At this split second, we had to take our chances and leap before the beams of the floodlights would fall on us. We jumped.

In November Polish Jews who had escaped the deportation to Treblinka organized a small group to protect those Jews who were in hiding. The news of executions in the labour camps in December stimulated plans for resistance in Warsaw. An eye-witness wrote: "The community wants the enemy to pay dearly. They will attack them with knives, sticks, carbolic acid; they will not allow themselves to be seized in the streets, because now they know that labour camps these days mean death."

In December, in the labour camp at Kruszyna near Radom, Jews decided to resist with knives and fists. When they were ordered to assemble, they attacked the guards. Three weeks later four hundred Jews imprisoned in the Kopernik camp in Minsk Mazowiecki barricaded themselves into the building and resisted with sticks, stones and bricks. On 22 December in Cracow the Jewish Fighting Organization attacked a café frequented by the SS and Gestapo. In Czestochowa, on 4 January, members of the Jewish Fighting Organization wounded the German commander.

On 18 January 1943 the Germans entered the Warsaw ghetto determined to deport Jews to Treblinka. They did not expect any resistance, but preparations had been made in the ghetto for months. Pistols and grenades were obtained; those who had no weapons armed themselves with sticks, bottles and lengths of pipe. As Jews were being deported along the street, a small group began to throw grenades at the Germans. In the words of one of those who observed these events:

> The fighters set up a barricade in a little house on Niska street and held it against the German reinforcements which soon arrived. The Germans found it impossible to enter the house, so they set it afire. The fighters inside continued firing until the last bullet . . . though the unit was destroyed the battle on Niska street encouraged us. For the first time since the occupation we saw Germans clinging to the walls, crawling on the ground, running for cover, hesitating before making a step in the fear of being hit by a Jewish bullet. The cries of the wounded caused us joy, and increased our thirst for battle.

Several months later the Jews in Warsaw learned that the ghetto was to be destroyed. In response the Jewish community was determined to fight for its survival. The commander of the Jewish resistance group, Mordecai Anielewicz, declared: "He who has arms will fight. He who has no arms – women and children – will go down into the bunkers." As the Germans entered the Warsaw ghetto on 19 April, the Jews attacked. As one of the resistance fighters recounted:

All of a sudden they started entering the ghetto, thousands armed . . . And we, some twenty men and women, young. And what were our arms? The arms we had – we had a revolver, a grenade and a whole group had two guns, and some bombs, home-made, prepared in a very primitive way . . . When the Germans came to our posts and marched by us we threw those hand grenades and bombs and saw blood pouring over the streets of Warsaw . . . There was rejoicing.

The next day German soldiers shelled buildings and burned apartment blocks. Yet the Jewish fighters continued their battle. By the end of the first week of May the last stage of Jewish resistance was a bunker in which 120 fighters were assembled. For two hours the entrance was bombarded and then the Germans used gas against the Jews. According to the observer: "Aryeh Wilner was the first to cry out: 'Come, let us destroy ourselves. Let's not fall into their hands alive.' The suicides began . . . Then someone discovered a hidden exit, but only a few succeeded in getting out this way. The others slowly suffocated in the gas." Street by street the ghetto had been eliminated. In the fighting 7,000 Jews lost their lives, and 30,000 were deported to Treblinka.

The Final Stage of Terror and Christian Responsibility

Reports of resistance in Warsaw spread throughout Europe, but pressure against the Jews continued. The advance of the Red Army on the eastern front since early 1943 led to the decision to dig up the corpses of Jews and burn them. On 15 June at the Janowska death pits in Lvov, hundreds of Jewish labourers were forced to dig up those who had been murdered and extract gold teeth and rings from the fingers of the dead. As a witness recounted:

The fire crackles and sizzles. Some of the bodies in the fire have hands extended. It looks as if they are pleading to be taken out. Many bodies are lying around with open mouths. Could they be trying to say: "We are your own mothers, fathers, who raised you and took care of you. Now you are burning us." If they could have spoken, maybe they would have said this, but they are forbidden to talk too – they are guarded. Maybe they would forgive us. They know that we are being forced to do this by the same murderers that killed them. We are under their whips and machine guns.

The pace of the killing was unchanging. On 4 October Himmler addressed his SS officers. The Jewish race was being eliminated, he explained:

> Most of you know what it means when one hundred corpses are lying side by side, or five hundred, or one thousand. To have stuck it out and at the same time – apart from exceptional cases of human weakness – to have remained decent fellows, that is what has made us hard. This is a page of glory in our history which has never to be written . . . we had the moral right, we had the duty to world peace, to destroy this people which wished to destroy us.

Several days later a number of Jews who were imprisoned in Warsaw in Pawiak prison attempted to celebrate the Day of Atonement. One of the inmates later stated:

> In a cell in the Pawiak prison, ruled by barbarians bent on exterminating world Jewry, stood a group of Jews deep in prayer. Atlasowicz was standing by a greenish-brown prison table which served as a makeshift lectern. His broad back swayed reverently in a constant motion as he recited the ancient prayer. Atlasowicz intoned the Psalm in a muffled voice, not quite his own.
> "Light will shine on the righteous."
> "And joy upon the upright of heart."
> For a moment he was silent. Then he turned to the others, and in a hushed voice, as though talking to himself, he continued: "Our *Kol Nidre* in this place is unique and symbolic. It is our continuation. Here we take up the golden tradition of sanctity handed down to us by generations of Jews before us. We are human beings and will not yield our souls to the barbarians; we defy our enemies by remaining true to our people and traditions."

During the winter of 1943 the murder of Jews continued without pause. At Birkenau on Christmas Day Jewish women who had been starved were brought from the barracks. Trucks drove up to the block where they were assembled, and women were piled into them. The victims knew they were going to the gas chamber and tried to escape and were massacred. According to an account of this incident, when the lorry motors started, a terrible noise arose – the death cry of thousands of young women. As they tried to break out, a rabbi's son cried out: "God, show then your power – this is against you." When nothing happened, the boy cried out: "There is no God."

As the months passed, Jews continued to be subjected to equally terrible events. In Kovno several thousand children were rounded up, driven off in trucks and murdered. As an observer of this action related:

> I saw shattered scenes. It was near the hospital. I saw automobiles which from time to time would approach mothers with children, or children who were on their own. In the back of them, two Germans with rifles would be going as if they were escorting criminals. They would toss the children in the automobile. I saw mothers screaming. A mother whose three children had been taken away – she went up to this automobile and shouted at the German, "Give me the children," and he said, "You may have one." And she went up into that automobile, and all three children looked at her and stretched out their hands. Of course, all of them wanted to go with their mother, and the mother didn't know which child to select and she went down alone, and she left the car.

By the summer of 1944 the last deportations took place. More than 67,000 were deported from the Lodz ghetto to Birkenau. Most were selected for the gas chamber, but some were chosen for medical experimentation. According to an account:

> When the convoys arrived, Dr Mengele espied, among those lined up for selection, a hunchbacked man about fifty years old. He was not alone; standing beside him was a tall handsome boy of fifteen or sixteen. The latter, however, had a deformed right foot . . . Father and son – their faces wan from their miserable years in the Lodz ghetto . . . I first examined the father in detail, omitting nothing . . . Before proceeding to the examination of the boy I conversed with him at some length. He had a pleasant face, an intelligent look, but his morale was badly shaken . . . Scarcely half an hour later SS Quartermaster Sergeant Mussfeld appeared with four *Sonderkommando* men. They took the two prisoners into the furnace room and had them undress. Then the Ober's revolver cracked twice.

At Birkenau the Day of Atonement was celebrated on 1 October with a note of religious exaltation despite the horror of the camp:

The moon shone through the window. Its light was dazzling that night and gave the pale wasted faces of the prisoners a ghostly appearance. It was as if all the life had ebbed out of them. I shuddered with dread, for it suddenly occurred to me that I was the only living man among corpses. All at once the oppressive silence was broken by a mournful tune. It was the plaintive tones of the ancient *"Kol Nidre"* prayer . . . When at last he was silent, there was exaltation among us, an exaltation which men can experience only when they have fallen as low as we had fallen and then, through the mystic power of a deathless prayer, have awakened once more to the world of the spirit.

Other Jews in Dachau on this Day of Atonement also prayed. But the experiences these faced had shaken their faith in God:

We gather closer to the cantor, a young Hungarian lad. Lips murmur after him – quiet muffled words hardly manage to pass, remain sticking in the throat. Here stands Warsaw's last rabbi, his face yellow, hairless, wrinkled, his aged body bent; his hands are rocking like reeds in the wind; only the eyes, sparkling stars, look out towards the cold sky above, and his lips, half open, murmur softly.

What does he say now, how does he pray, this last of the rabbis of Warsaw? Does he lovingly accept the pain and suffering, or does he, through the medium of his prayer, conduct a dispute with the Almighty, asking him the ancient question: "Is this the reward for faith?" Huddling to the cantor stands Alter der Klinger, the Kovno cab driver. His broad shoulders lean against a young tree and his mouth emits staccato sounds as if they were hummed out of his inside. No, he does not beg; he does not pray; he demands! He demands his rights, he calls for justice. Why were his children burnt by the Nazis? Why was his wife reduced to ashes?

What was the Christian reaction to such sufferings? During the war there were Christians who resisted this onslaught against the Jewish people. Prominent among the champions of Jewry were such figures as Patriarch Nikodemus, the head of the Orthodox Church in Rumania; the French Capuchin, Fr Marie-Benoit; Metropolitan Andreas Szeptycki, Archbishop of Lvov; Bishop H. Fuglsang Damgaard of Denmark. Yet many Christians simply refused to help Jews, including those in positions of ecclesiastical influence. For example when asked by the Vichy government in France about the anti-Semitic law promulgated in France on 2 June, 1941, the Vatican declared: "In principle, there is nothing in these measures which the Holy See would find to criticize." Again, when Dr Eduardo Senatro, the Berlin correspondent of *L'Osservatore Romano* asked Pope Pius XII whether he would protest against the extermination of Jews, the Pope is reported to have replied: "Dear friend, do not forget that millions of Catholics serve in the German armies. Shall I bring them into conflicts of conscience?" After the war the Vatican and others close to it helped thousands of war criminals to escape from Germany.

Within Germany itself the Nazis believed they were performing their Christian duty in advancing Hitler's anti-Jewish policies. Thus Heinrich Himmler declared that "by and large . . . we can say that we have performed this task in love of our people, and we have suffered no damage from it, in our inner self, in our soul, in our character." During the years of war the German Church did not issue a challenge to the activities of the Nazis, and only a few years after the war ended the German Evangelical Conference at Darmstadt proclaimed that the Jewish suffering which had occurred during the Holocaust was a divine visitation and a call to Jews to accept Christ as their Saviour. Such modern attitudes are not far removed from previous centuries of Christian contempt of Judaism and the Jewish people.

CHAPTER SEVENTEEN

Anti-Semitism in a Post-Holocaust World

After World War II Germany expressed little remorse or guilt for the destruction of six million Jews. Instead most Germans continued to harbour anti-Semitic sentiments. Although the radical left was critical of Fascism, it expressed little sympathy for the plight of the Jews. Such attitudes were also manifest in post-war Austria where a number of ex-Nazis were rehabilitated. More recently when Kurt Waldheim was criticized for his activities during the war years, many Austrians became contemptuous of the world Jewish community. Similar Judeophobia has been expressed in Britain where neo-Nazis and ultra-right groups advanced the theory of a world-wide Jewish conspiracy. In America as well, anti-Semitism has intensified, largely as a result of the conflict between the American Jewish population and the black community: such black activists as Louis Farrakhan have portrayed Jews and Judaism as an evil force in the modern world. French hostility toward the Jews after the war has also led to the condemnation of Zionism, the occurrence of a series of attacks on Jewish property, and the resurgence of a nationalist party under the leadership of Jean-Marie Le Pen. Poland too has witnessed the rise of anti-Semitism despite the absence of a sizeable Jewish community. Russian antipathy to the Jews has similarly resurfaced in the last few decades – today the policy of *glasnost* has unintentionally inflamed centuries-old Christian contempt for the Jewish faith.

The German and Austrian Reaction

As a result of the war, Ashkenazi Jewry largely disappeared from German soil – the crimes committed against Jews did not evoke remorse or guilt. Opinion polls undertaken in 1946–1947 revealed widespread indifference to the plight of the Jews. Thus in 1947 three-quarters of all Germans believed the Jews to belong to another race; in the following year 41 per cent of the population continued to approve of the Nazi seizure of power; in 1952, 88 per cent declared that they bore no responsibility for the mass exterminations.

From the late 1960s the German new left has reacted to what it regards as the philosemitism of the conservative establishment. Although anti-Facist and anti-capitalist in orientation, these reactionaries have castigated Israel for its policies regarding the Palestinians. Thus when the Green Party Euro MP Brigitte Heinrich was refused entry to Israel in 1984, she declared:

> The genocide of the Jews created the psychological pre-requisites for setting up Israel as an internationally recognized state. The expulsion of the Palestinians is therefore indirectly the result of the Nazi persecution of Jews . . . For the same reason that we – the generation which did not experience National Socialism – do not reject the moral guilt of our people for killing millions of Jews, we cannot keep silent about Israeli expansionist policy, occupation of foreign territories by Israeli troops, the repressive measures in the occupied territories.

In the view of the radical left, Israeli attitudes mirror those of the Third Reich. Recently the left has openly criticized Jews for their avarice. The play *Garbage, the City and Death* by Rainer Werner Fassbinder, for example, portrays a rich Jewish speculator who despoils Frankfurt, and various Christian anti-Semitic stereotypes are found throughout the script. More recently the controversy surrounding the Bitburg affair exemplified the lack of concern with Jewish sensitivities: in 1985, Chancellor Kohl requested that President Reagan pay homage to the German war dead at Bitburg cemetery where the Waffen SS were buried.

Open hostility to the Jews has also been expressed. Thus the Bavarian deputy Hermann Fellner from the Christian Social Union attacked Jewish survivors who were seeking compensation from the Flick concern. In North-Rhine Westphalia the mayor stated that the only way to solve his budget deficit would be to kill a few rich Jews. Again, the local chairman of the Christian Youth Union declared that Israel had made the democratic constitutional state responsible for the murder of Jews in the Third Reich. In the 1980s anti-Jewish sentiment was manifested even more widely. According to the researches of

Werner Bergman, six to seven million Germans could be classified as anti-Semitic; approximately two million of that number were characterized as hard-core anti-Semites. With the unification of Germany, the emphasis on the continuities of German history and national pride has led to the marginalization of the Jewish question: reminders of Jewish suffering at the hands of the Nazis tended to detract from the resurgence of patriotism and confidence in the future.

Post-war Austria has also witnessed the continuation of anti-Semitic attitudes. By 1949 many Austrian ex-Nazis had been re-enfranchised, and from 1955 prominent National Socialists had been fully integrated into political life. The two dominant political parties – the Socialists and the Catholic conservatives – competed for the former Nazi vote. In this context even the election of a Jewish-born socialist, Bruno Kreisky, as the Austrian Chancellor in 1970 did not undermine the traditions of Christian anti-Jewish hostility. Such attitudes surfaced when the former Secretary General of the United Nations, Kurt Waldheim, was attacked for his activities during the war. The campaign against Waldheim provoked a backlash of anti-Semitism, and after 1986 it was widely believed that international Jews based on the East Coast of the USA manipulated the media to defame Waldheim's character. Thus in 1987 the former vice-mayor of Linz wrote to the President of the World Jewish Congress, drawing an analogy between the persecution of Waldheim and Jews handing Jesus over to the Romans. This was Hitler's legacy to the land of his birth.

Judeophobia in Britain and America

After the war, Jewish antipathy was exacerbated by the Anglo-Zionist conflict over Palestine – pro-Arab attitudes in the Foreign and Colonial Offices tended to affect decision-making. None the less, in post-war Britain many Jews became affluent and took on prominent roles in the business world and the professions. In recent years Anglo-Jewry has drifted toward the policies of Thatcherite conservatism with such Jewish figures as Sir Keith Joseph, Sir Leon Brittan, and Nigel Lawson joining the Cabinet. Such attitudes have also been mirrored in the religious establishment, and the Chief Rabbi Lord Jakobovits repeatedly espoused views in harmony with the government's policies.

Yet despite the general prosperity of British Jewry, anti-Semitism has not disappeared from English life. From the 1970s, neo-Nazi and ultra-right groups promulgated Jewish conspiracy theories of the pre-war years. The National Front, for example, has promoted Fascism and racial bigotry. Its anti-Semitic publication, *Holocaust News*, attempts to demonstrate that the murder of European Jewry did not take place. These myth makers have recently been joined by the British historian David Irving, who contends that the gas chambers never existed. In the wake of such revisionist theories, there have been assaults on Jewish cemeteries, the proliferation of anti-Semitic graffiti, assaults on Orthodox Jews in north London, and verbal abuse directed at pupils of the Jewish Free School.

As in the United Kingdom, American Jews enjoyed considerable prosperity in the 1950s and 1960s. By the 1970s many reached the upper ranks of American society. Yet paradoxically, in the 1980s a considerable number of Jews believed that anti-Semitism was on the increase, due to resentment about Jewish political power and the growing hostility between blacks and the American Jewish population. In the 1960s tensions between the black and the Jewish communities led to the formation of a Third-World ideology among the black population, which linked the struggle at home with the exploitation of non-white peoples in other countries. In this context the black nationalist activist Malcolm X portrayed the Jews as expropriators: "Jews who with the help of Christians in America and Europe", he declared, "drove our Muslim brothers out of their homes where they had been settled for centuries, and took over the land for themselves." According to Malcolm X, American aid to Israel was taken from the pockets of black taxpayers to support aggression against the Third World. Further, Jewish businessmen in Harlem were regarded as colonialists who exploited the blacks, just as Western colonialists had previously violated the peoples of Africa and Asia. At the end of the decade the Black Panther Party equated racism with Israel.

Such a radical Third World policy became a dominant motif of the Presidential campaign of Reverend Jesse Jackson. Jackson's references to Jews as "Hymies" and his unwillingness to distance himself from the anti-Semitic black leader Louis Farrakhan intensified Jewish fears. Not surprisingly, pronouncements by Louis Farrakhan, who regarded Hitler as a great man and Judaism as a "gutter religion", had a profound impact on the Jewish community. Farrakhan's anti-Jewish attitudes (which were rooted in the Black Muslim faith of Elijah

Muhammad in the 1950s) have been overlaid by leftist national ideologies, Third Worldism, support for the PLO, and the acceptance of funds from Colonel Quaddafi of Libya. In 1984 a survey revealed that Jews in America believed that blacks were more anti-Semitic than any other group in the United States including Catholics, fundamentalist Protestants, big business, and the State Department.

According to recent research, 37 per cent of blacks as opposed to 20 per cent of whites are anti-Semitic. Although less than half of black anti-Semitics are more anti-Jewish than anti-white, anti-Semitism in the black community appears to increase with economic contact with Jews. Alleged exploitation by Jewish merchants, landlords and employers appears to be the cause of such hostility. In addition, resentment is expressed by blacks moving into positions below those of Jewish professionals. Tensions between the new black middle class and affluent Jews have also exacerbated community relations. Further, it appears that anti-Semitism rises with the educational level of blacks: among those who are college educated, ideological commitment has fuelled hatred of American Jewry.

Paradoxically, the anti-Jewish policies of Farrakhan have attracted the allegiance of hate groups and individuals, from the Californian racist Tom Metzger and the Liberty Lobby founder Willis Cato to neo-Nazis and Klansmen. Meetings between left-wing black nationalists and right-wing racists have occurred, condemning the Jews as a destructive force in modern life. Such attitudes are shared by a number of American Christian conservative fundamentalists who continue to hold Jews responsible for killing Christ. Thus it appears that America may prove to be less hospitable to the Jewish community than in the recent past.

French Hostility

After the war, French Jewry lost its confidence in the French state: under its auspices labour camps had been created in which thousands of Jews died; French gendarmes pursued Jews and crowded mothers and children as well as the sick and elderly into cattle trucks that transported them to the death camps; and identity cards were stamped with the word "*Juif*" while the press denounced the Jewish population.

In the decades following the war such activities were barely acknowledged in French textbooks, and it was commonly believed that Marshal Pétain sought to protect Jews despite the anti-Semitic legislation he introduced. In addition, the French government and judiciary attempted to obstruct the trials of important French officials such as Maurice Papon (the former Gaullist minister and Paris prefect of police) who helped deport Jews from Bordeaux during the war. Another figure who went unharmed was Réné Bousquet (a prominent French banker) who as secretary-general of the Vichy police co-ordinated the deportation of Jews from the Free Zone in collaboration with the Nazis.

An additional troubling legacy of the Vichy past has been the personality cult of Marshal Pétain among supporters of the National Front. Combined with the anti-Semitic literature sold in bookshops, the spread of revisionist history, and the fascination with the German SS, this resurgence of anti-Jewish sentiment inflamed public animosity and contempt for the Jewish nation. Such Judeophobia was the theme of Jean-Paul Sartre's analysis of Jew hatred in his *Réflexions sur la Question Juive*. Pondering the silence of his compatriots regarding Jews at the end of the war, he wrote:

> Today those Jews whom the Germans did not deport or murder are coming back to their homes. Many were among the first members of the Resistance; others had sons or cousins in Leclerc's army. Now all France rejoices in the streets . . . Do we say nothing about the Jews? Do we give a thought to those who died in the gas chambers at Lublin? Not a word. Not a line in the newspapers. That is because we must not irritate the anti-Semitics.

Such reluctance to discuss the plight of Jewry persisted for twenty years after the war. By the mid-1950s over half of those who identified with the Right denied that the Jews were authentically French. According to another poll in the mid-1960s, 20 per cent of the population was anti-Semitic in orientation. After the Six-Day War in 1967, the French President Charles de Gaulle referred to the Jewish people as an arrogant, élitist, and domineering group. Such views evoked the image of Jewish power and domination and fostered suspicion about Jewish loyalties. At the time the Jewish political commentator Raymond Aaron accused de Gaulle of making anti-Semitism respectable, yet the President was simply expressing a traditional prejudice deeply rooted in the French psyche.

During this period the Communist Party also expressed neo-Stalinist hostility to Zionism. In the 1970s left-wing media created new themes to manipulate public sentiment – Zionism was equated with racism and Nazism, and Israel was viewed as a terrorist state which sought the genocide of the Palestinian people. Leftist French Catholics amplified these views, expressing contempt for Jewish particularism. By the time of the 1982 Lebanon War, anti-Jewish discourse had become dominant, combining elements of Christianity, Marxism and Third Worldism. A further feature which inflamed public opinion was the emergence of Muslim fundamentalism among North African Arab immigrants.

In 1980 a bomb exploded outside a Paris synagogue on Rue Copernic, which was possibly the work of Palestinian terrorists or neo-Nazis. This was followed by attacks on synagogues, schools and other institutions. According to an opinion poll taken at the time, over half the respondents believed that anti-Semitism had become widespread. The 1982 terrorist assault on a Jewish delicatessen in the Rue des Rosiers resulted in six deaths and twenty-four injuries. During this period Jewish graves were desecrated throughout the country, resulting in the outrage which took place at Capentras on 9 May 1990: thirty-four graves were damaged or destroyed and a corpse was exhumed and impaled on an umbrella. This desecration was followed by a series of anti-Semitic incidents throughout the country, ending in a protest in Paris by prominent Jews as well as Christians and Muslims.

Despite such public outrage, a considerable number of French citizens have been drawn to the radical policies of Jean-Marie Le Pen, who has attacked *L'Internationale Juive* as well as Jewish control of the media. Publications of the National Front and the radical right support revisionist theories of the Holocaust, denigrate Jewish politicians and journalists, and accuse Jewry of dual loyalty. Such figures as Roman-Marie, a deputy of the European Parliament, have publicly endorsed the conspiratorial theories of *The Protocols of the Elders of Zion*. The rise of Le Pen and the success of neo-Fascism thus illustrate that the Christian myth of the demonic Jew continues to haunt contemporary French life.

Polish Anti-Semitism

Although a number of Poles attempted to save Jews during World War II, most remained passive in the face of the Nazi onslaught. In the years following the war thousands of Poles died in the Polish Civil War, including 1,500 Jews who were killed in anti-Semitic campaigns. Some of these assaults were carried out by the anti-Communist underground, who were persuaded that Jews were betraying the Poles to the Soviet occupying forces.

In 1946 a massive pogrom was carried out in Kielce, where forty Jews were killed and over seventy-five wounded. This pogrom, which was initiated by the ancient Christian blood libel charge, reflected the unstable atmosphere of the country. Right-wing activists as well as Catholic bishops viewed this massacre as the result of Jewish provocation; others maintained that the Communists were responsible for the attack so as to discredit their rivals and Fascist anti-Semites. The Communists, however, declared that the massacre was the work of ultra-nationalistic extremists. Yet whatever its cause, massive Jewish emigration ensued.

Those who remained in Poland were committed to the creation of a classless, Communist society. Within the party several Jews – such as Jakob Berman, Hilary Minc and Roman Zambrowski – became important officials in the party, the security services and economic planning. These individuals were detested by the populace both as Jews and as servants of an alien Communist regime. In the Polish October of 1956 these Jewish Stalinists became scapegoats: on a visit to Warsaw, Nikita Khruschev suggested they be purged from the party in order to restore its popularity.

After Gomulka rose to power in the late 1950s, Polish politics embraced a more nationalist ideology, and anti-Semitism which previously had been suppressed, was integrated into a neo-Stalinist version of Polish chauvinism. By the early 1960s, Jews were beginning to be removed from high positions in the party, state government, and the civilian and military security apparatus. Senior officers of Jewish origin came under surveillance, and a card index for Polish Jewry was compiled. By the Six-Day War of 1967, a purge of Jews from all positions of influence was being planned.

From 1966 to 1968 a campaign of anti-Zionism was initiated, and a witch-hunt of Jews in 1968 forced the majority of Jews to emigrate. In the political struggle between two Communist factions, those of Gomulka and General Moczar, the latter appealed to Polish nationalism, anti-Russian sentiment, and anti-Semitism that attracted young members of the party as well as those who belonged to the Veterans Association. In this campaign Gomulka's supporters proposed an even more nationalist Communism, devoid of Jewish cosmopolitanism and Marxist revisionism.

As party leader, Gomulka advocated a policy of anti-Semitism. On 19 June 1967 he accused Polish Jews of instigating an anti-Soviet campaign, working as agents of Western imperialism, and propagating Zionism. As a result, Jews were eliminated from the foreign ministry and other governmental departments, the universities, and the press and party schools. In addition, those individuals who had been lifelong Communists were regarded as cosmopolitans and aliens. Further, international Zionism was accused of inciting student youth during the anti-government protests of November 1968.

Jews were also accused of Trotskyism and Social-Democratic revisionism. Thus in an essay of 1968, the Polish Communist Party theorist Andrzej Werblan declared that it was necessary to correct the ethnic imbalance in governmental policy. This was vital because "no society can tolerate excessive participation of the national minority in the élite of power, particularly in the organs of national defence, security, propaganda and representation abroad, coming from an outside cosmopolitan background."

Such charges were followed by a campaign against Zionism and world Jewry. Initiated by Moczar and supported by the PAX organization of the pre-war Polish Catholic Fascist Buleslaw Piasecki, this onslaught led to a mass exodus of those Jews who had remained in Poland. Yet despite the disappearance of the Polish Jewish community, anti-Semitism continued to serve as a vital factor in Polish political life. In 1980–81 the Communists attempted to discredit Solidarity and the dissident organization KOR. In the Communist press Jews were accused of influencing Solidarity, and anti-Semitic pamphlets caricatured the Solidarity advisor Bronislaw Gieremek as a Hasidic Jew. A number of labour activists were also falsely accused of being Jewish. In the elections of 1990 the liberal Catholic prime minister, Tadeusz Mazowiecki, was smeared as a crypto-Jew and his government was depicted as being controlled by Jews rather than authentic Poles.

Such anti-Jewish sentiment was to a large degree based on previous Christian hostility towards the Jews. Many Polish peasants continued to believe in the medieval Christian blood libel; young Christians were still taught that all Jews killed Christ; and even university students tended to accept the validity of Jewish stereotypes. Such attitudes were reinforced by the pronouncements of the Primate of Poland, Cardinal Jozef Glemp, who criticized Jewish reservations about the existence of a Carmelite monastery at Auschwitz. Polish Christian anti-Semitism has thus persisted until the present, despite the absence of a Jewish population within the country.

Jewish Hatred in Russia

Between 1948 and 1953 there was renewed suspicion of the Jews in Russia, with the campaign against bourgeois Jewish nationalism and rootless cosmopolitanism. Nazi anti-Jewish propaganda influenced many sections of the Soviet population, particularly in the Ukraine, Belorussia, and the Baltic states. As the Cold War intensified, Stalin attempted to isolate the USSR from the West and promote a cult of Russian nationalism. In this atmosphere the Jews became a convenient scapegoat. Although Jewish Stalinists in eastern European countries expressed loyalty to Moscow, they were nevertheless sacrificed in show trials: Communists of Jewish origin were branded as crypto-Zionist traitors.

Within the USSR Jewish cultural organizations were liquidated in 1948. Yiddish writers and Jewish artists were arrested and sent to concentration camps in Siberia. In 1952 Soviet Yiddish intellectuals were executed or allowed to die in prison. In the following year nine physicians (including six Jews) were charged with attempting to poison the Soviet leadership under the direction of Western intelligence organizations and the American Joint Distribution Committee. As a result, Jews were dismissed from various institutions, and assaulted in the streets and schools.

Even though Stalin's successors dismissed these accusations against the doctors, they did not seek to curb Soviet anti-Semitism. In 1956 Khruschev denounced Stalin's policies in a report to the Twentieth Party Congress, but he did not condemn Stalin's policy toward the Jews. Rather, he denounced Yevgeny Yevtushenko for drawing attention to anti-Jewish attitudes in his poem "Babi Yar". Under Khruschev's regime atheistic campaigns were revived, and Judaism was portrayed in negative terms. During this period the Ukrainian writer Trofim Kychko published a tract, *Judaism without Embellishment*, which reflected the anti-Semitism of the time.

By the 1960s Jews had been removed from the Diplomatic and Foreign Service, leading positions in the army, and important Communist positions. In addition they were unrepresented in Soviet institutions as well as in universities. In 1967 the Six-Day War led to an official anti-Jewish policy which continued for two decades. Repeatedly Judaism was portrayed as a criminal religion which promulgated an ideology of racial superiority. Thus, during a debate on the Middle East in the United Nations Security Council in 1971, the Soviet ambassador stated that Zionism is Fascist and racist: "The chosen people: is that not racism? What is the difference between Zionism and Fascism, if the essence of the ideology is racism, hatred towards other peoples? The chosen people. The people elected by God. Where in the second half of the twentieth century does one hear of anyone advocating this criminally absurd theory of the superiority of one race and one people over others?"

During this period books by anti-Zionists appeared which criticized the Jewish concept of chosenness. Vladimir Begun, in *Creeping Counter-Revolution*, for instance, argued that Zionist aspirations are grounded in the Torah which he depicted as a "textbook of bloodthirstiness, hypocrisy, treason, and moral degeneracy". According to Begun and other critics, Zionism has become the central ideology of Jewish bankers in their quest for world domination – a view reminiscent of *The Protocols of the Elders of Zion*. More recently such anti-Zionists have become popular lecturers for the nationalist Pamyat organization, and the proliferation of their writings has revived latent anti-Semitic attitudes. In addition to such semi-official propaganda, there has been an outpouring of novels, essays and pamphlets which portray Jews as responsible for undermining Russian life.

During the Gorbachev years, chauvinist anti-Semitism has flourished, particularly within Pamyat, which spearheads the Movement for the Restoration of Monuments of Russian Culture, and the Russian Republic Culture Fund. Other organizations with similar views are the Patriot Society, Otchestvo in Novosibirsk, and Rossy in Leningrad. Publications which promote anti-Jewish hostility include *Nash*

Sovremenik (the journal of the Union of Writers of the Russian Republic), *Molodaya Gvardiya* (the Komsomol literary monthly), the weekly *Nedelya*, and the newspaper *Sovietskaya Rossiya*. Among the ranks of those who support Pamyat are intellectuals whose ideology is grounded in their disillusionment with Communism. Advocating patriotism and traditional values, they have attacked what they believe to be the destructive influences of Western cosmopolitanism. In *Russophobia*, for example, Igor Shafarevich contends that the Jews aim to destroy the Christian as well as natural foundations of Russian life. This new wave of national loyalty has reaffirmed the Stalinist myth of rootless cosmopolitanism. Symbolic of this new movement was an incident that occurred in January 1990 when members of Pamyat besieged the Moscow Writers Club, shouting: "You dirty Jewish mongrels, you're not writers! Get out to Israel! Now we are masters of the country and neither the Party, nor KGB, nor the militia are going to help you! Next time we'll come with machine guns!" Thus the paradox of *glasnost* is that it has unleashed fury against the Jewish population in the final decade of the twentieth century.

CHAPTER EIGHTEEN

Toward Reconciliation

Despite two millennia of Jewish persecution and suffering, in recent years there has been a major effort on the part of the Church to overcome Christian antipathy toward Judaism and the Jewish people. In the last few decades, for example, the Roman Catholic Church and the World Council of Churches have issued numerous decrees denouncing anti-Semitism and encouraging positive Jewish-Christian encounter. In addition, pioneering Christian scholars have attempted to understand the Jewishness of Jesus – modern Christology, they believe, must be purged of any anti-Jewish bias. God's enduring covenant with the Jewish nation has also repeatedly been emphasized, and various theories have been propounded to illustrate that Jesus' death and resurrection do not replace God's revelation on Mount Sinai. In this context the traditional idea of Christian mission has been replaced by the notion of Christian witness. No longer do most Christians feel compelled to convert the Jewish people to the one, true faith; rather Judaism is affirmed as a valid religious tradition with its own spiritual integrity. Christians have also been increasingly preoccupied with the religious implications of the Holocaust. Along with Jewish thinkers, Christian theologians have struggled to make sense of God's nature and activity in the light of the destruction of six million innocent victims. There are thus positive signs of hope as both Jews and Christians stand on the threshold of the twenty-first century.

Church Statements

Despite twenty centuries of Christian anti-Semitism, there has been a concerted effort in recent years to find common ground between Jews and Christians. In particular the Churches have been anxious to overcome centuries of hostility towards the Jewish people by issuing official pronouncements concerning Judaism. Thus in the Roman Catholic Church the decree *NostraAetate* was promulgated by the Second Vatican Council in October 1965. Its section on the Jewish religion begins by recognizing the spiritual bond that links the people of the new covenant to Abraham's descendants and affirms God's continuing covenant with the Jews: "God holds the Jews most dear for the sake of their Fathers; he does not repent of the gifts he makes or of the calls he issues." In the light of such an understanding, Jewish-Christian dialogue is recommended: "This Sacred Synod wants to foster and recommend that mutual understanding and respect which is the fruit, above all, of biblical and theological studies as well as fraternal dialogues." In addition, *Nostra Aetate* repudiates the ancient charge of deicide: "True, the Jewish authorities and those who followed their lead pressed for the death of Christ; still, what happened in his passion cannot be charged against all the Jews, without distinction, then alive, nor against the Jews of today."

In subsequent years various national and provincial synods have attempted to apply the teaching of this statement. In 1974 Pope Paul established a Commission for Religious Relations with the Jewish People which produced guidelines and suggestions for implementing its conclusions. This document insists that Christians should condemn anti-Semitism and view Jews "as they define themselves in the light of their own religious experience". In addition, the document encourages Christians to pray together with Jews: "In whatever circumstances as shall prove possible and mutually acceptable, one might encourage a common meeting in the presence of God, in prayer and silent meditation, a highly efficacious way of finding that humility, that openness of heart and mind, necessary prerequisites for a deep knowledge of oneself and others. In particular that will be done in connection with great causes, such as the struggle for peace and justice."

To celebrate the twentieth anniversary of *NostraAetate*, the Commission published *Notes on the Correct Way to present Jews and Judaism in preaching and catechesis in the Roman Catholic Church*. In this document the Church and Judaism are conceived as parallel ways of salvation; the permanent value of the Hebrew Scriptures as a source of Christian revelation is stressed; and Jesus is depicted as a faithful Jew. Further, it recognized that the "Gospels are the outcome of long and complicated editorial work . . . Hence it cannot be ruled out that some references hostile or less than favourable to the Jews have their historical context in conflicts between the nascent Church and the Jewish community.

Certain controversies reflect Christian-Jewish relations long after the time of Jesus." Finally, the permanence of Israel and its continuous spiritual significance for the Jewish people is assumed.

Similar views about Judaism and the Jewish people have been expressed by the World Council of Churches (WCC). At its first Assembly in Amsterdam in 1948, the WCC declared: "We cannot forget that we meet in a land from which 110,000 Jews were taken to be murdered. Nor can we forget that we meet only five years after the extermination of six million Jews." At the Evanston Assembly in 1954 the Jewishness of Jesus was emphasized as well as God's concern for the Jews. In 1961 at the New Delhi Assembly, the WCC condemned anti-Semitism and stressed that the Jewish nation should not be blamed for Christ's crucifixion: "In Christian teaching the historic events which led to the Crucifixion should not be presented as to fasten upon the Jewish people of today responsibilities which belong to our corporate humanity and not to one race or community."

In 1967 the WCC's Faith and Order Commission, and its sub-unit the Consultation on the Church and the Jewish People (CCJP) agreed on a joint report. This document affirmed that although God's revelation in the Hebrew Scriptures was fulfilled in Jesus Christ, God did not abandon the Jewish nation. In 1977 the British Working Group of the CCJP highlighted the theological significance of the Holy Land for the Jewish people:

> Judaism believes that there is a positive spiritual purpose in fulfilling as many of God's commandments as possible; the opportunity for this is at its highest in the Holy Land, where the commandments concerning the Holy Land and its produce may be observed, and where the sanctity to Judaism of worship in previous times is keenly felt . . . In modern times, many Jews have therefore seen a strong, religious purpose in the strengthening of Jewish settlement in Israel.

In 1982 the WCC statement *Ecumenical Considerations on Jewish-Christian Dialogue* was produced, which pointed out the need for Christians to abandon stereotypes. Judaism, it asserted, is not a fossilized religion of legalism, but a living tradition. Further, Christian responsibility for Jewish suffering was acknowledged: "Teachings of contempt for Jews and Judaism in certain Christian traditions proved a spawning ground for the evil of the Nazi Holocaust." More recently the

WCC has summarized the convictions which now guide most Churches in their dealings with the Jewish people:

1. The covenant of God with the Jewish people remains valid.
2. Anti-Semitism and all forms of the teaching of contempt for Judaism, especially teaching about deicide, are to be repudiated.
3. The living tradition of Judaism is a gift of God.
4. Coercive proselytism directed towards Jews is incompatible with Christian faith.
5. Jews and Christians bear a common responsibility as witnesses to God's righteousness and peace in the world.

Such pronouncements have repudiated misconceptions about Judaism and have paved the way for positive Jewish-Christian encounter – after centuries of persecution, the Churches have at last come to accept responsibility for the plight of the Jews.

Jesus the Jew

Through the centuries the Jewishness of Jesus was eclipsed by the Church's desire to differentiate between Judaism and Christianity. In recent years, however, a number of Christian as well as Jewish scholars have emphasized Jesus' connections with his ancestral faith. In this quest these writers have stressed the importance of dispelling the stereotyped pictures of first-century Judaism as portrayed in the Gospels. Rather, the Jewish tradition should be understood in terms of God's covenant with Abraham. In this light the Law should be seen as a gift, with Pharisaic Judaism as the logical continuation of God's relationship with his Chosen People.

As a product of the early Church, the Gospels reflect the disputes between the followers of Jesus and the Jewish community. None the less it is evident that Jesus had strong affinities with the Pharisees. His emphasis on reinterpreting the oral law is reminiscent of rabbinic teaching. Like the Pharisees he stressed the importance of love, adhered to belief in the resurrection, and rigorously observed Jewish festivals. Although Jesus did not follow all the Pharisaic prescriptions (such as those concerning washing before meals, ritual purity and table fellowship), his departure from strict Pharisaism may have simply been a reflection of internal disputes among the Pharisees themselves.

Like other Jews of this period Jesus was convinced that a new age was dawning. In declaring that the Kingdom of God is at hand, he was acting in line with Jewish eschatological expectations. The coming of this new epoch in human history would bring about a new Temple, the restoration of the twelve tribes of Israel, and an ingathering of the multitudes. For Jesus and traditional Jews alike the new age would not be an overturning of God's covenant with the Jewish people, but instead the outpouring of God's love to all. The advent of the Messiah would bring about a transformation of the world in which evil would be overcome. Jesus was thus a faithful son of the covenant, a Jewish messianic figure standing firmly within the Jewish heritage. Understanding Jesus in this way should enable Christians to revise their perception of Jewish life as well as of the Jews of Jesus' time.

As far as Jesus' titles are concerned, these too should be viewed within a Jewish context. Those who witnessed Jesus' resurrection believed that the Messianic age had dawned. According to contemporary biblical scholarship, the titles given to Jesus originated in the early Christian community to express their belief in Christ. Such expressions as "Messiah", "Son of Man", "Son of God", and "Lord" were drawn from the Jewish heritage to convey the significance of Jesus' life and teaching. Yet as the Church became increasingly gentile, such terms came to emphasize his divine status. The Christological declarations of Church Councils were intended to affirm the presence of God in Christ.

Unfortunately for the Jewish community, this development led to the Church's denigration of Jews and Judaism. However, in the light of a modern understanding of early Christology, it is possible to transcend such a negative perception of the Jewish faith. Given that the thought forms of the early Church were culturally conditioned, it is no longer necessary to portray credal formulations as metaphysical claims. Thus a number of modern Christian theologians have attemped to develop a systematic Christology devoid of anti-Judaism. Such a reconstructed theology is not tied to traditional Christocentrism and exclusivity; instead emphasis is placed on Christ's redemption of the entire world. In this light Jesus' resurrection should be perceived as validating the Jewish tradition. In the words of Jacobus Schoneveld (the General Secretary of the International Council of Christians and Jews): "The resurrection means the vindication of Jesus as a Jew, as a person who was faithful to the Torah, as a martyr who participated in Jewish martyrdom for the sanctification of God's name. What else can this mean than the validation of the Torah, and vindication of the Jewish people as God's beloved people?" Such a modern understanding of Jesus' ministry is far removed from Christian hostility of previous centuries: rather than placing the Jewish community outside of God's providential care, many Christian theologians today are seeking to affirm the continuing covenant between God and Israel.

God's Covenant and the Jewish People

In the past Christianity maintained that God's covenant with the Jews had been superseded by his covenant with the New Israel: through the centuries Christians believed that with Jesus' resurrection the Christian community had become the heir to promises made to Abraham and the patriarchs. By rejecting Jesus, Israel had shown itself unfaithful and had abandoned its covenantal obligations. As a punishment God destroyed Jerusalem, and banished the Jewish nation from its ancestral home.

Today, however, many Church bodies have rejected this view, affirming instead the continuing validity of God's covenant with his Chosen People. The Second Vatican Council, for example, implies such a view in *Nostra Aetate*: "God holds the Jews most dear for the sake of their Fathers; he does not repent of the gifts he makes or of the call he issues – such is the witness of the Apostle." In 1979 the Diocese of Cleveland, Ohio, quoting this passage, preceded it with an affirmation of respect for the Jewish faith: "Our respect and regard for Judaism, therefore, is not for an ancient relic of the distant past. It is God himself who made the Jewish people his own and gave them a divine and irrevocable vocation."

Again, the Churches in the Netherlands stated in 1981:

> The promises which the God of Abraham, Isaac, and Jacob has made to the Jewish people have never been revoked by their God, who is our God, too. Nor did God ever recall the covenant which he, through Moses, had made with them. We Christians call this covenant – by a term which has occasioned much misunderstanding – the "old covenant". This covenant was not abolished or replaced by the "new covenant" in and through the coming of Jesus Christ.

Likewise the 1982 statement of the Texas Conference of Christians decreed: "We acknowledge with both respect and reverence that Judaism is a living faith and that Israel's call and covenant are valid and operative today. We reject the position that the covenant between the Jews and God was dissolved with the coming of Christ."

According to some contemporary scholars, there is only one covenant into which gentiles are admitted through Jesus Christ. Such writers assert that Judaism and Christianity are complementary aspects of the same divine purpose. Thus the eschatological significance of Jesus' salvific work must be understood as a future event – even for Christians Jesus is not yet the Messiah. Messianic fulfilment is not a present reality, but rather a mission. God's single covenant is new after the Christ event only in that it embraces both Jews and gentiles. In this light, the Church can be seen as a community of gentiles who have been drawn to worship God and bring knowledge of him to the nations.

Such writers as Paul Van Buren stress that this does not imply any dilution of the Christian conviction that Jesus is the Christ and Son of God. According to Van Buren, for those committed to Jesus, what took place in Christ "marked a genuinely new beginning, a step out and beyond the circles of God's covenant with his people, the Jews. But it surely cannot and does not detract from, much less annul, that covenant." Other writers point out that Christianity has not replaced Israel in the divine drama of salvation – Israel's vocation still continues in the modern world. Thus the Church and the Synagogue are bound together within one covenant. As Jacobus Schoneveld explains:

When we look at the Church's life and teaching, has anything been added to the Torah? I have searched for a long time for anything new. In fact nothing new is there, which goes beyond a certain change of emphasis or a certain different nuance in comparison with Jewish teachings of the first century, except that through Jesus the gentiles have been admitted and the range of the teaching of the Torah has become much wider.

An alternative approach to this issue has been proposed by Christian writers who have formulated a two-covenant theory. James Parkes, for example, has written regarding the Sinaitic revelation and Calvary:

The highest purpose of God which Sinai reveals to man as community, Calvary reveals to man as an end in himself. The difference between the

two events, both of which from the metaphysical standpoint arise identical as expressions of the infinite in time, lies in the fact that the first could
not be fulfilled but by a brief demonstration of a divine community in
action; but the second could not be fulfilled except by a life lived under
human conditions from birth to death. Thus Jesus' death on the cross did
not replace Sinai: Judaism and Christianity are different but equally valid
responses to the Divine initiative.

These single and double covenant theories thus offer a means of
reconciliation between Christians and Jews – no longer is the Jewish
community being condemned for refusing to accept Jesus as "God of
God, Light of Light, Very God of Very God."

Christian Mission

In the past Christians were intent on converting Jews to the true faith:
such mission was the avowed purpose of Jewish-Christian encounter
and still continues in the modern world. However, today there has been
an attempt on the part of many Christians to reinterpret the concept of
mission. The former Archbishop of Canterbury, Lord Runcie, for
example, has declared:

> Whilst in the past the goal of Christian mission has mainly been the
> awakening of faith, the founding of churches, the growth and mainten-
> ance of Christian life, we now perceive more clearly . . . another goal as
> that of giving witness to the spirit of love and hope, of promoting justice
> and peace, sharing responsibility with others for the development of a
> caring society, especially where people are in need . . . This will mean
> some claims about the exclusiveness of the Church have to be renounced,
> but also that past and present prejudices about other religions have to be
> overcome, and ignorance and contempt actively resisted.

Another approach to Christian outreach focuses on the distinction
between proselytism as opposed to witness. The quest to win converts
from another faith characterized previous Christian attitudes, whereas
Christian witness is currently understood as a sharing of religious
experience. In this process there is no desire to pressurize others. In the
words of Lord Coggan, formerly Archbishop of Canterbury and Chairman of the Council of Christians and Jews, "The tragedy takes place
when mission or evangelism is interpreted in terms of proselytization.

That last word speaks of pressure, if not of force, of (at least would-be) compulsion – 'Believe this, or else!'"

Such a reorientation of Christian mission is based on the recognition of God's presence in all the world's religious faiths – a view which is increasingly being accepted by many Christians. This shift in perspective is grounded in the conviction that a God of love could not allow the mass of humanity to wallow in ignorance and darkness: as the providential Lord of history, God must provide a means of salvation for all people. Thus according to the Catholic priest Bede Griffiths – whose *ashram* in South India has attracted both Hindu and Christian visitors – God's cosmic covenant with humanity implicitly contains the revelation of God's presence in Christ. A similar inclusivist view has been expressed by the Catholic theologian Karl Rahner, who maintains that "Christianity does not simply confront the member of an extra-Christian religion as a mere non-Christian but as someone who can and must be regarded in this or that respect as an anonymous Christian."

Other Christian theologians have proposed an even more radical reorientation of Christology. The Protestant theologian John Hick, for example, speaks of a Copernican revolution in theology which involves a major transformation of the Christian view of religious pluralism. It demands, he writes, "a paradigm shift from a Christianity-centred or Jesus-centred to a God-centred model of the universe of faiths. One then sees the great world religions as different human responses to the one Divine reality, embodying different perceptions which have been formed in different historical and cultural circumstances." Similarly, the Roman Catholic priest Raimundo Panikaar endorses a new map of world religions. For Panikaar, the mystery within all religions is both more than and yet has its being within the diverse experiences and beliefs of the world's religions. "It is not simply that there are different ways of leading to the peak," he writes, "but that the summit itself would collapse if all the paths disappeared." Such a vision of the universe of faiths implies that no religion can claim final or absolute authority.

A similar position is advanced by Stanley Samartha of the World Council of Churches. God, he believes, is the Mysterious Other: "The Other relativizes everything else. In fact, the willingness to accept such relativization is probably the only real guarantee that one has encountered the Other as ultimately real." By relativizing all religious figures and revelations, Samartha does not intend to deny their necessity or reduce them to a common denominator. The Mysterious Other must confront humanity through various mediations, yet no particular manifestation is universally valid. A particular religion such as Christianity can claim to be decisive for some people, but no religion is justified in claiming that it is decisive for all.

Again, the Catholic theologian Paul Knitter argues that the theocentric model is a valid reinterpretation of Christian tradition and experience. Jesus should not be understood as God's complete revelation – exclusivist language in the New Testament should be seen as essentially confessional in nature. Such Christological language, he asserts, is much like the language a husband would use of his wife: "You are the most wonderful woman in the world", and so on. In the context of a marital relationship these claims are true, but only as an expression of love. Similarly it is possible for Christians to express their dedication to Jesus without adopting an absolutist position. Utilizing the analogy of marriage, Knitter writes: "The deeper the commitment to one's spouse and the more secure the marriage relationship, the more one will be able to appreciate the truth and beauty of others. Therefore, not only does commitment to Jesus include openness to others, but the greater the commitment to him, the greater will be one's openness to others." Such redefinitions of Christology provide a new basis for viewing the Jewish heritage. With God at the centre of the universe of faiths, Judaism can be seen as an authentic religious expression, and such a paradigm shift calls for a critical reassessment of the Church's attitude to the Jews.

The Holocaust

For Jews as well as Christians, the Holocaust or *Shoah* is of overwhelming significance. According to a number of Jewish thinkers the destruction of six million Jews by the Nazis was a unique event – the Final Solution was the first systematic genocidal assault in human history. Likewise a number of Christian writers have stressed the centrality of this tragedy. According to Alice and Royal Eckardt, for example, the Holocaust was "a truly transcending or metahistorical event, an event that twists our journey through space-time by 180 degrees."

How can one make sense of this modern calamity? From both the Christian and Jewish sides there have been a variety of theological responses. The British Jewish theologian Ignaz Maybaum, for example, contends that the Jews died in the concentration camps for the sins of mankind as God's suffering servant and sacrificial lamb. For Maybaum, Auschwitz is the analogue of Golgotha, and he sees the Nazis as instruments of God's will. On the analogy of Nebuchadnezzar, who in Jeremiah 27:6 is described as God's servant, Maybaum maintains that Hitler played a divinely instrumental role in the purification of a sinful world. God is pictured at Auschwitz in the role of a surgeon performing a necessary operation, cutting out a part of Israel for the renewal of the body of mankind. Jews therefore suffer in order to bring about the rule of God over the world and its peoples; their God-appointed mission is to serve the course of historical progress and bring mankind into a new era.

A second Jewish approach to the Holocaust is to see in the death camps a manifestation of God's will that his chosen people survive. Such a paradoxical view is most representatively expressed by the theologian Emil Fackenheim, who asserts that God revealed himself to Israel out of the furnaces and through the ashes of the victims of Auschwitz. Through the Holocaust, he believes, God issued the 614th commandment: "Jews are forbidden to grant a posthumous victory to Hitler." According to Fackenheim the commitment of faith is not called into question by any event of history, including the Holocaust; thus Fackenheim urges Jews to hold fast to the traditional covenant God who is present in and the Lord of history.

Another Jewish response to the Holocaust is to reject any kind of explanation – instead, the events of the Holocaust are seen as part of God's inscrutable plan. The Orthodox scholar Eliezer Berkovits, for example, argues that the modern Jewish response to the destruction of six million Jews should be modelled on Job's example. We must believe in God, he maintained, because Job believed. If there is no answer to the question of understanding God's silence in the face of the Nazi genocide, "it is better to be without it than with the sham of . . . the humbug of a disbelief encouraged by people who have eaten their fill at the tables of a satiated society." At Auschwitz God was hidden, yet according to Berkovits, in his hiddenness he was actually present. As Hidden God, God is Saviour; in the apparent void he is the Redeemer of Israel.

Paralleling such Jewish speculation, a number of Christian thinkers have formulated theories grounded in Christian theology. Among Christian writers one of the most important developments has been the desire to reinterpret the doctrine of Divine impassibility. As the German theologian Jürgen Moltmann explains: "To recognize God in the crucified Christ means to grasp the trinitarian history of God and to understand oneself and this whole world with Auschwitz and Vietnam, with race hatred and hunger, as existing in the history of God. God is not dead. Death is in God. God suffers by us. He suffers with us. Suffering is in God." Elsewhere he states:

> It is necessary to remember the martyrs, so as not to become abstract. Of them and of dumb sacrifices, it is true in a real, transferred sense, that God himself hung on the gallows as Elie Wiesel was able to say. If that is taken seriously, it must also be said that like the cross of Christ, even Auschwitz is in God himself. Even Auschwitz is taken up into the grief of the Father, the surrender of the Son and the power of the Spirit.

A similar Christological understanding of the Holocaust binding Jews and Christians together has been formulated by the Swiss theologian Clemens Thoma:

> For a believing Christian, the sense of the sacrificial way walked by the Jews under the Nazis ... is not too difficult to determine ... The approximately six million Jews killed in Auschwitz and elsewhere lead his (the Christian's) thoughts first of all to Christ, with whom these Jewish masses have become one in suffering and death. Auschwitz is the most eminent modern sign of the inmost relationship and oneness of the Jewish martyrs ... with the crucified Christ, although the Jews affected here could not have been aware of this. The Holocaust is thus, for the believing Christian, an important sign of the unbreakable unity, founded upon Christ crucified, of Judaism and Christianity in spite of all breaks, separate ways and misunderstandings.

While Jews would no doubt have difficulties with such Christological interpretations, these theories illustrate the current Christian sensitivity to the religious perplexities of the Holocaust. No longer is the Church prepared to stand by silently as the Jewish people endure persecution and death; instead, many Christian theologians are acutely aware of the horrors of the death camps and the Church's share of responsibility for these atrocities. Profound questions are being raised about human nature and religious belief, and in their common quest to understand God's ways Jews and Christians are reaching out to one another. In the shadow of the Holocaust, this is perhaps the most important cause of hope for the future.

Conclusion

Looking back over two thousand years, it is possible to isolate a number of causes of anti-Semitism: Jews have been detested because they were different, despised on account of their financial success, and feared for their connections with Jewry in other lands. In addition to the various social, economic, and psychological explanations for humanity's longest hatred, the Christian roots of Jewish antipathy run very deep. In the Greco-Roman world, the early Church utilized a number of Hellenistic ideas that had penetrated into the Jewish religion to denigrate Judaism itself: the allegorical interpretation of Scripture was transformed into a justification for separating religious meaning from ritual practice; revival movements served as a basis for the belief that the Christian faith was the fulfilment of biblical teaching; the quest to harmonize Hellenistic thought with the Jewish tradition led to the denigration of the God of the Old Testament; and the universalization of Judaism intensified the Christian conviction that the gospel should be spread to all people.

With the emergence of Christianity, the followers of Christ believed themselves to be the true heirs of the covenant. For these Christians Jesus' messiahship was understood as bringing about a new age in which the true Israel would become a light to the nations. Given this eschatological vision, the Jewish people were regarded with animosity. The writers of the Gospels depicted Jesus attacking the leaders of the nation, and the Church taught that circumcision of the heart – rather than obedience to the Law – was what God required. In proclaiming this message Paul stressed that the Jewish nation had been rejected by God and that the old covenant had been superseded. The Epistle to the Hebrews emphasizes the antithesis between the Jewish people and the Christian community, and this contrast is highlighted in the Fourth Gospel which differentiates between the spiritual universe of Christianity and the realm of darkness represented by the Jews. The New

Testament thus sowed the seeds of contempt for Judaism and the Jewish people.

In the light of this teaching, the Fathers of the Church developed an *Adversos Judaeos* tradition which vilified the Jews. According to the Fathers, Jews were guilty in the past of indecent actions, and they have continued to be a contemptible people. Given such behaviour, God's promises in future apply only to the Church. Basing their views on Scripture, the Church Fathers argued that the struggle between Judaism and Christianity was prefigured in Scripture. By rejecting Christ, Jews have been rejected and are doomed for eternity. Christians, rather than the Jewish Nation, thus constitute God's elect. As the religion of the Roman Empire, Christianity was to serve as an instrument for spreading the promise of God's redemption to humanity.

The tradition of Christian anti-Semitism as created by the Church Fathers continued through the centuries. In the fifth and sixth centuries the *Codex Theodosianus* and the Justinian Code denied Jews various rights. Later, during the time of the Crusades, Jewish communities were decimated throughout western Europe. Such hostility toward the Jews was intensified by various charges levelled against the Jewish population. Frequently Jews were accused of killing Christian children to use their blood in preparations for the Passover. Jews were also charged with blaspheming the Christian faith in the Talmud – as a result, this sacred text was cast to the flames. Further, Jews were blamed for causing the Black Plague by poisoning wells. Yet despite this onslaught on the Jewish community, many Jewish martyrs went to their deaths confident that their tormentors would be punished eternally for their sins.

Throughout the Middle Ages the Jew was represented as a dark, demonic figure; repeatedly Jews were accused of possessing the attributes of both the Devil and witches. As the personification of evil, they were regarded as sub-human. In addition, Jews were viewed as magicians, able to work magic against neighbouring Christians. On this basis, the Jewish population was accused of desecrating the Host for magical purposes and of committing acts of ritual murder. While it is true that Jews did engage in practices of a magical nature, such activities were dependent on the power of good rather than evil. Thus Christian allegations were based on ignorance and fear, and many Jews lost their lives as a consequence of such misunderstanding.

Not only were Jews despised and tormented by Christians, they were
frequently expelled from the countries where they resided. In the
fourteenth century Jews were driven out of France; nevertheless,
negative images of Jews continued to play an important role in French
culture. In various literary forms – such as catechisms, lives of Jesus
and canticles – Jews were portrayed as tools of Satan. Similarly in
England Jews were vilified despite the fact that they had been expelled
in 1290. German Jews were also despised, despite the fact that some
Jews attained important positions as court Jews throughout Germany.

In Spain the Jewish community flourished during the Middle Ages,
but by the fourteenth century Spanish Jews also came to be viewed with
grave suspicion. Numerous measures were taken against them, and as
a result many Jews converted to Christianity. Such apostasy, as well as
the Christian attack on the Jewish populace, led to a decline of the
aljamas. In the next century the Church instituted the Inquisition to
purge *conversos* who were suspected of continuing to practice Judaism.
Throughout Spain tribunals were established to extract confessions –
those who refused to confess were burned at the stake. Eventually, at
the end of the century, King Ferdinand and Queen Isabella issued an
Edict of Expulsion to rid their country of this accursed race.

As the Inquisition sought out Christian heresy in Spain, numerous
Marranos fled to Portugal. There they lived as Christians while
continuing to observe various Jewish practices. In 1536 the Portuguese
Inquisition was established to track down Marranos wherever they
lived. Those *conversos* who had escaped to other countries flourished in
the sixteenth and seventeenth centuries. In centres such as Antwerp,
Venice, Amsterdam and London, they returned to Judaism while
retaining many of their former cultural characteristics. During this
period some Marranos gained enormous political influence; others
awaited the coming of the Messiah to lead them back to Zion. Some
Marranos, however, distanced themselves from traditional Judaism
and advanced heretical ideas which unintentionally paved the way for
further Christian anti-Semitism in later centuries.

Turning to eastern Europe, Jews in Poland faced virulent anti-
Semitism in the seventeenth century. In 1648 Bogdan Chmielnicki
became hetman of the Cossacks and instigated an insurrection against
the Polish gentry which spread to the Jewish community. Thousands of
Jews were slaughtered in these revolts by Christian mobs. In the wake
of this massacre, the *Hasidim* fostered religious piety in the face of

rabbinic hostility to their new movement. The Jewish community was thus torn asunder from without and within. In Russia Jews were initially prevented from living in the country, but once Polish territories were annexed to Russia, Jews came to be regarded with contempt and were eventually expelled from the villages where they had previously settled.

In the early modern period, centuries-old Christian prejudice combined with commercial interests provoked antipathy toward the Jewish population in western lands. In Germany merchants protested against Jewish infidels, complaining that Jewish trade would destroy the economy and corrupt the Christian population. Similar antipathy was expressed in France, where the bourgeoisie resisted Jewish settlement. Jews were also subject to considerable hostility in Great Britain, where attempts to allow Jewish naturalization were met with great resistance. Although Jews in the United States were treated more tolerantly, Jewish life elsewhere did not alter radically from medieval patterns of existence. Stereotyped as foreign and corrupt, most Jews suffered discrimination, and even assimilated Jews were frequently unable to escape such sentiment.

The Enlightenment, however, brought about a dramatic alteration in the conditions of the Jews; none the less, a number of Christian writers continued to attack Jewry on rationalist grounds. In France, Protestants influenced by the Enlightenment sought to ameliorate the condition of the Jews, yet even they were unable to free themselves from Christian assumptions about Jewish guilt for killing Christ. During this period a number of major thinkers of the age sought to encourage Judeophobia. To escape from such denigration, enlightened Jews disassociated themselves from Judaism, and a number sought to gain social acceptance by banding together as a new Jewish-Christian sect.

By the end of the eighteenth century the spirit of the Enlightenment encouraged Christian Europe to improve the condition of Jewish existence. With the establishment of the Napoleonic era, Jewish life changed dramatically. In France the summoning of the Great Sanhedrin heralded Jewish emancipation. In such a climate Jewish reformers attempted to adapt Jewish worship to modern conditions. Reform temples appeared throughout Germany, yet ironically many Jews influenced by the Romantic movement were indifferent to such alterations to Jewish practice. Instead of providing a basis for the improvement of Judaism, the Reform movement undermined traditional Judaism and intensified Christian antipathy to the Jewish faith. In Russia the official government policy of modernizing Jewish existence was driven by traditional Christian antipathy to the Jewish populace. From the Jewish side such changes evoked considerable unease among the Orthodox, who feared that such reforming steps would undermine Torah Judaism. Despite such reservations, liberal Christians continued to campaign for equal rights for the Jewish community. Yet their actions evoked widespread fears and at the end of the second decade of the nineteenth century attacks against Jewry spread from country to country.

In the nineteenth century a number of Jewish apologists endeavoured to ameliorate the condition of the Jewish population. In England the Tory Prime Minister advocated Jewish emancipation – such activity provoked a hostile response from various critics who denigrated Judaism in terms reminiscent of previous centuries. In France the Damascus Affair stimulated anti-Jewish feelings and revived the medieval Christian charge of ritual murder, giving rise to widespread anti-Jewish sentiment. At this time the Christian legend of the Wandering Jew, who was destined to roam the earth for having rejected Christ, became a major theme of French literature. French Judeophobia was further intensified by the writings of socialists. Similarly in Germany advocates of racism as well as philosophers vilified the Jewish people and their traditions.

During the second half of the nineteenth century, the Jewish community suffered further outbreaks of hostility. In Germany various racist publications attacked Jews, and the researches of Christian biblical scholars undermined the traditional belief that the Torah was given by God to Moses on Mount Sinai. Similar attitudes were expressed in France by a variety of Christian writers who denounced Judaism and the Jewish nation. At the end of the century the Dreyfus Affair raised fundamental questions about the viability of Jewish life in the diaspora. Inspired by a vision of a Jewish homeland, the Zionist Theodore Herzl sought to convince world leaders of the necessity of a Jewish state. During this period Russian Jewry underwent widespread persecution, and many Jews emigrated to distant lands. Others sought to improve their life through revolutionary struggle. Such activities alarmed the Russian authorities, who became increasingly perturbed by the publication of *The Secret of Judaism* and *The Protocols of the Elders of Zion* which depicted a Jewish conspiracy to achieve world domination. At the beginning of the next century the revival of the Christian ritual murder charge further inflamed Russian hatred of the Jews.

In the years leading up to World War I, Jews were viewed as scapegoats for the problems that beset German society. Although Germany prospered after the war, widespread unemployment occurred from 1930 to 1933. Such a situation led to the rise of Nazism, with its anti-Semitic policies. In Russia anti-Semites also accused the Jewish community of betraying national interests. With the onslaught of the Revolution, Jews were charged with international conspiracy, and attacks on Jews occurred throughout the country. After the war a series of forgeries was produced to implicate the Jews with revolutionary activity. During this period British writers also criticized the Jews for their dishonesty and participation in revolutionary causes. After the war the publication of *The Protocols of the Elders of Zion* reinforced such sentiments. The United States also witnessed the growth of anti-Semitism, which gave rise to the establishment of various bodies which sought to protect Jewish interests. French Judeophobia was also animated by the perception of Jewish influence on the world situation.

Such racial hatred crystallized in Adolf Hitler's view of the Jewish people as an evil nation that sought world domination. Once the Nazis gained power, they instituted a series of anti-Jewish policies. During *Kristallnacht* in 1938, Jewish property and buildings were destroyed, and in the following year the invasion of Poland resulted in the massacre of the Jewish population. The next stage in the Nazis' plan of Jewish extermination occurred with the invasion of Russia, where mobile killing battalions were used to destroy the Jewish populace. This method of slaughter was supplemented by the death camps at Auschwitz, Chelmno, Belzec, Sobibor, Majdanek, and Treblinka, where Jews were systematically killed. Although Jewish resistance did take place during this period in Warsaw and elsewhere, the Nazis continued with their policy of terror and death without pause. During the war most Christian leaders remained aloof from the horrors of the Holocaust, and once the war drew to a close the Vatican and others close to it aided a number of war criminals to escape.

After World War II, Germany did not express great remorse for its deeds; instead most Germans continued to harbour anti-Jewish feelings. Although the radical left was critical of Fascism, it was not principally concerned with Jewish suffering. In Austria similar attitudes prevailed. Similar Judeophobia was also expressed in Britain, where neo-Nazis and the ultra Right have advanced the theory of a world-wide conspiracy. Likewise in America anti-Semitism intensified in recent years, largely because of the conflict between the black and white communities. French antipathy toward the Jews after the war has also led to the condemnation of Zionism, attacks on Jewish property, and the resurgence of a national party. Poland too witnessed the rise of anti-Semitism in recent years, and in Russia the policy of *glasnost* has inflamed centuries-old Christian prejudice.

For twenty centuries, then, Jews have suffered at the hands of anti-Semites. The injustices and pogroms inflicted on the Jewish community have been to a large degree the result of Christian contempt. Anti-Jewish attitudes in the history of the Church were not accidental – rather they were the direct consequence of Christian teaching about Judaism and the Jewish nation. In modern times secular anti-Semitism was not always fuelled by such religious convictions, yet the previous Christian denigration of Judaism and the inheritance of negative stereotypes of the Jew provided the basis for hatred and attack. Today, however, ways are being sought to transcend this legacy of Christian anti-Semitism. Both the Roman Catholic and Protestant Churches have issued decrees condemning anti-Semitism, and Christians have been encouraged to understand Jesus in a Jewish context. God's continuing covenant with the Jewish people has also been recognized, and Christian mission has been largely curtailed. Further, Judaism has been affirmed as a valid religious tradition, and many Christians have come to accept responsibility for the Holocaust.

Anti-Semitism has thus been a constant feature of the history of Christendom. As we reach the end of the second millennium of this era, it is vital that both Christians and Jews affirm that they are heirs of a fearful tradition. It is only through this realization and through the recognition that both traditions emerge from a common source, that harmony can be achieved. We live in a troubled and troubling world. Humanity, as never before, has the technological capacity to destroy both itself and its environment. If the human race is to continue, we must all play our part in contributing to world peace. It is for both the Christian and the Jewish communities to liberate themselves from their destructive tradition of hatred. By working together on projects for the common good and through studying their mutual heritage, the long habit of

Christian anti-Semitism may at last be overcome: only then will Christians and Jews fully appreciate the promise in the Psalmist's words:

> Behold how good and how pleasant it is for brethren to dwell together in unity! It is like the precious ointment upon the head, that ran down upon the beard, even Aaron's beard; that went down to the skirts of his garments; as the dew of Hermon, and as the dew that descended upon the mountains of Zion: for there the Lord commanded the blessing, even life for evermore.

Further Reading

Almog, Shmuel (ed.), *Antisemitism Through the Ages*, Oxford, 1988.

Arendt, Hannah, *Antisemitism*, New York, 1968.

Barbarosa Da Silva, A., *Is There a New Imbalance in the Jewish Christian Relationship?*, Uppsala, 1985.

Berger, David (ed.), *History and Hate: The Dimensions of Anti-Semitism*, Philadelphia, 1986.

Braybrooke, Marcus, *Time to Meet*, London, 1990.

Brockway, A., *Learning Christology Through Dialogue with Jews*, 1985.

Byrnes, Robert, *Antisemitism in Modern France*, New Brunswick, 1950.

Cargas, Harry James, *Shadows of Auschwitz*, New York, 1990.

Cohen, Jeremy, *The Friars and the Jews: Evolution of Medieval Anti-Judaism*, Ithaca, 1982.

Cohn-Sherbok, Dan, *Holocaust Theology*, Lamp, 1989.

Cracknell, Kenneth, *Towards a New Relationship*, London, 1986.

Croner, Helga (ed.), *Stepping Stones to Further Jewish-Christian Relations*, New York, 1977.

Croner, Helga, (ed.), *More Stepping Stones to Jewish-Christian Relations*, New York, 1985.

Curtis, Michael (ed.), *Antisemitism in the Contemporary World*, Boulder, 1986.

Davies, A. T. (ed.), *Antisemitism and the Foundations of Christianity*, New York, 1979.

Dinnerstein, Leonard, *Uneasy at Home: Antisemitism and the American Experience*, New York, 1987.

Eckhardt, A. L. and Eckhardt, A. R., *Long Night's Journey into Day*, Detroit, 1982.

Ettinger, Shmuel, *Antisemitism in the Modern Age*, Tel Aviv, 1978.

Flannery, Edward H., *The Anguish of the Jews*, New York, 1985.

Forster, A. and Epstein, B., *The New Anti-Semitism*, New York, 1974.

Freedman, Theodore (ed.), *Anti-Semitism in the Soviet Union, its Roots and Consequences*, New York, 1984.

Friedlander, Albert, *Out of the Whirlwind*, New York, 1976.

Gager, John, *The Origins of Antisemitism: Attitudes Towards Judaism in Pagan and Christian Antiquity*, Oxford, 1985.

Gilbert, Martin, *The Holocaust*, London, 1986.

Glassman, Bernard, *Anti-Semitic Stereotypes Without Jews: Images of Jews in England 1290–1700*, Detroit, 1973.

Hay, Malcolm, *The Roots of Christian Anti-Semitism*, New York, 1981.

Further Reading

Hay, Malcolm, *Europe and the Jews: The Pressure of Christendom on the People of Israel for 1900 Years*, Boston, 1990.

Holmes, Colin, *Anti-Semitism in British Society 1876–1939*, New York, 1979.

Isaac, Jules, *Genèse de l'Antisémitisme*, Paris, 1956.

Isaac, Jules, *Has Anti-Semitism Roots in Christianity?*, New York, 1961.

Isaac, Jules, *The Teaching of Contempt: Christian Roots of Anti-Semitism*, New York, 1964.

Katz, J., *From Prejudice to Destruction, 1700–1933*, Cambridge, Mass., 1980.

Katz, J., *The Darker Side of Genius: Richard Wagner's Antisemitism*, London, 1986.

Klein, Charlotte, *Anti-Judaism in Christian Theology*, London, SPCK, 1975.

Korey, William, *The Soviet Cage: Anti-Semitism in Russia*, New York, 1973.

Kushner, Tony, *The Persistence of Prejudice: Antisemitism in British Society During the Second World War*, Manchester, 1989.

Langmuir, Gavin, *History, Religion and Antisemitism*, Berkeley, 1990.

Lebzetter, Gisela, *Political Antisemitism in England 1918–1939*, London, 1978.

Lendvai, Paul, *Antisemitism Without Jews: Communist Eastern Europe*, New York, 1971.

Levinger, Lee, *Anti-Semitism Yesterday and Tomorrow*, New York, 1936.

Lewis, B., *Semites and Antisemites: an Inquiry into Conflict and Prejudice*, New York, 1986.

Littel, Franklin, *The Crucifixion of the Jews*, New York, 1975.

Litvinoff, B., *The Burning Bush: Antisemitism and World Jewry*, London, 1989.

Mehlman, Jeffrey, *Legacies of Antisemitism in France*, Minneapolis, 1983.

Mosse, G., *Towards the Final Solution: A History of European Racism*, New York, 1978.

Oberman, Heiko A., *The Roots of Antisemitism in the Age of Renaissance and Reformation*. Philadelphia, 1984.

Oxaal, I. *et al* (eds), *Jews, Antisemitism and Culture in Vienna*, London, 1987.

Parkes, James, *The Conflict of the Church and the Synagogue*, London, 1934.

Parkes, James, *Judaism and Christianity*, Chicago, 1948.

Parkes, James, *Antisemitism*, London, 1963.

Pawlikowski, John, *What Are They Saying About Jewish-Christian Relations?*, New York, 1980.

Pawlikowski, John, *Christ in the Light of Christian-Jewish Dialogue*, New York, 1982.

Peck, Abraham, *Jews and Christians after the Holocaust*.

Perlmutter, N. and R., *The Real Anti-Semitism in America*, New York, 1982.

Pinson, Koppel S. (ed.), *Essays on Antisemitism*, New York, 1942.

Poliakov, Leon, *A History of Antisemitism*, London, 1974.

Pulzer, P. G. T., *The Rise of Political Antisemitism in Germany and Austria*, London, 1988.

Quinley, Harold and Clock, Charles, *Anti-Semitism in America*, New Brunswick, 1983.

Reinach, Theodore, *Textes des auteurs Grecs et Romains relatifs aux Judaisme*, Paris, 1895.

Rubenstein, Richard L. and Roth, John K., *Approaches to Auschwitz*, London, 1987.

Ruether, Rosemary, *Faith and Fratricide: The Theological Roots of Antisemitism*, New York, 1974.

Sandmel, Samuel, *Anti-Semitism in the New Testament*, Philadelphia, 1978.

Saperstein, Marc, *Moments of Crisis in Jewish-Christian Relations*, London, 1989.

Sartre, Jean-Paul, *Antisemite and Jew*, New York, 1976.

Schoeps, Hans J., *The Jewish-Christian Argument*, New York, 1963.

Seidel, Gill, *The Holocaust Denial: Antisemitism, Racism and the New Right*, London, 1986.

Seltzer, Robert, *Jewish People, Jewish Thought: The Jewish Experience in History*, New York, 1980.

Talmage, F. E., *Disputation and Dialogue, Readings in Jewish-Christian Encounter*, New York, 1975.

Thoma, Clemens, *A Christian Theology of Judaism*, New York, 1980.

Trachtenberg, Joshua, *The Devil and the Jews: The Medieval Conception of the Jew and its Relation to Antisemitism*, New Haven, 1943.

Trachtenberg, Joshua, *Jewish Magic and Superstition*, New York, 1961.

Valentin, Hugo, *Anti-Semitism*, London, 1936.

Van Buren, Paul, *Discerning the Way*, Part I of *A Theology of the Jewish-Christian Reality*, New York, 1980.

Van Buren, Paul, *A Christian Theology and the People of Israel*, Part II of *A Theology of the Jewish-Christian Reality*, New York, 1983.

Weinberg, Meyer, *Because They Were Jews: A History of Anti-Semitism*, New York, 1986.

Williamson, C. M., *Has God Rejected His People? Anti-Judaism in the Christian Church*, Nashville, 1982.

Wilson, S., *Ideology and Experience: Antisemitism in France at the Time of the Dreyfus Affair*, London, 1982.

Wistrich, Robert (ed.), *Anti-Zionism and Antisemitism in the Contemporary World*, London, 1990.

Wistrich, Robert, *Antisemitism: The Longest Hatred*, London, 1991.

Yassen, L. C., *The Jesus Connection: To Triumph Over Anti-Semitism*, New York, 1985.

General Index

accusations against Jews, of:-

apostasy 19, 25, 79, 97, 98; avarice 211; blasphemy xiii, xv, 26, 38, 46, 71, 73, 76, 127, 235; blindness, spiritual 8, 36, 37, 118, 127, 131; blood, Christian, use of 38, 43, 55, 57, 76, 107, 119, 178, 217, 235; blood rituals, xv, 44; cannibalism 27, 57, 161; conspiracy, international Jewish xix, 177, 179, 183, 184, 188, 189, 193, 194, 210, 212, 213, 216, 239; corrupting Scripture 127; deformity, physical 54, 55, 122, 157, 187; deicide (see killing Christ); demonism 27, 61; depravity 25, 26, 27, 30; destroying racial purity 196; disease 2, 54, 55, 57, 178; espionage xix, 179, 182; genocide 216; hardheartedness 33; Host, profanation of xv, 43, 44, 45, 51, 53, 57, 65, 86, 102, 109; idolatry 26, 27, 34, 35, 73, 148; infanticide xv, 27, 38, 43, 44, 45, 57, 86, 109, 177, 235; killing Christ xix, 18, 19, 24, 27, 29, 32, 33, 35, 65, 115, 128, 161, 175, 177, 214, 219, 223, 224, 237; magic 43, 51, 55–7, 62, 63, 86, 131, 178, 235; murder, ritual xv, xviii, 38, 43–5, 51, 52, 57, 65, 86, 102, 109, 117, 152, 156, 161, 165, 166, 173, 177, 178, 235, 239; nihilism 175; poisoning Christians 47, 56, 57, 62, 101; poisoning wells xv, 38, 49, 56, 235; racism 216, 220; rejecting Christ 11, 22, 32, 33, 45, 157, 227 (see also killing Christ); revolution, conspiring for 168, 169, 183, 184, 185, 187, 190, 196; sacrifice, human xiii, 130, 156; sacrifice, of children 27, 57; satanic activities xv (see also demonism); sorcery (see magic); subhumanity 45, 55, 235; treachery 53, 64, 115, 181, 182, 183, 219; tsaricide 174, 175, 183; usury 62, 64, 73, 116, 134, 140; world domination xix, 165, 168, 174, 177, 180, 181, 184, 188, 191, 193, 196, 220, 238, 239

Acts of the Apostles 18
Adrianople 97
Adversos Judaeos tradition xv, 25, 235
Albania 97
Albi 41
aljamas 77, 80, 82, 236
allegorization of Scripture 4, 234
Allgemeine deutsche Burschenschaft 161
Alliance Israélite Universelle 168
Alsace 76, 116, 117, 140, 146, 147, 150
America 183, 210, 213–4, 240 (see also United States)
Amsterdam 89, 98, 110, 236
amulets 60f
Ancona 89, 95
Andalusia 89
Anti-Christ 61, 82, 150
Anti-Defamation League 179, 189
Anti-Semitic League 166
Antisemitische Volkspartei 167
Antwerp 89, 236
Aphikomen 60
apocalyptic 6, 7, 8, 11
apostates 77, 79, 80, 81, 84, 155, 190, 236
Aragon 46, 79, 81, 86
Archives Israélites 157
Aryan race 45, 162, 167, 169, 181, 196
Ashkenazi 103, 108, 119, 210

assimilation of Jews xviii, 111, 133, 135, 139, 141, 145, 146, 147, 182, 189, 237

Auschwitz 195, 199, 200, 219, 232, 233, 239

Austria xix, 45, 108, 113, 156, 166, 184, 196, 210, 212, 239

Austrian Christian Party 167

autos-da-fé 45, 61, 88, 91, 161

Avignon 46

'Babi Yar' 220

badge, distinctive Jewish 45, 46, 81, 102 (*see also* clothing, insignia)

Baltic States 219 (*see also* Lithuania)

baptism 7, 20, 83 acceptance by Jews 79, 81, 82, 98, 138, 145, 147; forced 40, 41, 82

Barcelona 81, 86

Bavaria 122, 164, 211

Bayonne 64

Bayreuth 166

Belorussia 219

Belzec 195, 199, 202, 239

Berlin 135–8, 142, 147, 150, 166, 174

Bessarabia 112

Béziers, Council of 62

Bialystok 203

biblical scholarship 223, 225, 226 Christian xviii, xx, 15, 132, 165, 167, 222, 238

Birkenau 195, 199, 206, 207

Bitburg 211

black Americans xix, 121, 210, 213f, 240

Black Death (*see* Black Plague)

Black Muslims 213f

Black Panther Party 213

Black Plague 48–50, 52, 54, 56, 63, 77, 117, 235

Blois 44

Board of Deputies of British Jews 119

Bohemia 73, 75, 76, 122, 150

Bolsheviks 179, 181, 183, 189, 190, 192, 193, 194, 198

book burnings 46, 161, 197

Book of the Kahal 173

Bordeaux 41, 64, 89, 215

Brabant 41

Brazil 120

Britain xix, 172, 179, 180, 184, 185–8, 193, 210, 212–3, 224, 231, 239, 240 (*see also* England, Great Britain)

Brussels 44

Burgos 80

burning at the stake xvi, 45, 77, 85, 86, 87, 88, 110

Capentras 216

Castile 46, 77, 79, 81, 84

Catalonia 79

Catharism 54

Catholics (post-Reformation) 68, 168, 169, 209, 214, 216, 217, 230

cemeteries, desecration of 213, 216

census of Jews 166

Charleston 122

Chelmoo 195, 199, 239

Chmielnicki Massacre 105–7, 236

Christ, Christian doctrines of xv, 4, 8, 11, 12, 14, 19, 21, 22, 23, 24, 28, 29, 31, 33, 34, 35, 36, 37, 226, 228, 230

Christian Social Union 211

Christian Socialist Workers' Party 166

Christian Youth Union 211

Christology redefined 226, 231, 233

Church, early 12, 28, 225, 226, 234

Church Fathers xv, 3, 5, 25–37, 38, 43, 110, 125, 236

circumcision 3, 5, 6, 20, 30, 34, 35, 82, 100

'circumcision of the heart' 12, 20, 35, 234

Clermont Ferrand, Council of 39

Clothing, Jewish, distinctive 45, 46, 81, 93, 144, 146, 168 (*see also* badge, insignia)

Codex Theodosianus 38, 235

Committee for the Reorganization of Jewish Life 145

Committee of Deputies of British Jews 119

Communism 181, 184, 216, 217, 218, 220

complaint books 140

concentration camps, Nazi (*see under* death camps, and individual names) Soviet 219

Connecticut 120

Constantinople 82, 91, 94, 96f, 106, 185

conversion, forced 39, 43, 79, 81
conversion, from Judaism,
    to Christianity xvi, 70, 77, 79, 80, 81,
    98, 110, 112, 120, 122, 136, 137, 145;
    to Islam 92, 97
conversion, to Judaism 10, 11, 70, 86,
    109
conversos 77, 80, 82–7, 89, 91, 96, 236
Cortes of Toro 78
Cossacks xvii, 101, 105–7, 236
Council of Christians and Jews 229
Council of the Four Nations 103, 106,
    107, 152
court Jews 64, 75, 76, 133, 236
covenant xx, 7, 10, 17, 18, 19, 22, 30, 223,
    225, 226, 227–9, 234, 240
covenant, 'new' xv, 20, 22, 34, 35, 223,
    227
covenant, 'old' xv, 21, 22, 23, 227, 234
Cracow 102, 105, 199, 203, 204
Crimea 106
Crusades xv, 38, 40, 41, 43, 107, 235;
    First 39; Second 43; Third 40;
    Albigensian 41; Shepherds' 41, 77
Czestochowa 204

Dachau 208
Damascus Affair xviii, 152, 155–7, 173,
    238
Daniel, Book of 13f, 33
death camps xix, 195–209, 214, 231, 232,
    233, 239
death trains 200–1, 202, 214
demonic image of Jew xv, xvii, 4, 24, 28,
    51–63, 73, 119, 127, 139, 140, 157,
    184, 216, 235
demons 21, 27, 31, 51, 54, 56, 58, 59f, 97
Denmark 150, 208
deportation by Nazis 199–205, 207, 215
Devil 24, 41, 51, 53f, 61, 73, 74, 235 (*see
    also* Satan)
diaspora 2, 8, 11, 32, 33, 96, 238
dietary laws 3, 5, 20, 35, 84, 85, 88,
    123
Disputation of Tortosa 81
Doenmeh 97
Dominicans 46, 54, 80
drama, anti-Jewish 53, 211

Dreyfus Affair xviii, 165, 170–73, 185,
    238
dualism 9

Edict of Expulsion xvi, 77, 88
'Edict of Grace' 84
education 103–4, 142, 145, 146, 188;
    exclusion of Jews from 166, 176, 218,
    220
Egypt, ancient 2, 26; modern 96,
    157
Einsatzgruppen 198, 199
emancipation xvii, 139–51, 152, 162,
    169, 173, 180, 237, 238
emigration xviii, 175, 176, 217, 218,
    238
England, medieval, 40f, 41, 43, 44, 46,
    51, 102; post-medieval xvi, 64, 70f,
    236; early modern 113; Enlightenment
    xvii, 125–7; 19th-century xviii, 152,
    156, 238; 20th-century 172; (*see also*
    Britain, Great Britain)
Enlightenment xvii, 125–38, 139, 143,
    148, 237
eschatology 7, 11, 23, 226, 228,
    234
Essenes 7, 9
Esther, Prayer of 90
Eucharist 36, 57
exile xv, 10, 11, 25
Exodus 2, 6, 26, 171
expulsion of Jews xvii, 57, 72, 79, 101,
    112, 141, 145, 235, 237; from
    Bohemia 73; from England (1290)
    64, 70, 236; from France 64, 73,
    116, 236; from Germany 91, 135; from
    Kiev 145; from Portugal 91, 92; from
    Russia 111; from Spain 73, 88, 91, 92;
    from Vienna 113
extermination, Nazi policy of 195, 197,
    206, 209, 211

Fascism 210, 213, 216, 217, 218, 220,
    239
'Final Solution' 74, 231
flagellants 48f, 61
Flanders 94
foetor judaïcus 54, 123, 127, 128

forgeries xix,165, 169, 170, 171, 177, 179, 183, 184, 188, 239
Fourth Gospel xv, 12, 23f, 234
Fourth Lateran Council 45
France, medieval 39, 40, 41, 44, 45, 46, 47, 51, 61, 102, 236; post-medieval xvi, 64, 70, 94, 95; early modern xvii, 113, 116–8, 237; Enlightenment 125, 127–32, 237; Napoleonic 139–42, 150; 19th-century xviii, 146, 147, 152, 154–60, 238; modern xix, 165, 168–71, 184, 185, 192–4, 208, 210, 214–6, 239, 240
Frankfurt 48, 76, 115, 141, 148, 211
Freemasons 168, 169, 188
free-thinkers 125–6, 129–32
Freiburg, Council of 57

gas chambers 164, 195, 199, 201–2, 206, 207, 213
Gascony 81
Gaza 96, 97
German supremacy myth 160 (*see also* Aryan race)
Germany, medieval 40, 46, 48, 49, 51, 53, 54, 56, 61, 102; post-medieval xvi, 64, 71–2, 75, 76, 98; early modern xvii, 113–16, 237; Enlightenment 125, 132–8, 139, 141, 237; 19th-century xviii, 142–4, 147, 150, 152, 160–64, 165, 166–8, 170, 174, 238; early 20th-century 179, 180–2, 184, 187, 190, 193, 239; Nazi era 195–208, 239; post-Nazi 210–12, 239–40
Gestapo 197, 204
ghettos 63, 79, 102, 122, 141, 195, 199, 203, 204, 207
glasnost 210, 221, 240
Gnosticism 1, 8–9, 58, 126
God-fearers 3
Gospels xv, 12, 13, 15, 223, 225, 234; Fourth xv, 12, 14, 15, 23f; Synoptic 12, 14–19
Graf-Wellhausen hypothesis 167
Gransdorf 198
Great Britain xvii, 113, 118–20, 150, 156, 191, 237 (*see also* Britain, England)

Great Sanhedrin xvii, 119, 139, 140, 149, 150, 237
Greece (modern) 96
Greeks (ancient) xiv, 1–3, 10, 12

Halberstadt 114
Hamburg 76, 89, 115, 142f, 147, 199
Hasidim 6, 7, 108–9, 173, 236
hat, distinguishing Jewish 46, 146 (*see also* clothing)
Hebrew language 173
Hebrew Scriptures 11, 28, 44, 100, 120, 130
Hebrews, Epistle to xv, 12, 22f, 234
Hellenism xiv, xv, 1, 2, 4, 8, 10, 234
Hellenistic Judaism xiv, 4
Holland 92, 98 (*see also* Netherlands)
Holocaust xiv, xix, 197–209, 210, 224, 231–3, 239; Christian reaction to 208–9, 222, 232–3, 240; denial of 213, 216
Holocaust News 213
holy days, Jewish 83, 85, 88, 90, 91
homeland, Jewish xviii, 10, 11, 89, 95, 165, 171, 172, 186, 192, 238 (*see also* state, Jewish)
Hoveve Tzion 176
humanism 140
Hungary 75, 105, 122, 143, 184

incantations 59f
Infamous Decree, the 141
Inquisition xvi, 46, 54, 57, 59, 61, 236; Brazilian 120; Portuguese 88, 89, 90, 236; Spanish 79, 84–8, 90
insignia, wearing of 69, 76, 78, 102 (*see also* badge, clothing)
International Council of Christians and Jews 226
Isaiah, prophecy of 13, 14, 15, 28, 36
Islam 92 (*see also* Muslims)
isolationism 173
Israel, 'new' 18, 21, 227
Israel, state of (modern) xiii, 211, 216, 224
Israel, 'true' 1, 6, 8, 10, 11, 12–15, 19, 20, 22, 34, 234
Italy 45, 46, 51, 52, 61, 94, 95, 97, 141, 168
Ivanhoe 157

Janowska 205
Jena 161
Jerusalem 3, 10, 11, 12, 18, 27, 31, 36,
  39, 41, 65, 96, 227
Jerusalem 'spiritual' 22
'Jew-Devil' 62, 63, 159, 235
Jew of Malta, The 95
'Jewish-Bolshevik Conspiracy' 190, 192f,
  198
Jewish-Christian dialogue 223, 224
Jewish Emancipation Bill 120
Jewish Fighting Organization 195, 203,
  204
Jewish Statute 112
Joint Distribution Committee 219
Judaism, spiritualization of 1, 4–6, 10–
  11, 23, 32, 35, 36
Judenstaat, Der 171
Judeo-Christian sects xvii, 125, 137, 227
Judgement, Day of 13f
Justinian Code 38, 235

kaballism 71, 96, 97, 98, 108
kahal 102f, 107
Kaluszyn 202
Kharkov 172
Khazars 101
Kielce 217
Kiev 145, 174, 177
killing batallions, mobile, Nazi 195, 199,
  229
Kingdom of God 13, 14, 17, 18, 23, 226
Kopernik 204
KOR 218
Korzec 202
Kovno 207, 208
Kruszyna 204
Kristallnacht xix, 195, 197, 239
Ku Klux Klan 214

labour camps 203, 204, 214
law, of conscience 35; Jewish 3, 5, 11, 15,
  44, 47, 225; (Christian attitudes to) 12,
  17, 20, 21, 25, 28, 34, 35, 234; Mosaic
  16, 17, 21, 26, 34, 35, 88; natural 4, 5,
  10, 20; Noachian 3; oral xiii, 10, 11,
  225
Lebanon War 216

Leghorn 93
Leipzig 115
Leningrad 220 (*see also* Petrograd)
literature, anti-Semitic 47, 51f, 65, 191,
  238; English 26, 52, 95, 126, 153, 185;
  French xviii, 42, 47, 51, 65, 66f, 130,
  131, 152, 155, 158–60, 169, 215, 216;
  German xvii, 72–4, 162–4; Polish 109;
  Russian 220; Spanish 78; (*see also*
  publications)
Lithuania 56, 102, 107, 108, 111
Lodz 199, 207
London 40, 70, 71, 89, 118, 156, 186,
  187, 213, 236
London Committee of Deputies of Brit-
  ish Jews 119
Low Countries 41, 52
Lublin 102, 105, 203, 215
Lukow 203
Lusitania 186
Lvov 105, 205, 208

magic xvi, 55–61, 62, 63, (*see also* sorcery
  and under accusations)
Mainz 39, 40, 41, 42
Majdanek 195, 199, 239
Malleus Maleficarum 54
Marcinkance 203
Marconi Affair 185
Marranos xvi, 64, 70, 71, 82–3, 89–100,
  118, 148, 236
Marxism 216, 218
Maryland 120
Massachusetts 120
massacres, of Jews xiv, xv, 38, 39, 40, 41,
  42, 48, 56, 77, 79, 105–7, 165, 195,
  197, 198, 207, 236, 239 (*see also* pog-
  roms)
mass executions 198
Meis Kampf 196
Merchant of Venice, The 96, 153
Messiah xvii, 6, 7, 11, 13, 14, 82, 96, 150,
  226, 228, 236; Christian 5, 8, 12, 13,
  14, 18, 20, 25, 30, 31, 32, 33, 71, 81,
  132, 178, 228, 234
Messiahs, false 89, 90, 96–7
messianism xv, 6, 11, 13, 14, 25, 31, 226,
  228

Metaphysicians 152, 161
mezuzah 56
midrash 11, 107
military service 121, 141, 145, 146, 147, 170, 183, 217
minnesingers 47
Minsk Mazowiecki 204
Mishnah xiii, 10, 107
mission, Christian xx, 222, 230
mitnagdim 108
Montpellier 46, 117
Moscow 109, 110
Munich 181, 195
Muslims 216;
    Black 213f

National Front, British 213;
    French 210, 215, 216, 246
naturalization 119
Nazaraioi 6
Nazis xiv, xix, 45, 152, 159, 195–209, 210, 211, 212, 215, 217, 231, 232, 233, 239
Nazism 164, 179, 181f, 194, 216, 219, 224, 239
Nemirov 107
neo-Nazis 210, 213, 214, 216, 240
Netherlands 150, 227 (*see also* Holland)
New Christians 77, 83, 88, 90, 91
'new Israel' 20, 30
New Jersey 188
New Testament 1, 9, 12–24, 25, 31, 43, 53, 231, 234
New York 120, 122, 184, 188, 189, 190
North Africa 82
Northwest Ordinance 121
Norwich 40, 143
Nostra Aetate 223, 227
Novgorod 109
Novosibirsk 220
Nuremburg trials 199, 201

Odessa 174
Old Christians 77, 84, 91
Old Testament 1, 9, 120, 234
Oliver Twist 153
Orthodox Church 208
Orthodox Jews xviii, 139, 143

Osservatore Romano 209

pagans xiv, 1, 3, 4, 10
Palatinate 76
Pale of Settlement 112, 144, 145, 146, 172, 175
Palestine, ancient 2, 3, 6, 9
    modern 95, 96, 172, 173, 176, 184
Palestine Liberation Organization 214
Palestinians (modern) xiii, 211, 212, 216
Pamyat 220, 221
Paris 46, 56, 62, 117, 147, 156, 161, 168, 169, 170, 200, 216
Parliament, Jews in 120, 153
Patriarchs 7, 25, 35, 227
PAX 218
Pentateuch 6, 10, 35, 98, 167
Petrograd 183, 187, 190, 192 (*see also* Leningrad)
Pharisees 1, 7, 10–11, 12f, 15, 37, 225f
Philadelphia 122
pogroms 165, 168, 174, 175, 179, 183, 190, 193, 240 (*see also* massacres)
Poland xvii, xx, 46, 56, 101–9, 111, 112, 118, 122, 135, 144, 173, 236;
    in World War II 195, 197, 199, 203, 238; post-war 210, 217–19, 240
Polish Civil War 217
Polish October 217
political parties, anti-Semitic xviii, 165, 166, 167, 211
Portugal xvi, 82, 88, 89–91, 94, 236
Prague 73, 143
priesthood 5, 7, 10, 19, 23, 36
propaganda, racist 169
prophets, Hebrew 6, 14, 15, 17, 19, 23, 28, 31
proselytism 229
Protestants xvii, 68, 98, 122, 125, 127–9, 132, 140, 160, 214, 230, 237, 240
Protocols of the Elders of Zion, The xix, 165, 177, 179, 184, 188, 189, 191, 196, 216, 220, 238, 239
Prussia 76, 114, 135, 156, 186
Psalms 13, 14, 28, 31, 241
publications, anti-Semitic xvi, 52f, 64, 65; American 181, 191; English 52, 79, 186, 187, 188;

French xvi, xviii, 68–70, 156, 157–60, 168f, 192, 193, 194, 216; German xvii, 71, 74, 76, 162, 166, 167, 179, 180; Russian 173f, 176f, 178, 183, 184, 220, 221, 238; (*see also* literature)
Puritans 70, 120

reconciliation, Jewish-Christian xx, 222–33
Reformation, Protestant 68, 160
reformers, Jewish xviii, 140, 237
Reform temples 139, 142, 237
Religious Opinions Relief Bill 120
Resistance, Jewish against Nazis 202–5, 215
revival movements 1, 6–8, 234
revolution 165, 175–8; French 117, 140, 143, 168, 169; Russian xix, 179, 181, 183f, 187, 190, 238, 239; Turkish 185
Rhineland 49, 56
Roman Catholic Church (modern) 222, 223f, 240 (*see also* Catholics)
Roman Empire 25, 31, 32, 38, 235
Romans (ancient) 1, 2, 3, 10, 12, 18, 19
Romantic movement 139, 143, 237
Rumania 208
Russia, Tsarist xvii, xviii, xix, 56, 101, 106, 108, 109–12, 139, 144–6, 156, 165, 169, 172, 173–8, 179, 182, 189, 236f, 238; Communist xix, xx, 179, 183–4, 192, 193, 195, 196, 198, 202, 210, 218, 219–21, 239, 240

Sabbath 2, 3, 4, 6, 12, 16, 20, 27, 35, 36, 47, 57, 83, 87, 119
sacrifice xiii, 5, 6, 23, 28, 32, 34, 35, 36
Salonica 89, 92
Samaritans 6, 7, 18
Saragossa 61, 83, 86
Satan 16, 48, 54, 55, 57, 58, 59, 64, 65, 155, 236 (*see also* Devil)
Savoy 48, 54
scholarship (*see* biblical)
scholarship, Jewish 103–5, 107, 167
Scribes 15, 19, 37
Secret of Judaism, The 165, 238
seder 60

Sephardim 104, 119, 120
Sepher Yetsirah 107
Seville 79, 84, 85
Shabbatean Movement 96–8
Shammai, school of 12
show trials, of Jews 219
Shulham Arukh 104, 107
Six-Day War 215, 217, 220
Smolensk 106, 111
Smyrna 96
Sobibor 195, 199, 239
Social Democratic Movement 174
socialism 152, 159, 181, 194, 212, 238
Solidarity 218
sorcery 51, 55–61, 63 (*see also* magic)
South Carolina 121
Spain xvi, 41, 46, 61, 77–88, 89, 90, 94f, 102, 118, 236
Speyer 39, 40, 49
Stalinism 216, 217, 219, 221
state, Jewish 165, 171, 172, 184 (*see also* homeland)
Stutthof 198
Suffering Servant 13, 28, 232
Sweden 106
Switzerland 48, 54, 140, 148, 162
synagogue 7, 10, 16, 25, 27, 29, 33, 71, 119, 182, 228
synagogues, burning of 73, 166; destruction of 61, 79, 114, 150, 197, 216; turned into churches 61, 80
Syria 156

Talmud xiii, xv, 44, 45, 46, 47, 59, 60, 61, 71, 79, 81, 104, 107, 140, 142, 235; opposition to 38, 72, 73, 108, 146, 148, 235
Temple 6, 7, 10, 11, 16, 18, 23, 27, 32, 33, 34, 36; allegorization of xv, 5, 11, 12, 16, 23, 36, 226; Second 3, 9, 10, 128
Third Reich 76, 211
Third Worldism 213f, 216
Tiberias 95
Toledo 61, 84
Torah 1, 4, 6, 7, 11, 12, 20, 21, 23, 26, 32, 61, 83, 104, 108, 139, 141, 220, 227, 228, 238

Toulouse 41, 54
Treblinka 195, 199, 201, 203, 204, 205, 239
Trent 45
Trotskyism 218
Turkey 82, 87, 91, 111, 185

Uganda 172
Ukraine 105–7, 108, 110, 173, 184, 219, 202, 203, 220
United Nations 220
United States xix, 113, 120–22, 176, 179, 188–92, 212, 227, 228, 237, 239 (*see also* America)

Valencia 61, 81, 82
Vatican xix, 195, 208, 239
Vatican Council, Second 223, 227
Velladolid, Statute of 81
Venice 89, 93, 94, 95, 236
Vichy government 208, 215
Vienna 49, 62, 75, 76, 167, 171; Congress of 141
Vienne, Council of 62
Vilna 105, 107, 108
Virginia 120
Vitebsk 183

'Wandering Jew' xviii, 25, 29, 34, 76, 152, 155, 157–60, 238
war criminals xix, 209, 239
Warsaw 102, 195, 202, 203, 204f, 205, 206, 208, 216, 239
Weimar Republic 181
witchcraft 51, 53–4, 58f, 235
World Council of Churches 222, 224f, 230
World Jewish Congress 212
World War I xix, 180, 181, 182, 184, 185, 189, 239
World War II 195–209, 210, 217, 239
Worms 39, 41, 48
Würzburg 40, 41, 43, 150

Yaroslav 103
'year of apostasy' 81
yeshivot 103–5
York 40

Zionism xiii, xviii, 172, 176, 184, 185, 210, 212, 216, 217, 218, 219, 220, 238, 240
Zionist Organization 172
Zohar 96, 107

Index of Names

Aaron, Raymond 215
Abel 28
Abraham 18, 20, 21, 23, 30, 34, 36, 225, 227
Adams, James 120
Agobard, Archbishop 39
Aksakov, Ivan 173
Albert of Aix 40
Albert the Great 47
Alexander I, Tsar 145
Alexander II, Tsar 174
Alexander III, Tsar 173, 175
Alexis, Pope 109
Amolon, Archbishop 39
Amos 36
Anielewicz, Mordecai 204
Antiochus Epiphanes 6
Aphrahats 27, 29
Apollonius Molon 2
Aquinas, Thomas 53
Arndt, Ernst Moritz 160
Augustine 28, 29, 34, 37

Baal Shem Tov (Besht) (*see* Israel ben Eleazer)
Baer, Dov 108
Balfour, Lord 186
Ballin, Albert 186
Barrès, Maurice 192
Basnage, Jacques 128, 129
Bauer, Bruno 162
Begun, Vladimir 220
Beilis, Mendel 177f
Belloc, Hilaire 190
Benedict XII, Pope 54
Benedict XIII, Pope 81
Bergman, Werner 212

Berkovits, Eliezer 232
Berman, Jakob 217
Bernard of Clairvaux 40
Bernardino of Feltre 62
Bernardo of Siena 62
Boccaccio 48
Boehm, Max Hildebert 180
Boleslav V, King 102
Bontoux, Eugène 169
Börne, Ludwig 147, 155
Boulanger, Nicholas 131
Bousquet, René 215
Brafman, Jacob 169, 173f
Brittan, Sir Leon 212

Cain 28, 29, 34, 157
Capet, Hugh 62
Caro, Joseph 104
Carto, Willis 214
Casimir IV, King 102
Cassel, Sir Ernest 185
Catherine I, Empress 111
Catherine II, 'The Great' 111, 114
Cecil, Lord Robert 187
Chamberlain, Houston Stewart 167, 180
Chamberlain, Joseph 172, 187
Charlemagne 62
Charles V, Emperor 90, 94
Charles the Bald 62
Chateaubriand 155, 158
Chaucer, Geoffrey 52
Chéradame, André 194
Cheremona 2
Chmielnicki, Bogdan xvii, 101, 105–7, 108, 236
Chorin, Aaron 143
Christ (*see* General Index; *see also* Jesus)

253

Chrysostom, John 26, 27, 28, 31, 33, 36
Cicero 2
Clemenceau, Georges 192
Clement VI, Pope 48
Clement VII, Pope 90
Coggan, Lord (Donald) 229
Conrad von Megenberg 49
Constantine 31
Coryat, Thomas 93
Crémieux, Adolphe 154, 156-7
Crescas, Hasdai 81
Cromwell, Oliver 70, 71, 118
Cyprian 29

Dahl, Vladimir 173
Damgaard, H. Fuglsang, Bishop 208
d'Argens, Jean-Baptiste, Marquis 128
David, King 16
de Aragon, Francisco 94
de Arbues, Pedro 86
de Ayala, Lopez 78
de Berry, Duchesse 155
de Bottens, Polier 132
de Châteauroux, Eudes 47
de Gaulle, Charles 215
de Guzmán, Fernán Pérez 83
de Jaucourt, Chevalier 131
de la Caballería, Pedro 83
de la Varenne de Saint-Saulieu, Abbé 118
del Campo, Elvira 87-8
de Ligne, Prince Charles 117, 122
de Luna, Beatrice (*see* Nasi, Gracia)
de Luna, Brianda 94
de Mirabaud, Jean-Baptiste 132
de Montfort, Grignon 66
de Montoro, Antonio 83
de Nicolay, Nicholas 92
Denis, Pope 109
de Pinto, Isaac 92, 93
Derzhavin, Gabriel 144f, 173
de Saint Martin, Claude 149
de Sévigné, Mme 127
Deutz, Simon 155
Dewey, Melvil 188
de Wolski, Calixte 168
Dickens, Charles 153
Diderot, Denis 131

Diognetus 34
di Ragusa, Bonifazio 95
Disraeli, Benjamin xviii, 152-4
Dostoevsky, Fëdor 174, 180
Dreyfus, Alfred 165, 168
Drumont, Edouard 165, 169
Dühring, Karl Eugen 167

Eckart, Dietrich 195
Eckhardt, Alice 231
Eckhardt, Royal 231
Edward VII, King 185
Eisenmenger, Johann Andreas 76, 166
Eliezer of Triesch, Rabbi 143
Elijah ben Solomon Zalman 107
Elizabeth, Empress 111
Ephrem 26, 27, 29, 31
Erasmus 72
Eugenius III, Pope 40
Eusebius 31, 32, 33, 35

Fackenheim, Emil 232
Farrakhan, Louis 210, 213, 214
Fassbinder, Raines Werner 211
Felner, Hermann 211
Ferdinand of Aragon xvi, 77, 84, 86
Fernán Pérez de Guzmán 83
Ferrer, Vincent 61, 81
Feuerbach, Ludwig 161
Fichte, Johann Gottlieb 125, 135
Fiorentino, Giovanni 52
Fitzgerald, F. Scott 191
Fleckeles, Eleazer 143
Fleury, Abbé, 65
Ford, Henry 191
Förster, Bernhard 166
Fourier, Charles 159
Franco, Yuce 86
Frank, Jacob 97f
Frederick II, Emperor 44
Frederick II, 'the Great' 115
Frederick William, Elector 114, 115
Freret, Nicholas 132
Friedlander, David 138
Fruitolf 41

Gans, Eduard 147
Gerondi, Jonah 46

Ghillany, Friedrich Wilhelm 161
Gieremek, Bronislaw 218
Glagau, Otto 166
Glemp, Jozef, Cardinal 219
Goedsche, Hermann 169
Goethe, Johann Wolfgang von 115
Goldsmid family 120
Gomulka, President 217, 218
Gorbachev, Mikhail 220
Gougenot de Mousseaux, Chevalier 165, 168
Graf, Karl Heinrich 167
Grant, Madison 189
Grant, Robert 120
Gregory IX, Pope 66
Gregory X, Pope 44
Griffiths, Bede 230
Gumpertz, Aaron Salomon 133

Hagar 21f, 29
ha-Kohen, Nehemiah 97
Halevi, Solomon 80
Halorki, Joshua (*see* Jeronimo de Santa Fé)
Harding, W. G. 192
Hegel, Georg Wilhelm 125, 135, 192,
Heine, Heinrich 147, 148, 156
Heinrich, Brigitte 211
Henry II (France) 94
Henry III 80
Henry VII (England) 70
Henry VIII (England) 70
Henry of Trastamara 77f
Henry, Major H. J. 170
Herschel, Moses 136
Herz, Henriette 137
Herzl, Theodor xviii, 165, 171f, 238
Heydrich, Reinhard 198
Hick, John 230
Hilton, John 188
Himmler, Heinrich 197, 206, 209
Hindenburg, Paul von 180, 197
Hippolytus 27, 33
Hitler, Adolf xix, 74, 180, 195–7, 209,
212, 213, 232, 239
Hosea 29, 31
Hugh of Lincoln 52, 57
Hugo, Victor 155, 158

Innocent III, Pope 45
Innocent IV, Pope 44
Innocent VIII Pope 54
Institoris 54
Irenaeus 36
Irving, David 213
Isaac 18, 22, 23
Isaac of Antioch 30, 35
Isaac of Troyes 50
Isabella, Queen xvi, 77, 83, 84
Isaiah 13, 14, 15, 28, 36
Israel ben Eleazer 108
Issacs, Rufus 185
Isserlein, Israel 63
Ivan III 109, 110
Ivan IV, 'the Terrible' 56, 110

Jackson, Jesse 213
Jacob 18, 23, 28, 29
Jacobovitz, Lord 212
Jacobson, Israel xvii, 139, 142
Jahn, Friedrich Ludwig 160
Jean d'Outremeuse 43, 48
Jeronimo de Santa Fé 79, 81
Jesus xv, 8, 12, 13, 14, 15–17, 18, 21, 24,
25, 30, 32, 35, 47, 57, 65, 66f, 71, 212,
226, 227, 228, 231
Jesus as Jew 222, 223, 224, 225–7, 240
John III, King 90
John XXII, Pope 54
John Casimir, King 106
John Damascene 27
John of Capistrano 61
John the Good, King 46
Joly, Maurice 177
Joseph 23, 29
Joseph Jacob of Polonnoye 108
Joseph, Sir Keith 212
Juan I, King 79
Judas Iscariot 64, 65, 74, 155
Justin Martyr 34

Kant, Immanuel 125, 134
Karitzin, Feodor 109
Khruschev, Nikita 217, 219, 220
Kipling, Rudyard 185
Kitchener, Lord 186
Knitter, Paul 231

Knox, Alfred 184
Knox, Robert 152, 154
Kohl, Helmut 211
Konrad von Wurzburg 47
Kostomarov, Nikolai 173
Kriesky, Bruno 212
Kychko, Trofim 220

Labat, Brother 93
Lamartine, Alphonse de 158
Lambelin, Roger 194
Lavater, Pastor 133
Lawson, Nigel 212
Lazare, Bernard 170
Lenin 184, 189, 192
Leo XIII, Pope 167
Leopold I, Emperor 75, 113
Leopold of Lorraine, Duke 116
Le Pen, Jean-Marie 210, 216
Leroy-Beaulieu, Anatole 174
Lessing, Gotthold Ephraim 133
Levi, Nathan Benjamin 96, 97
Levin, Rahel 137, 147
Lilienthal, Max 146
Lissauer, Ernst 180
Liszt, Franz 164
Lloyd George, David 185
Londres, Albert 193
Louis IX 46
Louis XIII 116
Louis XIV 130
Louis XVI 117
Louis Philippe 155
Lueger, Karl 167
Lushchinsky, André 177
Luther, Martin xvi, 56, 64, 72–4, 149
Lutostanski, Hippolytus 173
Lysimachus of Alexandria 2

Macaulay, Thomas Babington 120
Maimon, Solomon 135
Maimonides, Moses 46
Malachi 32
Malcolm X 213
Manesseh ben Israel 58, 70
Manetho 2
Marcion 9
Marie-Benoit, Father 208

Marlowe, Christopher 95
Marr, Wilhelm 166
Martin V, Pope 82
Martinez, Ferrant 79
Marx, Karl 162
Mather, Cotton 120
Maximilian, Emperor 71
Maziminus 28
Maxse, Leo 186
Maybaum, Ignaz 231f
Mazowiecki, Tadeusz 218
Mehmet Ali 157
Mehmet Effendi (*see* Tzevi, Shabbatai)
Meir, Rabbi 63
Méline, F. J. 171
Mendelssohn family 136f
Mendelssohn, Moses 113, 124, 133f,
    136, 138, 145
Mendes, Diego 94
Mendes, Francisco 94
Mengele, Josef 207
Metzger, Tom 214
Meyerbeer, Giacomo 163f
Micas, Juan (*see* Nasi, Joseph)
Michael the Neophyte 109
Michaelis, Johann David 133
Miczynski, Sebastian 105
Minc, Hilary 217
Moczar, General 218
Mohammed II, Sultan 91
Molcho, Solomon (*see* Pires, Diego)
Moltmann, Jürgen 233
Montefiore, Moses 157
Montesquieu 130
Morgan, Thomas 126
Moses 2, 6, 10, 17, 21, 23, 34, 35, 36, 45,
    227, 228
Moses of Coucy 47
Muhammad, Elijah 214
Munk, Solomon 157

Napoleon Bonaparte 140, 141, 142, 149,
    150
Napoleon III 177
Nasi, Gracia 94, 95
Nasi, Joseph 89, 94–6
Naxos, Duke of (*see* Nasi, Joseph)
Newcastle, Duke of 119

Nicholas I, Tsar 145, 146
Nicholas II, Tsar 176, 183, 189, 192
Nidder 54
Nietzche, Friedrich Wilhelm 166
Nikodemus, Patriarch 208
Noah 3, 23

Oppenheimer, Samuel 75

Panikaar, Raimundo 230
Papon, Maurice 215
Paris, Matthew 57
Parkes, James 228
Pascal, Jacob of Toledo 48
Paul xv, 12, 20–22, 29, 30, 34, 234
Paul I, Tsar 145
Paul IV, Pope 95
Paul VI, Pope 223
Pedro the Cruel, King 77
Pegna, Francesco 85
Penn, William 120
Pétain, Marshal 215
Peter I, 'the Great' 110
Pfefferkorn, Johannes 71f
Philip II, King 95
Philo 4, 5
Piasecki, Buleslaw 218
Picquart, Georges 170f
Pires, Diego 90
Pius IX, Pope 168
Pius XII, Pope 209
Plato 2, 4
Pompeius of Trogus 2
Pope, Alexander 119
Proudhon, Pierre 159f
Prudentius 26, 29
Prynne, William 70

Quddafi, Colonel 214
Quinet, Edgar 158

Rachel 29
Rahner, Karl 230
Rampolla, Cardinal 167
Reagan, Ronald 211
Rebekah 28
Reubeni, David 90
Reuchlin, Johann 71f

Richard I, King 55
Riesser, Gabriel 148
Robespierre 140
Rohling, August 166
Rothe, Richard 161
Rothschild family 120, 169, 171
Rothschild, James de 115, 156
Rousseau, Jean-Jacques 130
Ruge, Arnold 162
Runcie, Lord (Robert) 229
Russo, Baruchiah 97

Samartha, Stanley 230
Samuels, Herbert 185
Sarah 21f, 23, 29
Sartre, Jean-Paul 215
Sassoon, Reuben 186
Schemann, Ludwig 164
Scheurer-Kestner, Auguste 171
Schiff, Jacob 189
Schlegel, Friedrich 137
Schleiermacher, Friedrich 138
Schoneveld, Jacobus 226, 228
Schwartz, Peter 71
Seligman, Joseph 188
Selim II, Sultan 95
Semyonov, Eugen 183
Senatro, Eduardo 209
Shafarevich, Igor 221
Shakespeare, William 96, 153, 157
Shammai 12
Shaprut, Shemtov, Rabbi 79
Sigismund Augustus, King 56, 110
Simeon ben Yohai, 47
Simons, George A. 190
Sisson, Edgar 183
Solomon ben Abraham 46
Solomon bar Simeon 40, 49
Soury, Jules 165, 169
Spener, Philipp Jacob 115
Spengler, Oswald 180
Spinoza, Baruch 89, 97–100, 169
Sprenger 54
Stalin, Josef 219
Stephen 17f, 19
Stiles, Ezra 121
Stoecker, Adolf 116
Sussex, Duke of 120

Sverdlov, Jacob 183
Swedenborg, Emmanuel 148
Swift, Jonathan 119
Szeptycki, Andreas, Metropolitan 208

Taft, W. H. 192
Teller, Wilhelm 138
Tertullian 26, 28
Thoma, Clemens 233
Thomas of Cantimpre 57
Tigre, Piccolo 168
Tindal, Matthew 126
Toland, John 123, 125, 126
Tolstoy, Ivan 176
Torquemada, Tomas de 86
Treitschke, Heinrich 166
Trotsky, Leon 190, 193
Tzevi, Shabbatai 89, 96–7

Urban II, Pope 39

van Buren, Paul 228
van Oven, Bernard 156
Veit, David 137
Veit, Simon 137
Voltaire 92, 130, 132
von Hameln, Glückel 75
von Hutten, Ulrich 72
Voshtchilo, Basil 108

Wagner, Richard xviii, 152, 162–4, 166
Wahl, Saul 101
Waldheim, Kurt 210, 212
Warburg, Max 113
Washington, George 121
Weill, Alexandre 148
Weizmann, Chaim 187
Wellhausen, Julius 167
Werblan, Andrzej 218
Wesley, John 120
Whiston, William 126
Wiesel, Elie 233
Wilhelm II, Kaiser 172, 180
William, Saint 43
Wilner, Aryeh 205
Wilson, Woodrow 192
Wittgenstein, Princess 164
Wolffsohn, David 172
Woolston, Pastor 127

Yehiel of Paris 47
Yevtushenko, Yevgeny 219
Yosel of Rosheim 75

Zalkind-Hourwitz 122, 123
Zalman, Solomon 107
Zambrowski, Roman 217
Zechariah 31
Ziyuni, Manahem 58
Zola, Emile 171